ETHICAL LONELINESS

published with a grant from

FIGURE FOUNDATION

comes an adjournment of sorrow

ETHICAL LONELINESS

the injustice of not being heard

JILL STAUFFER

COLUMBIA UNIVERSITY PRESS   NEW YORK

COLUMBIA UNIVERSITY PRESS

Publishers Since 1893

NEW YORK   CHICHESTER, WEST SUSSEX

cup.columbia.edu

Library of Congress Cataloging-in-Publication Data

Stauffer, Jill, 1966–
Ethical loneliness : the injustice of not being heard / Jill Stauffer.
pages cm
Includes bibliographical references and index.
ISBN 978-0-231-17150-2 (cloth : alk. paper)—ISBN 978-0-231-17151-9 (pbk. : alk. paper)—ISBN 978-0-231-53873-2 (e-book)
1. Loneliness—Philosophy.   2. Loneliness—Moral and ethical aspects.
3. Persecution.   4. Oppression (Psychology)   I. Title.

B105.L65S73 2015
172'.1—dc23
2015001677

COVER IMAGE: KÄTHE KOLLWITZ, *THE WIDOW I* FROM *WAR* © ARS
COVER DESIGN: CHANG JAE LEE

The tortured person never ceases to be amazed that all those things one may, according to inclination, call his soul, or his mind, or his consciousness, or his identity, are destroyed when there is that cracking and splintering in the shoulder joints.

—Jean Améry

The word *I* means *here I am*, answering for everything and for everyone.
—Emmanuel Levinas

But the difficultest rigor is forthwith,
On the image of what we see, to catch from that

Irrational moment its unreasoning,
As when the sun comes rising, when the sea
Clears deeply, when the moon hangs on the wall

Of heaven-haven. These are not things transformed.
Yet we are shaken by them as if they were.
We reason about them with a later reason.

. . .

We reason of these things with later reason.
And we make of what we see, what we see clearly
And have seen, a place dependent on ourselves.
—Wallace Stevens

Contents

Acknowledgments

In *Beyond Good and Evil*, Nietzsche wrote, "A thought comes when 'it' wishes, and not when 'I' wish, so that it is a falsification of the facts of the case to say that the subject 'I' is the condition of the predicate 'think.'" I think about that a lot. It means, among other things, that the ideas of this book owe much to many interlocutors—a large number of persons, the conditions in which I live, even the passing of time. Nietzsche's reminder is also reflected in the themes of the book, from Jean Améry learning in the hardest way imaginable that the life of the mind is not possible absent human community, to how, in the writing of the book, the ideas took their most interesting turns when I pushed myself to translate the argument for widely different audiences, to how none of this would have been possible absent the gift (and luxury) of time for writing.

It began when Oona Eisenstadt invited me to present a paper at a colloquium on contemporary Jewish philosophy at Pomona College in December 2010. I thought to myself, "I am not qualified for this." Oona insisted, and so I revised my thought and said to myself, "I suppose it is time for me to figure out how to put Jean Améry in conversation with Levinas." That paper was my first draft of the concept of ethical loneliness.

A second push came from Peter Rush at the Law School at the University of Melbourne in Australia, who asked me to give a plenary address at a July 2011 conference called "Affective States of International Criminal Justice." Looking at loneliness and legal response to violence through the lens of affect and its transfer helped me refine my argument about the self's intersubjective formation. The participants in the conference, a response to my paper by Shaun McVeigh, and the faculty and graduate students at Melbourne engaged with the work in progress in deeply helpful ways.

Then I was invited, in October 2011, to speak at a conference honoring the work of Linda Ross Meyer, where engaging with the serious challenge her work on mercy poses to the gut sense I was developing that resentment could also be restorative led me to begin to develop the ideas about hearing that are so central to this book's argument.

I owe singular thanks to James Martel, Claire Katz, and Gustavus Stadler, all of whom read the full manuscript and offered helpful support and critique—each showed me in different ways both what I knew I was doing with the book and what I didn't. Each moved me with the intelligence and generosity of their comments, and opened windows for me into my own thinking.

I am also indebted to two anonymous reviewers for Columbia University Press, whose vital comments advanced my thinking about some aspects of the project, and to Wendy Lochner and Christine Dunbar, for supporting this book and shepherding it through the publishing process. Donovan Schaefer, Raji Mohan, Tina Zwarg, Lisa McCormick, and Gus Stadler—all members of a faculty seminar on affect theory at the Hurford Center for the Arts and Humanities at Haverford College—read early versions of the chapters on ethical loneliness and revision, and their comments helped me think through the project during a key stage in my writing of it. Finally, most of the book came into being during a sabbatical leave provided by Haverford College. I used to think I could make writing happen no matter what constraints the outside world threw at me. Having a year to sink deeply into a demanding project taught me that some forms of thinking and writing need that buffer of space and time around them. To recast Nietzsche's counsel: thought doesn't come when I'm ready for it, it comes when it is ready—but that means one needs to provide a space where it might arrive.

During the years I worked on this book, I was invited to present work from it at Bard College's Human Rights Project lecture series, Yale Law School's Human Rights Workshop, a conference at McGill University on "The Art and Politics of Irony," Johns Hopkins University's WGS workshop on "Law and Loss," a colloquium on "Law's Counter-Archive" at the Birkbeck School of Law at the University of London, Rowan University's "Theorizing Rowan" series, and as a plenary address at the 2014 meeting of the North American Levinas Society. Every audience I encountered pushed the ideas along in productive and illuminating ways.

I also presented work in progress at meetings of the Association for the Study of Law, Culture and the Humanities, an interdisciplinary group that has been an important intellectual home for me; the Levinas Research Seminar, another rigorous and generative scholarly community; the Critical Legal Studies conferences in Stockholm, Sweden, and Belfast, Northern Ireland—so full of the best kinds of challenge to settled thought; the Society for Phenomenology and Existential Philosophy, a philosophical home; and the American Political Science Association, where I am always reminded of how far work in political theory can extend. Every meeting I attended illuminated for me how important it is for working scholars to talk to one another about matters large and small.

Further thanks go to Katie Ulrich, a student of mine at Haverford College, who engaged with this work very smartly in a senior seminar and then agreed to take on the thankless (but thankfully paid) task of hunting down, regularizing, and formatting the citations for the manuscript. She did a better job than I would have done and saved me an immense amount of time and stress in doing so.

Other friends and colleagues whose conversation and critique helped make this book what it is include Sara Kendall, Jennifer Culbert, Stewart Motha, Martin Kavka, Alison Young, Roger Berkowitz, Mark Antaki, Andrew Friedman, Sam Moyn, Linda Ross Meyer, John Drabinski, Diane Perpich, Joshua Ramey, Dave Eggers, Gayle Salamon, Anne Murphy, P. J. Brendese, Deborah Achtenberg, and Juliet Rogers, and the teachers and mentors who challenged and supported me as I made my way to this point: Marianne Constable, Judith Butler, Peter Fitzpatrick, Philippe Nonet, and David Cohen.

Early versions of this work appeared in print as "Speaking Truth to Reconciliation: Political Transition, Recovery, and the Work of Time," *Humanity* 4, no. 1 (2013): 27–48, and "A Hearing: Forgiveness, Resentment, and Recovery in Law," *Quinnipiac Law Review* 30, no. 3 (2012): 517–26. Ideas from those two articles appear throughout this book, and I've added a note corresponding to the first sentence of sections that rely heavily on earlier material to indicate my debt to those publications. A couple of themes from another article of mine, "How Much Does That Weigh? Levinas and the Possibility of Human Rights," originally published in the Turkish journal *MonoKL* 8–9 (2010): 661–74, also appear in the book (and also with a corresponding note where they appear).

It isn't just intellectual conditions—research money, library support, engaged students, generous colleagues, all of which I was lucky to have—that make a book possible but also the wider world that forms a backdrop to the life of the mind. And so I also owe immense thanks to the people I've long relied on most—those who actively contribute to building a shared world worth living in. My parents—Randy Stauffer (much missed) and Cheryle Stauffer—have always believed in me. The passing of time has shown me how much that matters. It has been a kind of strength, a well-built world I could fall back on, one that in no small measure made me who I am. My extended kin include my best-ever sister Natalie Kidder, Anne Stauffer, Evany Thomas, Liz Dunn, Heidi Pollock, Caroleen Beatty, Sunny Haire, Marilyn Fontenrose, Marco Baroz, Scott Kidder, and Ramsay Kidder. And then there is Gustavus Stadler, the one who arrived when I least expected, taught me how to rely on someone, and stayed.

Abbreviations

ANC	African National Congress
CONADEP	National Commission on the Disappearance of Persons (Argentina)
DRC	Democratic Republic of the Congo
EEEC	Extraordinary Chambers in the Courts of Cambodia
ICC	International Criminal Court
ICTR	International Criminal Tribunal for Rwanda
ICTY	International Criminal Tribunal for the former Yugoslavia
LRA	Lord's Resistance Army
MK	Umkhonto we Sizwe (armed wing of the ANC)
NAGPRA	Native American Graves Protection and Repatriation Act
SCSL	Special Court for Sierra Leone
TRC	Truth and Reconciliation Commission (South Africa)

ETHICAL LONELINESS

Introduction

> The experience of persecution was, at the very bottom, that of an extreme
> *loneliness*. At stake for me is the release from the abandonment that has
> persisted from that time until today.
>
> —Jean Améry, "Resentments"

Jean Améry wrote those lines in 1965, twenty years after he was freed
from the Bergen-Belsen concentration camp. He describes an abandonment that the passing of time, on its own, does not remedy. In what follows I want to distinguish that kind of loneliness from the solitude or
aloneness undergone by someone who can still rely on broad social support. Améry was subjected to an *ethical loneliness*. Ethical loneliness is
the isolation one feels when one, as a violated person or as one member
of a persecuted group, has been abandoned by humanity, or by those who
have power over one's life's possibilities. It is a condition undergone by
persons who have been unjustly treated and dehumanized by human beings and political structures, who emerge from that injustice only to find
that the surrounding world will not listen to or cannot properly hear their
testimony—their claims about what they suffered and about what is now
owed them—on their own terms. So ethical loneliness is the experience
of having been abandoned by humanity compounded by the experience of
not being heard. Such loneliness is so named because it is a form of social

abandonment that can be imposed only by multiple ethical lapses on the part of human beings residing in the surrounding world.

The main argument of the book is that this form of loneliness is widespread, that it is caused not only by dehumanization, oppression, and abandonment but also by the failure of just-minded people to hear well—from those who have suffered—what recovery or reconciliation after massive violence or long-standing injustice would require. Such failures of hearing haunt sites where the goal is political transition, reconciliation, or forgiveness. As such, unassuaged ethical loneliness has political ramifications. But beyond that instrumental concern, failure to hear will matter to those who do not listen and those who are not heard, not only because stories without an audience do not survive but also because being heard or ignored impacts how the past resonates in the present—it affects human processes of revision. "Revision" refers not to the lies of revisionist history but to how human beings live their pasts in the present moment, with different events carrying varying amounts of significance at different times. To take a mundane example: it may be devastating for a teenager to be unpopular in high school, but for someone who has aged well into adulthood, her independence and personal achievements have likely rewritten that history, finding in it some of the sources of strength she needed in order to succeed. Her vision of the past's meaning for the present will likely differ from that of someone who was a star athlete in college but who hasn't felt that much glory has been achieved since then. A history stays with both of them, though differently. This is also a common experience of aging, where dogmatic certainties of youth may become either more nuanced or less committed over time, or where things that didn't seem to matter at a younger age suddenly present themselves in an urgency that only collected years can put before us. In any of these cases, we may think we are the outcome of the choices we have made, but our choices will be only one part of the story of how we become the selves we are. Social conditions; friends, families, and strangers; cultural values; chance encounters; environmental factors—all of these and more will play a role. We are shaped by the worlds in which we subsist. Someone who lives among others who value athletic achievement, financial gain, or some other kind of fame higher than success at raising children may be more likely to devalue her current life (of raising children) than would one surrounded by people whose main aim is to be part of a thriving family. Someone who chooses a creative path that isn't well supported by capitalist market forces may feel that she is fortunate, brave, silly, or a failure—depending at least in part on how her choices resonate in her surroundings. Someone who has chosen to pursue an office job or the life of the mind without marriage or children may, if surrounded mainly by thriving families, find herself feeling that her life is simply invisible where she lives, especially if the past and present history of her social setting offers few guides and little support for an alternative path.

These are small things, tiny heartaches. I begin with mundane examples—and return to that level on occasion throughout the book—in order to demonstrate, and keep it firm in our minds, that this book full of stories of violence and injustice is also describing the human condition: our intersubjective reliance on one another. When I employ an everyday example to clarify a concept that then gets used to explain something much more dire, it is always to remind us that I am not describing things that can happen only to others or to people in desperate circumstances. It is part of the human condition that abandonments and abuses affect us as deeply as they do, and it starts with everyday losses that are less serious but that may underscore for us—if we take the time to look—our vulnerability, our false ideas about our autonomy, and what matters about the autonomy we do have. It is possible for each of us to think differently about how we come to be who we are, have what we have, and, accordingly, what we owe to the larger world. The mind-sets, views, and affective relations of human beings living in a shared world make a difference in what each of us thinks is possible, fitting, or just. A vast revolution can occur in that tiny space. It matters what stories we tell ourselves about these things. What is true in the preceding example about career choices is also true in cycles of violence, where even if retaliation is thought to be a "natural" response, what that will mean in a lived context—whether it will be violent, measured, world building, or world destroying—will be influenced by the attitudes of other human beings whose interactions make up the lived world we share for better and for worse.

Important aspects of how the past is lived in the present are beyond the capacity of an individual to choose or control. Where the stakes are higher, for a survivor of political oppression or anyone whose past is impacted by trauma, it will matter that current social and political conditions affect what kinds of revision are possible. Recovery may be easier for someone with broad social support, who knows both that, though she was once victimized, she is now safe and that her neighbors and the officials who enforce laws are committed to equal justice, than it is for someone who has survived brutal treatment but lives in a community where her harms haven't been addressed, are dismissed as part of a past that should be buried, or aren't widely declared to be harms worthy of redress. For those whose pasts are haunted by injustice, revision can be a life-saving human capacity. But some conditions make positive revisions possible, while others make negative ones more likely. Institutions may influence these conditions for better and for worse, but they cannot change them on their own.

It isn't only our choices that make us who we are. Selves and worlds are built by human interactions—affective, reasoned, chosen, and unchosen. Those forces are the backdrop to the worlds we build and in which we reside. Autonomy and liberty mean something only in spaces where they are respected. One aim of the book will be to show that this means responsibility for justice and recovery is, rather than a narrow legal concern, the very broadest of obligations. The past cannot be changed, but it can resound in the present moment in vastly different ways, some of them more hospitable to human thriving than others. It is everyone's job to author conditions where repair is possible.

In chapter 1 I develop an account of ethical loneliness. Using Jean Améry's reflections on being tortured and interned in concentration camps, Levinasian phenomenology, and evidence from various forms of testimony, I show how isolation and loneliness are part of the human condition, but particular uses of them actively remove some persons from that condition, dehumanizing them. The argument relies on an idea that selfhood is intersubjective, and thus it may come into conflict with the sovereignty of self assumed by some versions of liberal political theory, especially the tradition attached to institutional legality—which is the traditional site for theorizing reconciliation or transition after political violence. This is a tough line to tread, since I am concerned less with liberal political theory as it is practiced by careful thinkers of that tradition and more with widespread deeply held assumptions (almost bodily senses of truth) about what selves are, what responsibility is, and so on, that are inherited from a broad kind of Western liberalism. It's in the air and the water, you might say, to think that an uncomplicated autonomy is a natural and therefore nonnegotiable trait of human beings. I want to complicate that, allowing us to see autonomy as one outcome of the relation between human beings rather than as a predetermined boundary between them. Jean Améry's reflections on torture, abandonment, and the life of the mind set us on that path.

I use the work of Emmanuel Levinas to develop the account of ethical loneliness and the cooperatively authored self. The self's liberty still matters. But I'll argue that we cannot properly appreciate how that liberty is accomplished if we approach selves as if they were self-sufficient monads. Indeed there are harms—and remedies—that are rendered utterly inscrutable if we limit ourselves to thinking that a human self can experience meaningful autonomy separate from social conditions where many others recognize that self's autonomy. Selves are formed intersubjectively, in the presence of others, for better and worse and regardless of whether any of us would have willed it to be this way. Acknowledging that brings us closer to understanding how selves and worlds can be destroyed by human violence, and why human beings can be wounded—not only physically— in such deep and lasting ways. Being abandoned by those who have the power to help produces a loneliness more profound than simple isolation. That is why practices of political transition, reconciliation, or recovery should always aim to do more than rebuild the formal equality or political autonomy of persons. The "form" of equality offered in the context of individualist institutions cannot, on its own, remedy a harm made possible only by widespread neglect of human responsiveness.

Viewing recovery through the lens of ethical loneliness helps to balance a tendency to settle too quickly into ideas about autonomy, self-sufficiency, or sovereignty, formal equality, liberty as the capacity to choose one's commitments, all enshrined in what gets called the rule of law. Those assumptions find their way into the design of international institutions like criminal tribunals, international courts, and truth commissions. And they haunt the practices of political reconciliation and transitional justice.

The focus on ethical loneliness gives me a way to change the subject. Instead of talking about procedure, legality, and blame, I focus on how abandonment and loss are achieved and how they may be alleviated or compensated. In doing so I emphasize harms undergone more than wrongs inflicted. To set the context for the stakes of that shift, chapter 2 follows a tangent to the main argument, because its course is currently central to questions of reconciliation and recovery. In chapter 2, I discuss the retributive and reparative goals of postconflict trials and truth commissions. Courts focus on individual criminal responsibility—the culpability of the autonomous self—even for crimes that are possible only against a backdrop of widespread indifference and abuse. Truth commissions uncover the broader details of an unjust past but often get caught between the conflicting goals of nation building and individual recovery. Chapter 2 does justice to how important trials and truth commissions can be as local and international responses to grave harm but also shows the limits to thinking about the harms of dehumanization and abandonment only in terms of crime, individual responsibility, or nation building. It also uncovers a lack of substantial proof for the contention that these proceedings are cathartic or healing for survivors. My aim is, while acknowledging everything that is awe-inspiring about the responsive international, domestic, and hybrid institutions that have been created in the past few decades, to begin to focus also on what we don't know and what these institutions can't do.

And so I situate the discussion of trials and truth commissions in a larger conversation about repair. Whenever we settle on a course of repair, we ought first to consider what repair is, the ethics of how repair proceeds, who gets to decide what needs to be fixed, and whether there are things that cannot or should not be repaired. Repair, after all, is not a neutral practice. It is an intervention preceded by decisions made about value. It will matter whose voices get heard when those decisions are made.

Chapter 3 then turns its ear to hearing. In it I discuss how unintended ironies surface wherever institutions designed for hearing fail to hear well, and I show how the effects of those ironies tend to weigh most heavily on those with the least power to endure bad outcomes. Relying on testimony delivered in diverse settings—South Africa, Argentina, Holocaust archives, Native American dealings with U.S. legal proceedings, American prisons, the International Criminal Tribunal for the former Yugoslavia—I show failed attempts at listening and discuss some of the reasons why even a supportive audience might fail to hear well. The difference between communication—which always involves risk and uncertainty—and knowledge as fact emerges as key to understanding what is at stake in listening to the testimony of those who have been abandoned. Levinas's work will help here as well, showing how communication is rooted as much in our precognitive response to others as it is in its instrumental use to convey stable meanings. Described this way, responsibility appears not as a form of culpability but as a duty to respond not backed by the security of set rules. Responding well to others, especially survivors of wrongdoing, may require that we open ourselves to hearing something other than what we expect or want to hear, even when what we hear threatens our ideas about how the world is ordered—as listening to survivor testimony might do. Only a self capable of being jolted out of its mundane complacency is up to the task of both hearing what repair demands and helping to invent new responses to harms that no preexisting remedy fully comprehends. That form of listening may also more readily come to understand why the liberal story about culpability—that we are responsible only for acts we author and intend—cannot fix, or even adequately address, the most grievous harms human beings face (and create). And that will open a space where we might ask why Western legality so often fails to listen for its own failures. The stakes are high here, because when no one listens, stories get lost. But unaddressed harms do not disappear. They remain, and they color the affective relations between persons and communities, haunting the official sites of transition and reconciliation.

Chapter 4 looks at revision as a human capacity. As I mentioned earlier, by "revision" I mean the different ways in which a past can be lived in a present moment. For those struggling to rebuild selves, lives, and worlds after extended conflict or grave harm, some revisions render the present more livable than it otherwise would have been. Others fail to release the present moment from past harm, so that "now" seems to lack the capacity to offer a future. The chapter explores the relationship between resentment, forgiveness, time, and recovery for beings (such as ourselves) for whom revision is possible, defining "revisionary practice" as a way of making the past more livable in the present moment.[1] Key to chapter 4 is Jean Améry's refusal to forgive and his principled defense of his continued resentment against both forgiveness and the specter of Nietzschean ressentiment. His resistance helps us see the difference between reconciliation with other persons and reconciliation with time. Reconciliation with time reflects the desire, separate from any will to renew a relationship with an enemy, to be able to live with what the past has been. Nietzsche might say we can learn to "will backwards" on our own, but survivors of violence (and probably most of the rest of us) will likely need more than our own will to accomplish that. A survivor will need broad social support that functions as a promise that, though she was once abandoned by humanity, that will not be allowed to happen again. That is an aspect of world building, which is a cooperative enterprise, not a solitary endeavor. Accordingly, chapter 4 also shows why concepts of individual criminal responsibility and bystander innocence do not actively build worlds but rather, at best, reflect a world already built to support the liberal individual. Rebuilding destroyed selves and worlds requires more than that, which is only one reason why autonomous subjects with comfortable "self-sufficient" lives may also need to focus revisionary practices on their own selves before justice can be seen to be done.

Chapter 5 revisits retribution's roots in the Latin verb *tribuere* to recapture the word's wider history, arguing that calls for retribution always reflect a sense that something has been unjustly taken and that a balance must be put right. One must redo, offer again, something that should have remained intact. Retribution is thus a revisionary practice. In many circumstances the punishment of perpetrators is not sufficient to accomplish such a goal. That is why retribution needn't appear as an antonym of repair: in some cases its best goal is *tribuere*: to bestow, confer, grant, allow, or devote something deserved to one who deserves it. In this reading, "desert" applies not only to perpetrators but also to victims and the surrounding society. As such, "reparative retribution" repays those harmed for their harm. It offers compensation for loss. In addition to opening up our sense of the meaning of the word, defining retribution in this way also helps us understand why anger and resentment are not only negative affects: they express a person's righteous indignation at being treated unjustly and so may be important positive expressions of a relationship to the past, present, and future that is both reasoned and affective.

The chapter looks at cases from the United States, Argentina, Uganda, and South Africa where existing categories of response do not do justice to victims, to perpetrators, or to the larger unjust system in which those affected find themselves and considers alternatives to existing institutions that may be capable of addressing these harmful legacies more thoroughly. Each of the cases discussed shows that, though it will never be possible to hear everything—communication is fragile—what will matter in many settings is whether people who listen will, while paying attention to what is said, also watch out for what is not being heard. It will be important for those who listen to reflect on the limits to what they already know and how that affects what they are able to hear. Perhaps then people and the institutions they design will be able to listen for their own failures—and thus begin to live up to what justice after complex conflict or long-standing injustice demands.

The book then ends with a short meditation on how the relationship between selves, time, and other selves impacts our ideas and practices of justice and recovery.

I

Ethical Loneliness

Ethical loneliness is the experience of being abandoned by humanity compounded by the experience of not being heard. This chapter advances a phenomenology of sorts, describing how we are formed as selves and how this bears on ethical loneliness. Two thinkers who had deep experience of abandonment—Jean Améry and Emmanuel Levinas—are integral both to the philosophical structure of the argument and to its affective contour.

STORIES

We tell ourselves stories all the time about the kinds of selves we are. We're good at singing, bad at cooking. We are well loved by others, or maybe we are not. We are independent—no one's going to tell us what to do. Or we can't imagine who we would be separate from a loved one. We love cats, or dogs, or we think animals aren't meant to be domesticated. We are the type to nurture others, or maybe we tend to show them tough love. We need the help of others, or we don't. We identify with a gender, race, social class. We succeed. We fail. We belong, or we don't. We tell ourselves these stories. They may or may not be true. We may believe them whether or not they are true and whether or not they are good for us. In part these stories form who we are, again whether or not they are true or good for us.

Where do the stories come from? They come from our experience of the world, of course, and from our sense of who we are. But they also come from what other people say to us, from the values and truths produced by whatever cultures surround us, and from unspoken affective interactions between persons living alongside one another. For many of us, a deeply embedded story of who we are names us sovereign. We are autonomous selves, capable of consenting—or refusing to consent—to the conditions in which we live. Of course, many of us who tell ourselves that story also know that it leaves out part of the plot, since we didn't get to give birth to ourselves in a world we designed.[1] Instead, we landed, defenseless and in need of care, in a world already under way and as such full of rules, values, practices, and truths that we did not choose. If we are sovereign, it is in a dependent kind of way. Of course we know that.

In this chapter and those that follow I want to highlight moments when we may forget to know that. "We": a broad and large but not universal kind of first person plural made up of people who care about justice but whose lives have been lived mostly in a world safely taken for granted as benign—if not for everyone, at least for "us." I ask how well "we" know the limits to our autonomy not in order to rehearse another argument about free will or determinism but to draw attention to justice. Assumptions about the self's sovereignty are deeply embedded in prevalent ideas about justice. This is easily recognizable in the idea that we are responsible only for things we've done and intended, that we are blameworthy when we act with free will against standards we've accepted as our own, and that we lack culpability if we did not act freely or had no way of knowing what the rules require. There is nothing wrong with that idea on the face of it. But behind it lurk some problems, and I don't mean only the deservedly pervasively discussed ones about how social, political, and economic conditions undermine free will. There is something about the idea of autonomy that limits the stories we tell ourselves about who we are. And so we don't see very well who we are in certain circumstances. And so we may find ourselves developing strange ideas about how to proceed. That might be fine if all it meant is that we are deluded about our own selves. But I said I want to draw our attention to justice. I suspect that when we limit the stories we tell ourselves about what autonomy means for the kinds of beings we are, we miss something that matters more than a personal delusion might. If we misunderstand what autonomy is and what conditions its successful exercise requires, we may fail to comprehend how the selves and worlds of some human beings can be destroyed by other human beings. That might mean that we will have no idea how to listen to those who survive such harrowing loss. And, because we don't hear, we fail to learn something about the limits to our own autonomy and, more important, simply don't understand what conditions make successful recovery or reconciliation more or less likely after world-destroying events. Finally, we won't see how very unjust it is to believe, in some circumstances, that we are responsible only for what we've done and intended.

DESTRUCTION

At the beginning of his essay "At the Mind's Limits," Jean Améry admits that "the little word 'I' will have to appear here more often than I like, namely wherever I cannot take for granted that others have shared my personal experience."[2] How many of us have shared his experience? Raised in Austria, half Jewish and half Catholic by birth, a secular intellectual with a love of philosophy, he fled Austria in 1938 for France and then Belgium, where he spent time in the Belgian Resistance. Then came arrest, torture, and years in Auschwitz, Buchenwald, and Bergen-Belsen. Having changed his birth name, Hans Maier, to the Gallicized anagram Améry, after liberation he remained in exile, a writer composing in German but, for many years, refusing all German and Austrian outlets. Not many share his experience, not only because it is his own but also because it is made up of many layers of imposed isolation. It is that isolation—his ethical loneliness—that we need to understand in order to see what it was he sought to overcome in the postwar years, and what that search can tell us about the limits and possibilities of reconciliation.

At this historical moment some might not remember that there was a time after World War II when the Holocaust was not yet named or widely acknowledged for what it was.[3] Jean Améry committed suicide in 1978, at about the time Germany began to deal with its Nazi past in ways that stretched beyond the legalism of the Nuremberg and Auschwitz trials and into public consciousness by means of monuments, memorial sites, and civic education. Ruth Kluger, another survivor of the camps, describes in her memoir various of her experiences trying to communicate about her past in the United States in the years after World War II. Attending Hunter College in the 1940s, she found that in the consciousness of the Americans she encountered, "the Holocaust had no name yet, and hence it wasn't even an idea, only an event: among the other disasters of the Second World War, a lot of Jews had died."[4] It was not widely known that there had been a concerted effort to eliminate a group of people from the earth. Anton Gill shows how, between 1945 and the Eichmann trial (1961), even in Israel there was a tremendous silence around the Holocaust, an unwillingness to hear survivors' stories.[5] That puts Améry's struggle in a wider context: his resistance to forgiveness was in part a way to demand a wider recognition of the specific harms he had suffered, since no preexisting general term would capture adequately the horror of what he survived. As Kluger puts it, "A concept without a name is like a stray dog or feral cat. To domesticate it, you have to call it something."[6] Améry's resistance to the passing of time seeks a proper name for what happened to him.

What happened to Améry? I've already said that he was arrested, tortured, and interned in concentration camps. Readers understand what those things are. But those who have never been beaten, tortured, or otherwise dehumanized may lack the kind of understanding that brings to the fore the *harm* of these crimes. Améry himself admits that he thought he knew what was in store for him after his arrest. He had heard about beatings and torture and had prepared himself for the possibility that such things might befall him: "I regarded myself . . . as an old, hardened expert on the system, its men and its methods. . . . I thought there could be nothing new for me in this area. What would take place would then have to be incorporated into the relevant literature, as it were. Prison, interrogation, blows, torture; in the end, most probably death."[7] That police officers in both fascist and nonfascist states sometimes strike those they arrest is common knowledge, and often the public doesn't even protest, whether because they believe that those who get arrested are "bad guys" or they think physical abuse may be necessary to police interrogation, or they are certain such things could never happen to them. In all those cases, the *idea* of police brutality is just that—an abstraction. Améry thought his theoretical knowledge of what was in store for him had prepared him. But all that evaporated in the face of what he calls "the first blow":

Simple blows, which really are entirely incommensurable with actual torture, may almost never create a far-reaching echo among the public, but for the person who suffers them they are still experiences that leave deep marks. . . . The first blow brings home to the prisoner that he is helpless, and thus it already contains in the bud everything that is to come. (27)

Améry learned firsthand that no amount of knowledge can prepare a person for what physical abuse does. As he puts it, it turns a human being into a body. It does that in part by demonstrating to a person that he is powerless. That is why, though a gulf separates a punch in the face from torture, the first blow already begins to teach torture's lesson about power. For Améry, the reality of the first blow, rather than emerging as an interruption of the concrete everyday, reveals everyday life to be mostly a "codified abstraction," something that keeps us from standing "face to face with the event and, with it, reality" (26). The blow is real; daily life is abstract. He writes, "What one tends to call 'normal life' may coincide with anticipatory imagination and trivial statement" (26); the outcomes of our everyday actions tend to correspond with our expectations because of how mundane details get codified by our unreflective adherence to norms. As Jamie O'Connell points out,

most people possess a basic sense of security in the world: they go through daily life fairly confident that they will not be subjected to emotional or physical attack without warning, except perhaps in places they know to be particularly dangerous. Brutal abuse by another human being can shatter this, leaving the survivor constantly terrified of being subjected to the same torment again.[8]

For those who have never been left truly helpless, most of life passes without much demand that they confront the risks and responsibilities they incur simply by existing. For that reason, Améry takes issue with Arendt's thesis on the "banality" of evil: "When an event places the most extreme demands on us, one ought not speak of banality. For at this point there is no longer any abstraction and never an imaginative power that could even approach its reality."[9] Here Améry (like many others) misunderstands Arendt's meaning in using the term; he would likely agree that part of what was evil about how Nazis and many ordinary Germans treated Jewish

persons was its banality—the everyday ease with which they dehumanized people without applying moral categories. But Améry's point is that
the inescapable reality of violence cannot be called banal by those who
suffer it. He argues that, while it may have been initially shocking to him
that Gestapo officers possessed, in addition to pistols and leather coats,
ordinary faces, his treatment by those officers destroyed in him "all ab-
stractive imagination," converting them back into faces of evil because of
"how evil overlays and exceeds banality" (25).

He was beaten by the police officers who arrested him. He didn't give
up any information, at least in part because he had no information to give
up: his unit of the Resistance was organized in such a way that operatives
did not know the names or locations of other operatives. And so he was
transferred to Fort Breendonk, where he was tortured. Here is his initial
description of what happened:

> In the bunker there hung from the vaulted ceiling a chain that above
> ran into a roll. At its bottom end it bore a heavy, broadly curved iron
> hook. I was led to the instrument. The hook gripped into the shackle
> that held my hands together behind my back. Then I was raised with
> the chain until I hung about a meter over the floor. In such a position, or
> rather, when hanging this way, with your hands behind your back, for a
> short time you can hold at half-oblique through muscular force. Dur-
> ing these few minutes, when you are already expending your utmost
> strength, when sweat has already appeared on your forehead and lips,
> and you are breathing in gasps, you will not answer any questions.
> Accomplices? Addresses? Meeting places? You hardly hear it. All your
> life is gathered in a single, limited area of the body, the shoulder
> joints, and it does not react; for it exhausts itself completely in the
> expenditure of energy. But this cannot last long, even with people
> who have a strong physical condition. As for me, I had to give up
> rather quickly. And now there was a crackling and splintering in my
> shoulders that my body has not forgotten until this hour. The balls
> sprang from their sockets. My own body weight caused luxation; I
> fell into a void and now hung by my dislocated arms, which had
> been torn high from behind and were now twisted over my head.
> Torture, from Latin *torquere*, to twist. What visual instruction in
> etymology! At the same time, the blows from the horsewhip showered

down upon my body, and some of them sliced cleanly through the light summer trousers that I was wearing on this twenty-third of July 1943.

(32–33)

He points out that this is not the worst torture that can befall a captive. But he was broken, and not only because his shoulders were dislocated. Harm, when it is imposed by another human being, leaving neither hope of the self's resistance or another's assistance, may destroy a self: "You yourself suffer on your body the counter-man that your fellow man became. If no help can be expected, this physical overwhelming by the other then becomes an existential consummation of destruction altogether" (28).

Dehumanization is a common enough word, used to classify certain forms of bad treatment whereby human beings are deprived of their status as human beings, and it can describe many different kinds of bad treatment, so it may be necessary to describe further this particular denial of humanity, because understanding what dehumanizes also helps us determine what we take a human being to be. What Améry lost was his capacity to expect just treatment or help in the absence of such treatment. He writes that when harm is inflicted "against which there can be no defense and which no helping hand will ward off, a part of our life ends and it can never again be revived" (29). He calls what he underwent "the border violation of my self by the other, which can be neither neutralized by the expectation of help nor rectified through resistance" (33). He also names it a death—a death that was then drawn out over years of abuse and deprivation in concentration camps, where he was beaten, starved, forced to work without adequate clothing in freezing temperatures and to witness the deaths of his comrades. His humanity was denied consistently for years.

Améry tells us multiple times that his sovereignty was violated and that he never recovered: "Frail in the face of violence, yelling out in pain, awaiting no help, capable of no resistance" (33). But it is important to note that in the narrative he constructs, what is irreparable about what befell him is made up of equal parts loss of sovereignty and despair of all help. Human beings are always autonomous and dependent at the same time. If dehumanization destroys in a human being the capacity to expect help or just treatment, then part of what we take humanity to encompass is that the expectation of help or just treatment should be rewarded. That means that even beings who call themselves sovereign should know that they will need the help of others if that sovereignty is to be meaningful—sovereignty always relies on others who acknowledge its worth and thus observe its boundaries. Dehumanization is, in part, the refusal of that response. Sovereignty is dependence.[10]

DEPENDENCE

Améry writes, "I don't know if the person who is beaten by the police loses human dignity. Yet I am certain that with the very first blow that descends on him he loses something we will perhaps temporarily call 'trust in the world.'"[11] Trust in the world consists, for Améry, in "the certainty that by reason of written or unwritten social contracts the other person will spare me—or, more precisely stated, that he will respect my physical, and with it also my metaphysical, being" (28). He adds, "The expectation of help, the certainty of help, is indeed one of the fundamental experiences of human beings, and probably also of animals" (28).

Emmanuel Levinas points out that philosophers tend to think that truth consists in an "exhibition of being," the revelation of something that exists and is verifiably true. But, he continues, when philosophers stop there, they fail to ask *what shows itself* in truth and *who looks*.[12] This has something to do with the ability to make and hear cries for help. Levinas writes, "Why does research take form as a question? How is it that the 'what?' . . . becomes a demand and a prayer, a special language inserting into the 'communication' of the given an appeal for help, for aid addressed to another?"[13] Something exists; its existence is intelligible, truth, a given. And yet we still have questions about it. Such questions assume an interlocutor, someone who listens and responds and, in doing so, helps to confirm both the reality of the world and standards of shared living—everything from the "tiny ethics" of social etiquette to injunctions against murder and abuse. Questions and their assumed interlocutors thus open up a whole world beyond curiosity and research, leading us fairly directly to conditions necessary for human beings inhabiting a shared world. In a discussion of how he felt his intellectual life slipping away in the camps, Améry describes how some lines from Hölderlin's poetry occur to him during a march on a cold evening but no longer affect him as they once did: "Perhaps the Hölderlin feeling, encased in psychic humus, would have surfaced if a comrade had been present whose mood would have been somewhat similar and to whom I could have recited the stanza. The worst was that one did not have this comrade."[14] Améry's point was not that there were no other intellectuals in the camp but that for those who were there, it was difficult to sustain a belief in the reality of the life of the mind. Of the various poetic and philosophical sources of meaning that had once sustained him he writes, "Where they still meant something they appeared trivial, and where they were not trivial they no longer meant anything" (19). Améry had lost, among other things, the experience of intellectual inspiration that, for the person whose humanity has not been disregarded, seems private and, more significant, independent of others. His love of the life of the mind had gone missing not because he was kept from his studies but because the conditions imposed on him removed him from human community. Otherwise put, Améry is compelled to use the "little word 'I' " not because of an intellectual solitude, something he might have defined for himself in the work of thinking, such that he was in some way master of his own thoughts, his own inner life. What narrows his experience to an "I" is something more like a forced existential isolation. He had been abandoned by humanity.

Améry felt his love of the life of the mind slipping away in the camps. Levinas reveals that what feels like intellectual solitude to a free person is already a form of community: research takes form as a question, and a question addresses itself to others. That is an existential as much as an ethical truth.

EXISTING

It is easy enough to take one's own existence for granted. What would be the point or even the mechanism of "taking for granted" anything if I did not exist to do so? But there are conditions—or moods, or modes of attunement—that, if we examine them, reveal a human being's resistance to existence, to the fact that one *is*. Fatigue, weariness, indolence, these are positions taken with regard to existence. But the "taking" of a position, in these instances, doesn't feel like volition, as states like indolence and fatigue tend to arise against one's will. In *Existence and Existents* Levinas writes, "In weariness [*la lassitude*] existence is like the reminder of a commitment to exist, with all the seriousness and harshness of an unrevokable contract."[15] Self that I am, I'm stuck here in this body. Existence is a bond from which there is no release.

And yet we resist it. We look for escapes from being—and sometimes we find them for a moment in intoxication, aesthetic contemplation, sex, or other distractions. We find ways to release ourselves from the weight of existence. When Levinas points out that we all long to escape "being," he does not mean that we want to die. Death and suicide are ways out, of course. But for those who do live on, existing in the mode of resistance to that existence reveals something about the kinds of beings we are.

It's not that in every case of resistance we have *chosen* to resist. This isn't about rational or irrational choice. The refusal of existence is not a theoretical refusal—or is not only that. Not an autonomous decision, it is the *event* of refusal rather than the thought of refusal. Levinas describes the distinction as follows:

> When we take fatigue and indolence [*la fatigue et la paresse*] as contents [of thoughts], we do not see what is effected in them—or of what they are an impotent nonacceptance. Their whole reality is made up of that refusal. To take them as contents of the mind is to start by situating them in the flux of consciousness as "psychic realities," and then to ascribe to them, as a secondary property . . . an intention of refusal, a refusing thought. It is to interpret the event of refusal which they are in their very production . . . as a theoretical refusal.   (11)

When we think fatigue is the content of a thought, we give ourselves too much agency—we think we have fatigued intentions. But that mistakes what the event of fatigue is. An example: as most writers know, procrastination is not primarily the content of a thought but is rather the *event* of resistance to a weight one wishes to shed. I don't think to myself, "I am going to put off doing what I should be doing, what on some level I even want to be doing." Rather, I find myself in the midst of a refusal, failing to do what I aim to do. Procrastination is more mood than intention. If we think of weariness as the thought of weariness, and refusal to act as a decision we've made, that may help us blame ourselves and others for inaction. Such an account aligns nicely with retributive theories of justice and volitional theories of the subject, and both of those have important contributions to make to our ideas about selves and justice. But it leaves us with an incomplete picture of the kind of being a human being is. After all, how often do I get to *decide* to be tired of something? It's not that a weary being is lazy or has failed to make key decisions—or at least it is not only that—but that in moments of weariness, fatigue, and indolence, the weight of existence asserts itself.

Levinas takes the analysis a step further and says that when the weight of existence asserts itself, it allows us—if we take note—to *look* at existence rather than taking it for granted. Levinas writes, "Fatigue is not a cancellation of one's contract with being. The delay it involves is an inscription in existence, but what is peculiar to this inscription, its sort of hesitation, enables us to surprise it, to catch sight of the operation of assuming which the existence that is taken up already always involves" (25). If I pay attention to it, my lack of intention in the matter of my fatigue or procrastination might teach me something important about what a self is and how it is formed. When I am happy, full of energy, or simply up to the task at hand, existence does not strike me as a problem, does not strike me at all. It remains in the background. But I am not always happy or up to the task at hand, and in those moments I may experience existence as a weight—something that remains despite anything I will—but also as something that I must take up at every moment whether I will it or not. When I pause and consider that, I see existence: my resistance to it, the inevitable failure of that refusal, the need to take it up again each moment, and what, together, those things mean. There is a whole lot that is unchosen at the heart of a self's liberty. My sovereignty depends.

I might do nothing rather than the something demanded of the present instant: going to work, grading papers, cooking a meal, calling a friend, getting off the couch. In other words, I might lag behind the present moment rather than taking it up. But the moment will occur anyway. It's not that I somehow fail to be a self if I remain on the couch. When I am in the mode of fatigue, I may wish I didn't have to go on in the present moment. But life will go on—either in the mode of my taking it up or in the mode of my refusal to do so. If I remain in the mode of (willed or unwitting) refusal, indolence "may inhere in the act that is being realized, in which case the performance rolls on as on an ill-paved road, jolted about by instants each of which is a beginning all over again" (13). We all know such moments, sometimes making up whole days or weeks. We lag behind whatever present moment we are faced with, and so, rather than successfully avoiding our existence, we live it in the mode of bumbling, half-ass, wishful thinking or failure. Indolence "is a being afraid to live which is nevertheless a life" (17). Existence is mine, and each moment is a new beginning, beckoning me to take it on. That's freedom. But, again, my refusal to take up an instant is destined to fail. That's finite freedom. No escape.

Still, the sense of a freedom more than finite seizes us regularly. Levinas writes that "our first feeling, our ineradicable illusion, is a feeling or illusion of freedom" (44), and he suggests that this feeling comes from our relationship to intelligibility, the way things present themselves to us in the light of the world. What could be more obvious than my freedom to interact or not interact with objects in my surroundings? If I want to eat the apple sitting in a bowl in my kitchen, I'll reach out and do so. And if I don't, I won't, and so perhaps I am sovereign with regard to apples in my kitchen. Objects leave us room to reach toward them but also to withdraw from them. An object in light "comes from an exterior already apprehended and comes into being as though it came from us, as though commanded by our freedom" (41)—or so the Cartesian account assumes. "It is a way of relating to events while still being able to not be caught up in them. To be a subject is to be a power of unending withdrawal, an ability always to find oneself behind what happens to one" (42). Here we find the subject who is so confident that conditions will offer her a space of intelligibility that she does not even know that this belief requires confidence, or belief. She merely thinks that is what the world is.

It may be possible to live a whole life without having that confidence interrupted. One might call that the goal of liberal political theory, to provide or defend conditions where confidence in the intelligibility of the world may thrive. Those are not bad goals! We should note, however, that sites where such confidence remains secure are unequally portioned out across space, time, and other ways of dividing up worlds. What Levinas and Améry describe complicates the assumed inevitability of that security. If we pay heed, their descriptions may make it more difficult to take an easy autonomy for granted. We may see that the sovereign feeling sometimes possessed by human beings is not an essence but a product of human interaction. And that might open us up to recognizing a form of liberty—or even of law—that is a responsibility rather than an abstract freedom. If any of us has meaningful freedoms or legal protections—or if any of us lack them—that is the outcome not only of institutions but of a range of human relationships where responsibility is diffuse and not easily capturable in a story that focuses on consent to being governed and culpability for individual wrongdoing.

Groups of human beings can design just institutions, and they can also create dehumanizing conditions. Améry writes, "The Flemish SS-man Wajs, who—inspired by his German masters—beat me on the head with a shovel whenever I didn't work fast enough felt the tool to be an extension of his hand and the blows to be emanations of his psycho-physical dynamics."[16] What Améry means (in addition to making a jab at Heidegger's amoral phenomenology of tool use and perhaps also at his infamous membership in the Nazi Party) is that Wajs did not think of his actions in moral terms. He simply used a tool to do a job, and his job as he saw it was to beat a man over the head with a shovel.

Levinas composed most of *Existence and Existents* during his five years of captivity during World War II. He was more fortunate than Améry, but to say so strains the meaning of the word "fortunate."[17] Because he was naturalized as a French citizen and fighting in the French army, he was sent to the Jewish barracks of a forced-labor camp rather than to an extermination camp. He wasn't tortured, and he still had access to some books and to simple games played with fellow captives, but he writes, of that time, that "free" men, women, and children all "stripped us of our human skin. We were subhuman, a gang of apes."[18] He also describes his sense of abandonment and the attendant difficulty of retaining the life of the mind: "A small inner murmur, the strength and wretchedness of persecuted people, reminded us of our essences as thinking creatures, but we were no longer part of the world."[19] Emerging from captivity meant learning that his whole family in Lithuania had been murdered by Nazis with machine guns. He had lost the major part of what built his world. In such conditions it may be difficult to reclaim one's identity: who is left to corroborate it? His solace would be that his wife and daughter survived, and they were able to begin to rebuild a life together. He rarely wrote about this time of his life, but the dedication in French and English to *Otherwise Than Being* reads, "To the memory of those who were closest among the six million assassinated by the National Socialists, and of the millions on millions of all confessions and all nations, victims of the same hatred of the other man, the same anti-semitism."[20] Below that dedication is inscribed, in Hebrew, "To the memory of my father and master, Rabbi Yehiel son of Abraham the Levite, my mother and guide, Dvora daughter of Rabbi Moshe, my brothers Dov son of Rabbi Yehiel the Levite and Aminadav son of Yehiel the Levite, my father-in-law Rabbi Shmuel son of

Rabbi Gershon the Levite and my mother in law Malka daughter of Rabbi Chaim. May their souls be clutched in the link of life."[21] He prefaces his major work with both a general statement about victims of hatred or indifference and a personal record of the losses those forces imposed on his life. His philosophy is animated by the need to address the cause of those losses.

It is easy enough to take existence for granted if your life is easy enough that you are able to do so. Margaret Walker writes, "Some of us who have the good fortune to live in the safer parts of orderly societies in peaceful times are able to float down a stream of largely unreflective concern with implicit confidence that people will behave as they should in countless contexts."[22] That is how daily life can become what Améry called it—a "codified abstraction." Millions of human beings do not have that form of freedom. But even the easiest life will be punctuated by fatigue, weariness, and indolence. And those resistances may reveal to those who choose to look a relation to time and other beings that both redefines what a self is and helps us understand that selves and worlds are not essences but are, rather, cooperatively authored achievements and, as such, may be destroyed. That knowledge in turn clarifies a truth that is unintelligible if we define the self as simply autonomous: it shows why all of us—not only perpetrators of harms—*all of us* are responsible both for rebuilding destroyed selves and worlds and preventing their destruction in the first place.

The Self

Human selves differ in some respects from other objects in the world, which is why it is often harder to feel sovereign over another person than it is over apples in one's kitchen.[23] Other human beings might tell themselves different stories than I would tell, about themselves or about me. They might have different practices, resist my thoughts and plans, or they might challenge my assumptions about myself, others, and the world. We may tell ourselves we are sovereign selves because we wish that were true, or because we've been taught that it is true, but surely we also do that (when we do) because it is part of how we experience the world: most of the time, other people do not perfectly control us, and we do not perfectly control other people. Each of us has our own powers of liberty. In other words, our selves may be cooperatively authored, but we are also *auto-*

nomos: we "give the law to ourselves."[24] At any given moment, the law you give to yourself may not be one I have chosen. And we both may have to reckon with what that means. But that does not land us back in a site where autonomy amounts to the kind of self-sufficiency that gets to choose what will affect the self.

Levinas, in his later work *Otherwise Than Being*, describes the human self as compound, made up of parts we might call self, ego, and me, all residing in a bodily frame that is vulnerable and undeniably affected by others.[25] He theorizes that subjectivity is subjection to other human beings: the subject is a hostage, persecuted by the other, bearing infinite responsibility and owed nothing in return—an alarming set of assertions. Instead of describing an always-already autonomous being that is by definition free to make decisions about right and value unaffected by others, Levinas gives us a subject formed in heteronomy and responsive to others long before freedom is possible. His intent is not to deny our freedom but to draw attention to the vulnerability that defines us as embodied beings and thus bears on what freedom can be for us.

Here is roughly how self-formation "works" for Levinas: The "me" part of the self senses the demand of an other, responds despite itself, and thus is pressed by a responsibility it never chose. And so it tries to escape. It flees into itself to evade the demands of responsibility. But when the "me" retreats into the self, it finds the ego there already having taken up residence. That movement of the "me" into the self interrupts the sovereignty that the ego formerly thought it possessed. Note that this self-revelation occurs in interior space but is put in motion by what is not-me—"the other"—and thus I am "ego" and "me" and "other" all at once, deep within myself. I am separate and invaded at the same time. The ego will still insist on its existential solitude and will operate as if it were perfectly autonomous, owing nothing it didn't choose to owe. But the "me" will continuously interrupt the ego's assertion of independence, because it will keep trying to retreat inward to escape the demands placed on it by the presence of others—and all of this transpires fairly constantly in waves of affectivity wrought by human sense.[26]

Levinas's description of the human self helps to counter a tendency to accept an unproblematic autonomy as the defining feature of humanity. If the self just is defined as exposed, vulnerable, and formed in part in relation to others, it may make it more intelligible for us why human beings are able to destroy the selves and worlds of other human beings.

It also does justice to the depth of the attachments we form, since vulnerability is not only a negative asset: it may open us to abuse, oppression, and death, but it also makes possible friendship, solidarity, and love. It is deeply engrained in the Western self to define its relation to others in terms of its autonomy: others are out there and I choose to interact with them from within the protected site of my self. Levinas describes the encounter otherwise, arguing that the presence of others

> signifies not the disclosure of a given and its reception, but the exposure of me to the other, prior to every decision. There is a claim laid on the same by the other in the core of myself, the extreme tension of the command exercised by the other in me over me, a traumatic hold of the other on the same, which does not give the same the time to await the other.[27]

It isn't that I find myself at the start fully self-sufficient and capable of deciding for or against solidarity with others. Rather, others have already laid claim on me, called me to respond to them before I am able to choose to be affected. Self-formation is like a trauma striking against a self that would be autonomous. That may give us a richer sense of what it means to be a human being in general, but it also speaks directly to the sense of self inhabited by survivors of violence, who may find it more difficult to give themselves the useful fiction of autonomy. As Judith Herman puts it, "Traumatic events destroy the victim's fundamental assumptions about the safety of the world, the positive value of the self, and the meaningful order of creation."[28] A trauma survivor's sense of the self's independence has been interrupted by violence. That sense is part of what should be restored by transitional justice or reconciliative efforts. But just as law cannot tell us whether or not we should obey law, autonomy cannot instruct us in how to restore it where it has been lost or never gained in the first place.

ETHICAL LONELINESS

Let's consider Levinas' description the self's finite freedom and its relation to others again, this time with a view to describing ethical loneliness. In *Existence and Existents*, Levinas begins by drawing our attention to the impersonality of what he calls the *there is*. It is the brute fact of existence, indifferent to human plans, and yet always there rumbling in the background. These are the conditions in which a human being becomes something substantive against the backdrop of impersonal existence. A human being, unlike a chair or a sandwich, can take on her own being and thereby become a substance that carries existence, a consciousness bearing stable attributes. Levinas writes: "It is this coming out of a self, this appropriation of existence by an existent, which the 'I' is [*qu'est le «je»*]."[29] So each of us attains possession of the first-person pronoun "I" by turning the event of our self into the substance of our self, by taking on the present moment freely: by doing something and being something other than a chair or a sandwich.

However, this assuming of Being is not a simple freedom, because the self finds itself stuck in an existential solitude. No matter how broad a freedom your consciousness might devise, it is unceasingly riveted to your own self. Self and ego, body and mind, these are one. As Levinas puts it, "the freedom which is accomplished in cognition does not free the mind from every fate."[30]

So, I am stuck with myself, alone in my human frame. But the formation of my self occurs as a desire for escape from that solitude. I want out. But every attempt at standing outside the self—say, in sex, intoxication, sleep, reading, or viewing art, and so on—leads one back to the self. Indeed, every attempt at *ec-stasis* is made by means of the materiality of the body, and so the means of escape is also the ultimate reminder of one's being riveted, without parole, to one's own existence: you finish, sober up, or wake up right there in the same inescapable location: your self. The desire to escape the self is endless because it is impossible.

But therein lies a hope. I am riveted to my own existential solitude. But the other, an other human being, opens doors that would not exist in a world without others. That is true because the other human being is exterior to me in a way different from the way a sandwich or a chair is exterior to me. An other human being has her own self, his own solitude, and thus the space between us is intersubjective space, freighted with a giving of signs that precedes communication in language, as well as the possibility of bringing "me" out of myself and into a world.

So, we have (1) the indifference of brute existence, (2) human beings transcending brute existence by taking on the present moment and becoming selves, (3) selves finding themselves stuck with themselves, unable to escape but desiring escape, and (4) a way out offered by the presence of others. A self is not truly in a world until consciousness becomes communication. Research takes form as a question.

In the camps Améry lost his intellectual solitude, his love of the life of the mind, but that was not the measure of his ethical loneliness. Torture, internment, and dehumanization forced on him a condition of existential solitude—stuck-in-himself—but one where the way out offered by another human being was refused to him. Ethical loneliness begins when a human being, because of abuse or neglect, has been refused the human relation necessary for self-formation and thus is unable to take on the present moment freely.

Stories, Part 2

In 1980 in South Africa, Charity Kondile's son was killed by Dirk Coetzee and members of a counterinsurgency unit of the police.[31] More than ten years passed between her son, Sizwe's, disappearance and her learning what had befallen him. One day Mrs. Kondile picked up a newspaper reporting on testimony at a commission put together to investigate that police unit. She read there that her son had been apprehended, tortured to the point of having a brain hemorrhage, given poison to kill him, which didn't work, then transported to a remote farm and shot, and finally burned in a fire. In her testimony before the South African Truth and Reconciliation Commission (TRC) she says,

> Well Dirk Coetzee goes on further to say that when he died, they put his body on a pile of wood with a tyre near the Komatiepoort River at night, where it took them nine hours to burn his body. Dirk Coetzee further states that twice they were burning his body, the flesh was smelling good, and they were having beers at the time. So it was like a *braai* [barbecue] to them.[32]

Her testimony also covers how the lives of her family were transformed by their loss: Sizwe's sister suffering from depressive psychosis, a brother so depressed he cannot take care of himself, a child left fatherless, and Mrs. Kondile herself, the mother, who, instead of being supported by the surrounding community, was treated like a traitor when her son disappeared because those who knew him too quickly assumed he had betrayed his cause. As she puts it,

I was very disappointed to learn that people who had been so friendly to my son about six months [before he disappeared] should have turned against him so soon, and according to Mark Antony, when he says, "Oh judgment thou art fled to brutish [beasts] and men have lost their reason," that's a quotation I taught, that it seems . . . when I'm so anguished, looking for him, these people would not sympathize with me, they would still think I was telling lies.[33]

It is a dynamic story of loss. Mrs. Kondile did not only lose a son. She lost the sense that she could expect that she and her loved ones would be protected from harm. She also lost the security of living in a community where she could trust that, if she were to be harmed, she would be helped, and her harms recompensed. Like Améry, she lost the sense both that she could expect just treatment and that she would be offered help if treated unjustly. She lost a world, and so she lost some of the conditions necessary for coherent self-formation.

Susan Brison took a walk by herself on a rural lane in France one day, where she was hit from behind, forced to the side of the road, beaten, and raped. Her attacker then tried to strangle her to death multiple times, dragging her into a ravine and leaving her there for dead. Recovery from such treatment is more than a nursing of wounds—and of those she had plenty: multiple head injuries, a fractured trachea, a body covered with scratches and bruises, and both her eyes swollen shut.[34] Brison writes of the experience, "I had ventured outside the human community, landed beyond the moral universe, beyond the realm of predictable events and comprehensible actions, and I didn't know how to get back" (ix–x). Extreme violence delivered a message to her: that her self's own sovereignty remains intact only as long as others observe its boundaries. And so she, like Améry, lost her trust in the world: "The fact that I could be walking down a quiet, sunlit country road at one moment and be battling a murderous attacker the next undermined my most fundamental assumptions about the world" (26). This is the trauma of loss of safety. In particular, it is the loss of the sense the lucky among us have that other human beings will treat us as human beings rather than as objects to be disposed of or abused at will.

Brison learned this from being attacked. But the message was delivered in all its complexity as she worked to recover. She discovered that her new self had to be one that was painfully aware that selves are "both autonomous and socially dependent, vulnerable enough to be undone by violence and yet resilient enough to be reconstructed with the help of empathic others" (38)—and that getting the help of others is a complicated thing. Not only in cases of rape but also in muggings, cancer diagnoses, and bad fortune in general there is a will in the human self to believe it could not happen to "me" and so a distancing of that self from a hard truth of any trauma story: that it could happen to anyone.[35] Schooled in the idea of personal autonomy, we don't easily receive lessons about "the limits of the individual's capacity to control her own self-definition."[36] We are vulnerable creatures prey to harm, and most of our fellow beings on whom these evils befall do nothing to deserve them. But we want to believe it could not happen to us, so we may look for "reasons" why it has happened to someone else, and we may even avoid those who have been mistreated. Brison mentions how various of her extended family and friends, who would surely have sent cards if she were hospitalized for an appendectomy, remained silent.[37] If asked to defend themselves, each one of them would, we can guess, surely say that she or he did not know what to say in response to such a grave harm. But if the murderous twentieth and twenty-first centuries have taught us anything, surely it is that saying or doing nothing is another harm. Brison writes, "Each time someone failed to respond, I felt as though I were alone again in the ravine, dying, screaming. And still no one could hear me. Or, worse, they heard me, but refused to help."[38]

Returning to the moment of trauma is a symptom of trauma. But if such trauma is caused in part by a failure of protection, and failure of protection indicts not only those who inflicted harm but also all those who contribute to the world where such harms happen in widespread or systematic ways, then we are all responsible—to varying degrees—for recovery from and prevention of such harms. Lack of response to harm is what rendered Améry unable to move forward. In particular he could not forget "the sight of the Germans on a small passenger platform where, from the cattle cars of our deportation train, the corpses had been unloaded and piled up; not on a single one of their stony faces was I able to detect an expression of abhorrence."[39] Those bystanders may have been bigoted and full of hatred, they may have thought Jews were subhuman, or they may instead have been afraid to show any discomfort with what was happening in a totalitarian state where whatever Hitler ordered was law. The point to take away from this, in this instance, is that it doesn't matter to Améry what drives their indifference, just as it may not matter to Brison what led some of her friends and family to ignore her injuries and fail to hear her story, or to Kondile what made her neighbors call her son a traitor and fail to help her through a terrible ordeal. Having undergone an unjust injury at the hands of other human beings, Améry, Kondile, and Brison needed to have the wrongness of what befell them confirmed and denounced, not mainly by legal institutions or perpetrators but by the surrounding society in which they would have to live henceforth. They all needed help rebuilding a destroyed world. Walker argues that "victims of wrongful harm often experience as much or more rage, resentment, indignation, or humiliation in response to the failure of other people and institutions to come to their aid, acknowledge their injury, reaffirm standards, place blame appropriately on wrongdoers, and offer some forms of solace, safety and relief as victims experience toward the original wrongdoer."[40] That is a way of saying that survivors seek release from ethical loneliness, the sense of having been abandoned by humanity. They want the harms they have undergone to be heard and the wrongness of them affirmed in a lasting way not only by the perpetrators but also by the surrounding society. They seek the help of others to reassure them that they are living in a world with others, one where they will be protected when they are under threat. Only in conditions such as those might they be able to take existence for granted, or take on the present moment freely.

The reasons why support systems failed in these three cases are of course very different given the different cultural and historical contexts. But we can observe something about the failures that caused feelings of abandonment in these differently situated persons. Each person testifies to having been pushed beyond the confines of the shared human world into a space of abandonment by violence or oppression. Each experiences a difficulty in getting the story she or he most wants to tell heard on its own terms. And each person, while singular and deserving of justice on that scale, surely stands for a wider experience of failure and abandonment that also requires redress. All of that will matter to a discourse of reconciliation. As the handbook *Reconciliation after Violent Conflict* puts it,

> Good democratic politics—even the best politics—only work when relationships between the various actors are positive enough to permit basic trust, respect and cooperation. Bad relationships—those still

built on distrust, suspicion, fear, accusation, even ignorance—will effectively and eventually destroy any political system based on respect for human rights and democratic structures.[41]

In every scene of reconciliation there is a complicated series of bad relationships. Trials, truth commissions, and like institutions can't change them on their own, and unless those relationships can be transformed, law and the truth are not sufficient to get the job of reconciliation done. Continuing ethical loneliness is one expression of a failure after grave harm to restore—or, in many cases, to build for the first time—social relationships or, at the very least, conditions of meaningful safety.

LONELINESS

Recovery from mass violence and historic injustice is a complex affair, especially since recent scientific and psychological research has also shown that what is true of trauma is also true of loneliness: it rewrites genetic codes and hormonal signals, causes illness, and slows ability to recover.[42] It negatively impacts one's trust in the world. In 1958 Frieda Fromm-Reichmann argued that loneliness was at the heart of most mental illness, but that loneliness is not the solitude of the writer, the isolation of the artist, or the seclusion of the person waiting to recover from illness—rather, it is the want of intimacy. Since then psychologists have shown that closeted gay men suffering from AIDS-related illnesses are more likely to die quickly than those who have a support system; that college freshmen are the most unhappy not when they have few friends but when they have no close friends; that social exclusion, even if it is only imagined, lights up the same part of the brain where physical pain is expressed; that babies who are not held and cared for show irregular brain development; that baby monkeys kept isolated from their mothers and all other monkeys do not develop the ability to mingle with other monkeys; that in monkeys kept from their mothers for the first four months of life immunity-related genes are suppressed; but that when those monkeys are delivered over to foster care, "about half of their genetic deviations vanished"; and so on.[43] There is something telling about this, that even once we have read the studies relying on listening to excluded persons or scanning the brains of people isolated by social forces, some would still want the kind of proof that comes from abusive treatment of animals—and all this, for what? To prove that we need one another.

And so, while I might agree with the conclusions of scientists who have shown that the dorsal anterior cingulate cortex of the brain lights up equally when we are rejected as when we are physically harmed—meaning that the affective component of pain is similar in both situations—I doubt we need to isolate baby monkeys in order to prove that we are caught in the sway of our relations to others both affectively and rationally. After all, "a study of 8000 identical Dutch twins found that, if one twin reported feeling lonely and unloved, the other twin would report the same thing 48 percent of the time. This figure held so steady across pairs of twins . . . that researchers concluded that it had to reflect genetic, not environmental influence."[44] But even if that study gives us an accurate picture of how genes might influence human loneliness, 52 percent of what makes twins (or anyone else) grow up lonely comes from the surrounding world.[45] And so, the surrounding world is likely to make all the difference.

There is a loneliness that comes from being alone, from losing love or a loved one, or from feeling out of step with one's surroundings. That loneliness, whether fleeting or desperate, still has a world. Other people may recognize it and offer help. Social support may compensate for loss. It would be a category mistake to equate such loneliness with the abandonment undergone by those whose selves and world have been destroyed by human violence. Améry and Kondile—and, to a lesser extent, Brison—had multiple layers of isolation imposed on them. The differences in extent come not from what harms befell them but from the surrounding world's response: for Brison, a successful court case and sexual violence support groups helped her rebuild a world where she could live, even if she would never fully regain the sense of safety she once had. But even Brison experienced what for Améry and Kondile truly compounded their devastation: the silence and inaction of others. There are layers of betrayal in all these cases. Some of Brison's friends and relatives stood by her, listened carefully to her painful story, and lent support over the long period required for recovery. But some did not. Kondile's loss was orchestrated not only by the police who killed her son and the government that authorized that killing but also by members of her community who believed he was a traitor and officials both of the government and of community organizations who did not apologize for treating her family unjustly. Améry's continuing resentment was aimed not only at those who participated in his destruction but also at those who stood by while it happened, the younger generation that seemed to him to be sick of hearing about what their parents had done, and even at the silence of many of his fellow camp survivors. In all three cases, many of those who acted wrongly—or who simply did not contribute to rebuilding selves and worlds—are not what the law would call perpetrators. Neighbors, friends, relatives, the next generation, even fellow survivors, most of them people who never intended harm—all implicated. And so all three cases point to why responsibility for rebuilding worlds and selves after conflict must fall widely rather than focusing narrowly on law's story about criminal culpability. I'll develop this point throughout the book.

Améry, Kondile, and Brison all have some choice in how they tell the stories of what happened to them, to themselves and to others. But they lack control over what stories will be heard and who will listen—even when they speak to themselves. That is true of all of us, but, as chapter 3 shows, how this affects us varies according to power and luck. If stories lack support, they may begin to seem unreal, even to those who lived them. Human life, even in its privacy, relies on a cooperatively authored world. For those whose world has been destroyed, the absence of a willing audience is a second harm compounding the original violation.[46] Ending up pinned to the wrong story or no story at all might make recovery impossible, tying futures to past injuries. As Levinas has shown, research takes form as a question. Even my capacity to own my own intellectual solitude relies on my ability to trust that I am part of a world and that I can expect just treatment and help when I need it; it is already a form of sociality. Barbara Hernnstein Smith has written that narrative consists of "someone telling someone else something that happened."[47] It is not accomplished by a person acting alone. Susan Brison adds that narrative "is a social interaction—actual or imagined or anticipated or remembered—in which what gets told is shaped by the (perceived) interests of the listeners, by what the listeners want to know and also by what they cannot or will not hear."[48] A survivor whose story cannot or will not be heard is likely also someone whose harms have not yet been addressed. And if that is true, it is likely also true that social conditions do not yet exist that would make successful political transition or societal reconciliation possible.

Nietzsche says a similar thing in a different way. He admits that we don't get to choose all our influences, and that those influences work on us in ways we do and do not consciously note. In *Daybreak* he writes, "Out of damp and gloomy days, out of solitude, out of loveless words directed at us, conclusions grow up in us like fungus: one morning they are there, we know not how, and they gaze upon us."[49] We aren't sole masters of who we are—we are molded by our relations to others. Those relations and the larger world form us, and then we find others within ourselves (as Levinas also describes), judging us for who we are and aren't, in ways that may or may not be fair. We tell these stories to ourselves at least in part because our selves and worlds are cooperatively authored things.

But Nietzsche also writes the following: "Woe to the thinker who is not the gardener but only the soil of the plants that grow up in him."[50] You can take what is given, what you didn't get to choose, and live with it in many different ways. As chapter 4 shows, this means that the past is subject to revisions that may make the present moment more—or less—livable for those whose unjust pasts should have been otherwise. Nietzsche would have each of us create new worlds by the sheer power of our individual wills. But capacity to do that may also vary according to power and luck. (Indeed, Nietzsche, Améry, and Brison all had deep experience of the kind of "unreflective concern" that allows a person to take existence for granted *before* they underwent harm—or, in Nietzsche's case, illness. Many survivors have never had the liberty of that experience, and so the stories they tell say different things—as we will see in chapters 3 and 5.) So maybe what we aim to do, when we undertake a revisionary practice like a truth commission, transitional justice, or any of the various alternatives to those that spring up wherever harm needs repair, is to create conditions where all have equal power, each to be gardener of her own self. But, as the analysis of ethical loneliness begins to show, and the next chapters demonstrate, it will take more than the rule of law, individual responsibility, or faith in the liberatory power of political autonomy to make that possible.

2

Repair

No one is immune from wanting a master narrative, from wanting to be comforted by coherence.
—Teresa Godwin Phelps, *Shattered Voices*

Many things need repair. We know that economies, structures of governance, communities, civil relationships, and individual persons may need repair after oppression or violence. Those whose lives have been lived at a distance from the shadow of those misfortunes may neglect to note that their own selves may need repair. I don't mean only that ethical loneliness happens everywhere, even in settings rife with affluence and privilege. Of course we should pay attention to practices that isolate and dehumanize persons wherever they occur. But there is another site of repair: the attitudes, ideas about responsibility, and the sense of self of the person who does not feel implicated in the breadth and depth of this world's widespread uses of oppression, violence, and social isolation to destroy human beings and the communities where they dwell.

The other chapters of this book draw our attention to ethical loneliness as a widespread problem, show how practices of hearing often fail—even in institutions designed to hear and staffed by persons who want to hear well—and discuss what is at stake in practices of revision and retribution for those who have been harmed and for those who have not. This chapter pauses for a moment in the path of the book's main argument, to accomplish two things. It explores the possibilities and limitations presented by trials and truth commissions as responses to mass injustice. And it shows why, though trials and truth commissions are forms of response that are worthy of support, it is important not to let the field of response to grave and widespread harm be utterly dominated by them.

Trials and truth commissions are central to most claims about transitional justice and political reconciliation. And so this chapter functions both as necessary background to my larger argument and as delineation of what this book does not set out to accomplish. This book is not about trials and truth commissions. That means, among other things, that thinking about response to violence from the standpoint of ethical loneliness allows us to change the subject. It is important to honor the achievements of the responsive institutions that have been created in the past few decades. But we must focus also on what we don't know and what these institutions can't do.

Approaching Repair

Political reconciliation, political forgiveness, and transitional justice, all of these big ideas are reparative: each in its own way seeks to mend significant harms. Their purposes for doing so may vary—across cultures and institutions and within a single organization. However, whether the aim be justice, a future less rife with conflict, improved personal relationships, political expediency, or any of the many other aspirations that may surface postconflict, the processes all rely on an assumption that repair is possible. The assumption may not hold in all cases.[1]

In order to discern whether repair is possible, we need to know what repair is. And, in the wake of oppression and violence inflicted on human beings by other human beings, in order to understand what repair is, we need to recognize what breaks selves and worlds. In turn, in order to comprehend what breaks a self or a world, we ought to know something about what selves and worlds are—how they are formed, what sustains them. Finally, we need to understand how to make judgments about what can be repaired, what should be repaired, what cannot be repaired, and, perhaps, what should be left broken.

In her book *Repair: The Impulse to Restore in a Fragile World*, Elizabeth Spelman lays out different approaches to repair.[2] A master mechanic might fix a car by thinking beyond the car's repair guide, using what she knows about the design and purpose of the machine to get it working again. With that kind of repair, consolation for loss may not be needed, because the car fills its function as well after the fix as it did before. But if that same car were of a rare vintage and in the hands of a fan of its authenticity, the aim of repair might not be simply to get the car running but to keep as closely as possible to the original design—perhaps using only original parts even if those might be difficult to find or less efficient overall. In that case, re-creating authenticity offers consolation for the inevitable change that time brings. It does its best to keep an irretrievable past intact. However, a collector faced with the breakage, or even simply the decay, not of a machine but of a priceless work of art might make different decisions, weighing the pros and cons of both intervention and letting be—after all, any intervention is a form of creativity. One might even call it authorship. An expert in art restoration thus works to avoid leaving signs of her own work and makes judgments about what kinds of change can be responsibly introduced. She might even decide to let time's effect on an artwork stand. In that case, repair's consolation may be that not every change that time brings about is bad, or that damages can be mitigated if not fully erased. For Spelman, what all these possible orientations toward repair elucidate is that repair is not neutral. It is an intervention preceded by decisions made about value. About such decisions people are likely to disagree. And so, when we consider repairing human relationships and human damages, it is prudent to proceed thoughtfully and carefully, working in tandem with all stakeholders, because, as Spelman reminds us, "just because something is broken or damaged doesn't mean it should be fixed or that anyone or everyone is entitled to fix it."[3]

I sometimes suspect that some portion of the tremendous weight of hope tethered to forgiveness and reconciliation in the international justice community is symptomatic of a lack of reflection on, for instance, what people are being asked to forgive. I don't intend that as an accusation against anyone who writes about forgiveness but rather as a reminder that forgiveness, for all of us but perhaps especially for survivors of grave harm, may be easier said than done. Forgiveness is a tremendous gift and opportunity for any person, community, or polity that can manage it. But those who focus solely on that goal may neglect to dwell long enough on other questions, such as, What other old or new ways are there of redressing harm? What set of conditions would make forgiveness a goal worth reaching, or capable of being sustained (and what conditions render it less meaningful)? When might resentment and resistance be vital political expressions that should be heard alongside the discourse of repair? Might resentment and other negative affects even be, on occasion, more restorative than forgiveness? While these questions (to which we return in chapter 4) clearly evince a skepticism about some trends in the theory and practice of political reconciliation and transitional justice, my larger argument simultaneously makes a claim on behalf of the goals of those fields. We do owe something to the human beings whose selves, lives, and worlds have been torn apart by human violence and indifference. By "we" I mean the diffuse and large but not universal "we" of those who care about justice. It is important to think about what trials, truth commissions, and like institutional responses can *and cannot* achieve for recovering persons, communities, and nations.

JUSTICE AND TIME

Embedded in the argument about what best gets the work of transitional justice or political reconciliation done is a disagreement about time. On the one hand, the aim of a just proceeding is retributive, aimed at the past. For the retributive approach, past harms must be recognized, and those guilty of them punished or censured in some way to do justice to past harms, rebalance the scales. Retribution grants just deserts to those who have failed to live up to minimal legal standards. Proponents of that idea insist that it is the only way to end impunity for those who abuse the human rights of others. They often attach to that claim a hope that retributive proceedings will offer healing, catharsis, or closure for victims.

But there is also the other hand, reaching toward the future with arguments of restorative justice. For that hand, the aim is to rebuild community or to build it anew where it never before existed. That might mean replacing retributive legal proceedings with a different kind of institution, such as a truth commission or a set of reparative measures that may even include amnesty for some perpetrators. The goal is to begin to create a world that all parties might hold in common. It is widely believed that some combination of truth and forgiveness contributes to that goal.

Roughly put, retribution is about the past; restorative approaches focus on the present and future. Of course both approaches have a more complicated relationship to temporality than that—restoration does deal with a past as much as retribution seeks to create a certain kind of present moment and future. In the lived world where these approaches get used, the categories often blur and then combine themselves with theories of deterrence and rehabilitation. So, even though trials are usually thought to be the best sites for giving alleged criminals what they deserve, some argue that truth commissions that name names also mete out "just deserts" even if amnesty is awarded, since offenders will henceforth have to live in a society where everyone knows what they did. That is a different way to approach retribution and the problem of impunity. If everyone knows you tortured and murdered people, your daily life may not leave you feeling like you "got away" with something even if political amnesty keeps you out of prison. In turn, though truth commissions are thought to be the more restorative approach, many scholars and activists argue that trials do as good or better a job as do truth proceedings at building or rebuilding a shared world. The idea here is that court cases help to bring into being a society governed by the rule of law where all are treated with equal respect, and also help to establish the truth of what happened. "Retributive" trials can be restorative and "restorative" truth commissions can mete out retribution. The categories blur. All approaches are imperfect. And every nation or community struggling to move forward after violence or historic injustice will have a different set of limitations and possibilities to work with. And yet, despite the overlap, these forms are not the same.

TRIALS

When they work, criminal trials help to establish the rule of law, demonstrate to those who were victimized that crimes will not go unpunished, and begin to set up a societal expectation that justice is both possible and owned equally by all. Juan E. Méndez argues that after a long period of violence and inequality trials are preferable to truth commissions because the strict processes for obtaining *legal* truth produce a trustworthy record: if courts can show that irrefutable evidence was obtained under fair conditions, then others can't dispute the truth of the findings as subjective. That will matter in a setting where some portion of the injustice comes from people denying truths or subscribing to conflicting accounts of what happened.[4] Méndez suggests that wherever a truth proceeding replaces criminal prosecution, there is danger that it will be seen as a disguise for impunity—especially where amnesty is offered to perpetrators. Letting by-gones be bygones is morally wrong, he argues, "because it fails to recognize the worth and dignity of each victim. It is also politically wrong because it sets the new political order on the weak foundation of privilege and the denial of the rule of law."[5]

He is not alone in thinking this. Muhamed Sacirbey, former Bosnian foreign minister and ambassador to the United Nations, argues, "War and diplomacy have been the instruments defining our regional and global relations, and more often than not leaving much wanting. Increasingly though, it is becoming recognized that no conflict is truly dowsed and no peace and reconciliation is lasting without the rule of law and at least the impression that justice prevails."[6] Sacirbey voices a common belief that justice must be seen to be done and attaches it to a hope that law will accomplish that. Along those lines, a group of psychiatrists studying forgiveness in South Africa found that, though forgiving attitudes correlated with fewer symptoms of PTSD (post-traumatic stress disorder) and depression, "the perceived absence of justice (i.e., punishment of perpetrators and compensation of survivors) in the TRC process, about which many have protested, may have been a barrier to recovery. If justice is done, and seen to be done, psychological healing may be facilitated."[7] These researchers suggest that truth without justice does not achieve a full recovery. In turn, in Argentina, legal punishment of state terrorism seems to have solidified for both elites and survivors of political violence that henceforth all would be equal before the law.[8] Douglas Johnson, executive director of the Center for Victims of Torture, observes that the trials that did succeed in being held in Argentina had a "very salutary effect for victims."[9] Jamie O'Connell, citing a conversation with Johnson, points out that the trials "documented the extent of the dictatorship's human rights violations and their impact on victims, and firmly placed the blame on the military's top commanders," adding that such awareness might not have come about if the trials had not happened.[10] For some nations and individuals, an end to impunity accomplished by legal trials can help begin to free the present and future from determination by past harms. It can begin the work of repair.

Whether or not a trial will "work" will depend on social context as well as institutional capabilities. That is why Mariane Ferme argues that scholars need to stop arguing about whether tribunals are "a good idea" and instead ask "what difference they make."[11] That will mean understanding local context and listening well to those most impacted by the abuses. If there aren't enough judges or lawyers who can do the work, as was the case in Rwanda after the genocide, the system won't function.[12] If the judges and lawyers who are available are known to have been involved with a past criminal regime, people will not trust in the fairness of the proceedings and may even fear participating in them.[13] If social upheaval has not traditionally been handled in legal proceedings, legal judgments may not succeed in renewing the sense of community that was lost.[14] If courts use laws or procedures that are unfamiliar to the communities most affected by the violence, the people may not see justice being done.[15]

For instance, when the International Criminal Tribunal for the former Yugoslavia (ICTY) started accepting plea bargains, the confessions that followed helped establish the truth of crimes that might otherwise have remained hidden.[16] When Serbs who planned or participated in massacres confessed to what happened, that actually helped many in Serbia and Croatia accept the tribunal as unbiased rather than dismissing it as a witch hunt. That made "the continuing denials and revisionism about the war more difficult and the tribunal more acceptable."[17] But plea bargaining is not native to the judicial systems of the former Yugoslavia and so is often misunderstood or rejected as unfair by victims who hear about the trials' outcomes. Activist Lepa Mladjenovic reported that "the polls say that most of the population (93 percent) do not know that Plavšić was responsible for ethnic cleansing in 32 communities in Bosnia, for which she pleaded guilty. But they know that there is a sauna in her prison."[18] Rather than being happy about the confessions and the closing of cases, many survivors were distressed at the lighter sentences handed out. There were also concerns for fairness: "Relatives of wartime prison camp victims were furious when a guard who pleaded guilty to killing five inmates was sentenced to eight years, whereas lower-level guards who went to trial got twenty."[19] Serge Brammertz, prosecutor at the ICTY, related on a conference panel that when the charges in the case against Ratko Mladić were reduced to speed the case along, that decision had to be explained to victims' groups, who weren't happy about it—after all, in a domestic court system every murder is prosecuted.[20] (In a domestic system each case is considered separately—even if not prosecuted—while in international proceedings a reduction of charges in cases of mass murder may leave large numbers of unjust deaths unaddressed.) So even if plea bargaining helped some Serbs accept the ICTY as legitimate, it disappointed some Bosnian

Muslims who wanted more consistent outcomes from the trials. And the continuing legacy of distrust of the ICTY in Serbia speaks to how even truths arrived at using legal procedures may fail to convince a broader audience.

A criminal trial is focused mainly on perpetrators; in a court of law victims' stories matter only if they help to establish the narrow facts of a case as it is perceived by a prosecutor or defense attorney. Adversarial processes may fail to respect the experience of victims or even reawaken their trauma, leaving them worse off than before in terms of their feelings of recovery and of support from the surrounding society. Even processes that are less adversarial, such as inquisitorial systems that allow victims to play a role as *parties civiles*, or victim participants, may be hard-pressed to do justice to the distinction between wrongs inflicted and harms undergone. When we punish perpetrators we mete out judgment about wrongs inflicted, and in those cases victims matter only if in their capacity as witnesses they help build a case. But punishing a perpetrator does not rebuild the selves and worlds destroyed by human rights abuses, and so the retributive approach may leave entire communities' experiences of harm unaddressed.

The disjunction between wrongs inflicted and harms undergone finds its way into criminal trials at multiple sites. The first is in the area of numbers. In any legal proceeding after long-standing oppression or massive crime, trials will only ever cover a very limited number of individuals, most of whom will be part of a much larger (and often complex) story of wrongdoing and victimization. Teresa Godwin Phelps describes the problem:

> In situations faced by transitional democracies after massive oppression, many perpetrators and victims will never enter a courtroom, will never have an opportunity to tell or hear the truth. While a trial can name some specific conduct as wrong and to some extent educate the citizenry about the nature and extent of prior wrongdoing, it is focused in such a way so that the individual wrongdoing may not be adequately put into the context of the practices and ideologies of the oppressive regime.[21]

We might say that Phelps agrees with Méndez that a trial may, because of its rigorous standards of proof, contribute to decreasing the number of falsehoods that can be believed about past harms. But in doing so, she adds, only a very narrow version of a story will emerge, "starring" only the witnesses called to court and one or a few perpetrators. That story will cover only the range of crimes that count within the court's jurisdiction and can be proven beyond a reasonable doubt using legal procedures. And it will leave untouched a whole universe of harms that are not legally recognized (or cannot be proven using legal standards and procedures), as well as failing to cover the widespread effects of policies and laws that left people in desperate poverty or otherwise without protection—but that do not count as crimes punishable by law. Rigorous standards of proof cut both ways, and sometimes even what is widely known outside court cannot be conclusively established within its walls.

If ethical loneliness is the outcome not only of being abused but also of not being heard, then criminal trials, with their limited capacity to hear, are not likely to assuage, on their own, the kind of loneliness caused by social abandonment. Still, victims may be helped by successful trials even against perpetrators other than their direct abusers. "Criminal or civil actions against perpetrators whom survivors see as connected or analogous to their tormentor, or as indirectly responsible for their suffering, may also have a psychological impact," writes O'Connell (while also admitting that the "sparse evidence available on the reactions of survivors to judicial proceedings does not yet permit evaluation" of that hypothesis).[22] Where it is impossible to find all responsible, finding some guilty where before all acted with impunity may be tremendously reassuring—even vindicating— to those who have been affected by state violence. Even failed criminal trials may help: James A. Goldston of the Open Society Justice Initiative, writing about the failed domestic trial against General Efraín Ríos Montt in Guatemala, points out that, despite his conviction being overruled on appeal, "the very act of bringing Ríos Montt to trial has already accomplished much: in allowing victims to speak openly about what they suffered, stimulating public debate, and methodically setting forth in a 700-page opinion the extensive record of criminality."[23] On this reading, a trial may help recovery even when a perpetrator is not convicted.

I have remarked that in criminal trials, only a very few witnesses will ever have their day in court. Jeremy Sarkin, writing about the International Criminal Court (ICC), describes the same problem from the standpoint of offenders: "Even where the ICC has jurisdiction to act it can only do so in a very limited number of cases. . . . In places where thousands (or hundreds of thousands) of atrocities have occurred and the ICC prosecutes only a few of the most responsible, while nothing happens to the rest of the perpetrators, justice cannot be said to have been done."[24] Kamari Clarke makes a similar point about the first case brought before the ICC: Thomas Lubanga Dyilo (Lubanga) was convicted of enlisting and conscripting child soldiers in a civil conflict in the Democratic Republic of the Congo (DRC). Some say Lubanga is a warlord who used child soldiers to spread terror, murder, rape, and mutilation throughout the Ituri region of northeastern DRC. Others say he is a freedom fighter violently trying to even the scales of extremely unequal access to the country's mineral wealth. Clarke's analysis of the case shows how convicting Lubanga under standards of individual criminal responsibility and command responsibility tells one possible story about the conflict in the DRC. But it does not tell the larger story about poverty, a history of European colonization that left behind corruption, elites who hold all the wealth, a majority of the rest of the population living in desperate and unsafe conditions, all of that causing or exacerbating ethnic conflict—and creating conditions where someone like Lubanga could operate successfully. International legalism finds a few warlords or leaders criminally responsible, which helps create and codify a new regime of justice that "concerns itself with some crimes and not others and that celebrates the achievement of punishment and its symbolic potential to deter future crimes rather than addressing some of the contests at the heart of violent struggles."[25] Stephen J. Rapp, head of the Office of Global Criminal Justice in the U.S. State Department and former prosecutor at the Special Court for Sierra Leone (SCSL) and the International Criminal Tribunal for Rwanda (ICTR), makes a similar point when he observes with regard to the DRC that hundreds need to be tried but only six or seven will, which, for him, is a clear indicator that *more* is needed than legal trials.[26] Brenda Hollis, a prosecutor at the SCSL and ICTY, adds, speaking of recovering victims, "these people have so many needs, and a criminal court is one response to one need."[27]

Legal trials produce a narrow showing for victims, and also for offenders. When one or five or fifteen politicians, soldiers, or commanders end up in court but thousands return to their homes, justice starts to resemble gambling or scapegoating. No one is going to say that Eugene de Kock, a former South African police colonel, called Prime Evil for his role in a significant amount of killing and torture, should be left unpunished for his crimes—he was denied amnesty, put on trial, and sent to jail. But a number of people who committed crimes as heinous were awarded amnesty through the TRC (Truth and Reconciliation Commission) proceedings.[28] If the job of a system of incarceration is to impose retributive punishment, then perhaps it is simply justice that de Kock ended up in prison. But it isn't the kind of equal justice vanquishing all impunity that we imagine when we think about rule-of-law legal institutions in the abstract. De Kock, like anyone else who moved up the ranks of the police in apartheid South Africa, was acting on orders. The apartheid regime was set up to hide the responsibility of those at the top, leaving people acting on orders to end up in prison or fight for amnesty. Pumla Gobodo-Madikizela, a commissioner on the South African TRC, adds, "It is this component of the crime, the one that resides at the systemic, institutional, and policy levels rather than at a personal level, that is notoriously difficult to substantiate within the strict evidentiary rules of a purely judicial process."[29] So, after massive political violence or long-standing conflict, trials will give voice to some victims, but not many. And they will find guilty some offenders, but not many.

For those reasons Sarkin argues, about trials, that "if no other process occurs in the state, then it is likely that victims will not receive a truthful accounting or other elements such as reparations."[30] At stake here, then, is a definition of meaningful truth. Trials provide what Phelps calls "microscopic truth." One hopes that the worst of the worst will be caught and tried, "but the guard who raped and murdered someone's daughter, the low-level functionaries who ambushed and killed a group of peasants, these and many, many others, will never be 'brought to justice.' The stories of the harms that befell thousands of people are never heard or acknowledged—never even given a setting in which they might be heard."[31] As Sarkin points out, if trials aren't combined with other, more reparative efforts at the state or community level, most victims will not benefit in meaningful ways from international criminal cases.

Still, even if the numbers don't add up to a thorough accounting of past harms, trials do begin to demonstrate, not only to the offenders and victims who participate but also to the surrounding society and possibly the larger world, that there are now institutions in place that are ready and able to punish those who grievously abuse the human rights of others. That kind of reversal, where impunity is replaced with accountability, censure, and punishment, may play a powerful role in how people think and feel about possible futures and what the past means in the present moment.[32] It is one form of repair.

TRUTH COMMISSIONS

There are as many different kinds of truth commissions as there are truth commissions—some make their proceedings public, some don't; some are aimed at uncovering truth for the sake of reconciliation, others are aimed squarely at truth for the sake of the historical record or a justice that isn't entirely reconciliatory; some are state sponsored, some aren't; some are widely accepted by the public as an important institution, some aren't; some have a huge impact on public perception of past abuses and some don't.

Proponents of truth commissions argue that, in a setting where many long-standing harms come not (or not only) from discrete criminal action but the effects of violence, poverty, oppression, or silence, the stories collected by truth commissions can build a more comprehensive narrative of harms. And they can do so even if the kind of evidence needed for legal conviction of perpetrators is lacking, and even if the perpetrators cannot be found. Truth commissions can, in a way, liberate victims from the past by giving them a voice that *does not rely on*—that is set free from—perpetrators and legal institutions (though truth commissions are themselves often creatures of law). They may, if well designed, shift the site of power to those who before were powerless. Speaking about the South African TRC, Gobodo-Madikizela writes,

> The narratives of trauma told by victims and survivors are not simply about facts. They are primarily about the impact of those facts on victims' lives and about the painful continuities created by the violence in their lives. There is no closure. The lived experience of traumatic memory becomes a touchstone for reality, and it tells us more than facts about how people try to lead a normal life after such a trauma.[33]

A legal process will bring together and verify a selection of facts about crimes that were committed. But trials are about who did what illegal thing to whom, and thus many stories simply cannot be told (or heard) in a trial setting. Gobodo-Madikizela suggests that collecting stories not only of harm but also of context, and of the drawn-out effects of violence and unjust systems, may in some settings shed more light on what the problems are and how they might be addressed and redressed than would a legal trial. Spelman concurs, arguing that retributive approaches "fail to locate and properly attend to the multiple ruptures" caused by any conflict.[34] That's another way of saying that legal trials redress wrongs that were inflicted but may not fully address harms undergone. With regard to any survivor, "there may be not just the physical harm done to her or her property, but the resulting fear and anxiety over the victim's loss of a sense of control over her life."[35] Because court settings focus narrowly on legal culpability, they will inevitably leave many harms unredressed or fail to find all the sites where repair is needed. If being heard helps alleviate feelings of abandonment, then truth commissions may be the right choice where airing diverse truths and finding out what happened matters more than legal culpability. Most truth commissions cannot recommend punishment or lead to a trial, and some even trade truth for amnesty, but the widespread belief of those who argue in their favor is that being given a place to speak is as meaningful a step forward for many survivors as would be participation in a court case. And a court case, as we've seen, will leave many pertinent facts uncovered, not only because of the narrow focus on legal culpability but also because an adversarial process does not tend to produce a full confession. With regard to truth commissions, Phelps points out that

> storytelling settings can provide a different kind of truth than a mere recitation of facts. . . . These settings can reveal the truth about what oppression did to people—not just the recitation of events, but what the oppression felt like, how it changed and destroyed lives, even lives not touched by a specific crime. Because so many stories can be told, a larger picture emerges in which individual victims can see their place in a community of survivors.[36]

For Phelps that matters more than that those who testify may misremember key events due to trauma or simple memory failure, or even lie and not be found out because of a lack of rigorous fact-checking. From the kind of stories produced by a truth commission we learn more than what can be said in statements verifiable as true or false. In other words, there are certain truths that simply could not be established if we subjected them to the standards of what legalism calls truth.

But truth commissions also have their limits and are inevitably not open to all truths. In South Africa, the TRC focused on "grave violations" of human rights. The only crimes that counted as "grave violations" (and thus would qualify victims to testify and to request reparations) were killing, torture, severe ill-treatment, and abduction. "It meant that victims of forced removals or of Bantu education or any other of a myriad of laws passed by the apartheid government, or of the effects of those laws including hunger, poverty and the lack of basic health care, would not be deemed victims according to the Truth and Reconciliation Commission," Tristan Borer points out.[37] Every institution has a design, and every design has its limits. So, though Gobodo-Madikizela is right that more expansive stories could be told (and were told) before the TRC, it is also true that very many stories were not told there, and a large number of victims of apartheid did not qualify to testify. According to Borer, "while the TRC certified only approximately 20,000 individuals as victims and fewer than 10,000 individuals as perpetrators," surely there were more than 30,000 persons who gave and received harm under apartheid.[38]

The South African TRC also ignored important distinctions such as the difference between direct and indirect perpetrators (meaning, for instance, that a low-level functionary—a direct perpetrator—might have to apply for amnesty, but someone at the top of the chain of command would simply be able to deny that he ordered any unlawful actions), and created no space for group perpetrators. If we can't look at institutions such as police forces or political parties as perpetrators, there is something very important about the injustice of apartheid that we will not see. And if we can't look at the supportive roles played by the health, legal, media, business, and religious sectors, we will also miss something about a wider responsibility for justice and injustice.[39] The TRC did hold hearings focused on the response to and participation in apartheid of key sectors of society—religious community, law, business, labor, health, media, prisons—but brevity, lack of publicity or preparation time, and other factors made these hearings less than effective. It is certainly not the case that every member of, for instance, a political party or business practice that facilitated the success of apartheid bears direct (or legal) guilt—some may even have voiced opposition. What matters here is that without a sense of how much support these diverse groups lent to apartheid's structures, we will not have an accurate picture of how deep and broad the injustices were. That means that observers, victims, bystanders, and beneficiaries may find it harder to put their finger on what was wrong with official tolerance of violations or bystander complicity. And that means that an institution designed as the TRC was to transcend the limitations of legal blame would still fail to mark well the difference between ethical and legal responsibility. That failing is in keeping with Panu Minkkinen's reminder about truth commissions that "even if they operate at the fringes of law, there is nothing radically new about the way they function. It is still a more or less formalized encounter between an offender and a victim before a seemingly neutral third party that endorses the objectified outcome through its authority."[40] If, on some important level, the TRC is another juridified process focusing on the power of institutions to find individuals responsible for harms with complex social causes, the majority of those who care to pay attention to the TRC process may not see just how widely the weight of responsibility for past injustice ought to be felt. As Borer states (citing Mahmood Mamdani), "The narrow legalistic definition employed by the TRC has serious implications for how the injustices of apartheid will be historically remembered as well as implications in the practical realm of reparations and restitution."[41] Borer and Mamdani remind us that, though truth commissions begin as alternatives to legalistic responses to past harm, most of them are creations of law as well as complex institutions with rules and procedures that determine what counts as harm and what counts as truth.

That is true not only of South Africa. In Argentina, the National Commission on the Disappearance of Persons (CONADEP) was limited in its mandate to reporting on those who had disappeared. That meant that those who were tortured and then survived were not heard. (The same is true of Chile's National Commission on Truth and Reconciliation.) The work of the commission did help to give voice to the void where the loved ones and comrades of so many had simply vanished. That is why many believe that truth commissions are a better choice after a period where truth is hidden or denied. Aryeh Neier argues that "truth became the essential means to combat disappearances and death squad killings" because "in confronting crimes of repression that were invented to be deniable, it was necessary for the human rights movement in the first instance to prove that they had taken place and, in the second instance, to demonstrate who was responsible."[42] Since truth commissions separate truth from determination of punishment, they are more likely to get a more thorough truth, and that may be what people need—more than punishment of the guilty.

That each truth commission is slightly different is a positive attribute. Each institution is designed to respond to the very different contexts in which truth and justice matter after past injustice. Sometimes legal justice is more important than truth, and sometimes truth is more important than legal justice, and it will always be the case that not everyone affected by past crimes will agree with the decision that is taken by a government or community: note, as an example, that three prominent families of victims challenged the constitutionality of the South African TRC's power to grant amnesty.[43] They wanted trials and punishment.

Even if it is clear what part of the justice and truth continuum "matters" more to a transitioning society, political context will impact what is and is not possible after entrenched conflict. Amnesty was accepted as part of the South African TRC as a compromise, not as an ideal design. With response to past harm, what is possible and desirable in each case will vary. Pertinent factors include the past of the institutions and the society; local traditions and methods for dealing with the past; whether there are prospects for community building; how much time has passed since conflict or violence; numbers involved in the conflict; whether conflict was one-sided or complex; whether the current governing power is new or comprises members of an old regime; continuing distribution of minority and majority groups, victims, and perpetrators; and the involvement of international institutions and NGOs—these things all affect what is possible, and vary from site to site.[44] Ferme discusses the case of a young soldier "trained" to tell his story by participation in Sierra Leone's TRC, only to return to his community and find that, for them, silence and forgetting were the chosen means for dealing with the past—and were much more native to the region as coping mechanisms: "In his pursuit of individual attention for his story, he was undermining their own collective hopes for moving beyond their suffering."[45]

Truth commissions can fail in as many ways as can legal cases: they may, for example, cover only a select kind of crime, leaving many abuses unheard; they may lack the power to compel testimony from those most responsible; they may fail to set a deadline for publishing a report, fail to publicize the report, fail to write a report, or may lack the power to get official recommendations taken seriously by government actors; they may fail to live up to their promises. But when they succeed, they start to build a shared narrative that may make repair possible for those who most need it.

TIME AND RECOVERY

The notoriety of the South African TRC has had an impact on how people imagine truth commissions.[46] A form that was once thought to have truth seeking or investigation as its main goal (as was the case in Chile, Argentina, El Salvador, and Guatemala) is now widely seen as a site for truth telling or performance and a mechanism for achieving peaceful societal reconciliation. However, even if the form of truth telling/performance *were* the right fit for every postconflict society, we are still in the midst of a historical arc in which the success of South Africa's TRC is undecided. South Africa is still largely a divided society: one part success story consisting of a stable political system, honest courts, and a growing economy, and the flip side of that success, a society plagued by impoverishment of 45 percent of the country, a 40 percent unemployment rate, and a Gini coefficient (a statistical measure of inequality) of 0.6, marking it, alongside Brazil, as "the most unequal society in the world."[47] Continuing inequality, along with a failure of the government to live up to promises attached to the compromise measure that offered amnesty in exchange for truth at the initial moment of transition, have led to a sharp decline in approval of amnesty, decreased acceptance of its necessity, and more demands for accountability. In longitudinal studies conducted by David Backer, 91 percent of respondents in 2002–2003 accepted amnesty as a necessary compromise to avoid civil war. By 2008, acceptance numbers had dropped to 70.5 percent.[48] In turn, in 2002 57.5 percent approved of amnesty as a practice, whereas in 2008 that number had fallen to 20.4 percent. Backer argues that this change in attitude shows us at least two things: (1) a high rate of acceptance does not necessarily mean a high rate of satisfaction—especially when it involves enormous compromise—and so we should be mindful of what is promised and what is delivered, and (2) what a government does in the wake of an initial compromise, and how its decisions impact the lives of people over time, will determine how stable the settlement is. The original high rate of approval was, Backer suggests, attached to reluctant acceptance of political realities paired with an expectation that the government would live up to its promises to prosecute those who did not receive amnesty, make meaningful economic changes, and compensate victims with reparations. In the time between surveys, reparations were made only begrudgingly (with South Africa's president Thabo Mbeki arguing that the liberation struggle was not fought for money[49]) and at lower levels than promised. Also during that time, the National Prosecuting Authority policies around prosecution were modified, allowing enough discretion in prosecuting cases that many thought it amounted to a second amnesty, this time without hearings.[50] All of that may have led to a widespread perception that promises were not being kept. Yazir Henry, a survivor of the ANC's (African National Congress) armed struggle against apartheid, makes this observation: "Legal and political apartheid has gone but social, economic and psychological apartheid remains and will for a long time to come. . . . Not only do we live with serious post-war trauma, we carry this condition in a context of continued social and economic oppression."[51] That is why Backer concludes, about transitional justice in general, that

> the immediate consequences of any measure do not necessarily represent a durable status quo. Instead, these outcomes are contingent, subject to ongoing scrutiny and reassessment by interested stakeholders and therefore vulnerable in the event of altered conditions, including the introduction of new policies and the lack of follow-through on existing policies.[52]

Attitudes toward reconciliation are always subject to revision over time. Social norms and surroundings, institutional rules and procedures, and government policies will impact how persons hoping or struggling to get beyond an unjust past will experience that past in the present moment.

Reconciliation of past with present has not been a settled matter in Argentina either. CONADEP, created by President Raul Alfonsín in late 1983, gathered testimony on forced disappearances in Argentina's Dirty War, covering the years 1976 to 1983. An official summary report was delivered to Alfonsín in late 1984, and that opened the door to prosecutions of the military junta. The military had granted itself amnesty before handing over power to Alfonsín, but Alfonsín overturned the self-amnesty law, and nine heads of the military junta were convicted in 1985. The military rebelled, so in 1986 and 1987 Alfonsín passed laws restricting further prosecutions. In 1989–1990, Alfonsín's successor, Carlos Menem, pardoned those who had been convicted but also passed laws authorizing reparations for those who had been detained by the military. In 1996, when a retired navy officer admitted to throwing live political prisoners out of airplanes into the sea, "Argentina discovered how much of its difficult past was still unresolved, both emotionally and factually," with months' worth of newspaper articles and crowds protesting in the streets demanding more truth.[53] In June 2005, under pressure from an organized public campaign, Argentina's Congress overturned the law that had restricted the prosecutions of the military. Transitional justice has taken many turns in Argentina.[54]

CONADEP documented that 8,960 persons had been kidnapped by the military or the police and never seen again. Human rights organizations usually place the number much higher, around 30,000 persons. However, in the course of offering reparations to families of the disappeared, the human rights office of the government of Argentina "was able to document many more cases and a wider array of victims than the truth commission could."[55] As I mentioned, the truth commission focused on the disappeared, leaving to the side those who had been killed or who had disappeared but whose bodies had turned up and been identified, or who had been detained and tortured but survived. That meant that the truth unearthed by the truth commission was about one narrow slice of Argentina's violent history. The evolving policies on reparations allowed a wider truth to surface. In response to cases brought before the Inter-American Commission on Human Rights (an organ of the Organization of American States), the Argentine government developed a program to award up to $220,000 (depending on amount of time held) to petitioners who had been detained as political prisoners.[56] That program then expanded to include prisoners who had been detained and then released and forced into exile. Reparations of $220,000 were then made to family members of the disappeared. Further reparations may be awarded to new cases not included in *Nunca más*, the truth commission report. So, though CONADEP operated with a limited mandate, work that continued after the commission's end uncovered other truths and helped assuage the ethical loneliness of, for instance, torture survivors whose voices were left out of the truth proceeding. Unmet needs for justice fueled innovation in awarding reparations.

What many consider to be as important for Argentina as CONADEP's uncovering of truth and the government's offer of monetary reparations is an expansion of available categories for describing loss. The creation of a new legal category, "forcibly disappeared," meant that families could process wills, distribute inheritance, and take up other matters having to do with a person's estate but still stop short of declaring a person dead.[57]

Before the "forcibly disappeared" category was created, the only way to access inheritance, insurance, or other comforts or procedures associated with the passing of a loved one (including closing a bank account or selling property) was to have the missing person declared "presumed dead." But the death, declared on those terms, would not carry with it an acknowledgment that it was state inflicted. David Becker and his coauthors describe the impossible choice faced by families of the disappeared: "If family members choose to accept the death of a loved one, they [feel like they] 'kill' him or her. If they choose to maintain hope, they deny their everyday experience of the loved one's absence."[58] When that is the case, families may remain unable to take up processes of mourning or commemoration that may make loss more bearable.[59] In conditions such as this, some psychiatrists have found that "some families may fall into a limbo of 'ambiguous loss,' torn between hope and grief, unable to return to the past or plan for the future."[60] "Forcibly disappeared," as a category, allows families to move forward without embracing a lie about the conditions of their loss.[61] This marks a site where a legal innovation responds reparatively to how loss doesn't disappear but transforms over time. It is a revision that makes the present moment more rather than less livable.

EVIDENCE OF REPAIR

Let's return to where the chapter began—the importance of repair.[62] Legal trials and truth commissions both respond reparatively to past harms, and their different strengths and weaknesses suit them to different post-conflict settings. But what, precisely, are they engaged in repairing? Social institutions, the rule of law, civil relationships, social infrastructure, all are likely to be in need of repair in the wake of long-standing injustice. It is complicated but not impossible to fix those things. But what about the people who were harmed?

In the past twenty years many law review and other academic articles have asserted that testifying in criminal trials or truth commissions is healing or cathartic for survivors, and that criminal accountability facilitates political reconciliation, or that the truth of truth commissions does. Many of the assertions about the healing power of testimony and the reconciliative effect of truth were authored anecdotally or hopefully, without backing from empirical data. I don't state that as an accusation, because such data largely did not exist. Empirical studies did not exist because these forms of justice are relatively new and because, as Eric Stover points out, the experiences of witnesses have not always been important to larger political debates.[63] Oskar Thoms, James Ron, and Roland Paris argue, regarding transitional justice, that, "given the paucity and contradictory nature of the empirical findings to date, there appears to be an urgent need for more sustained, systematic, comparative analyses, and for greater attention to fact-based rather than faith-based claims";[64] Jamie O'Connell asserts that we need to replace anecdotal evidence or the mere hope that trials are cathartic with empirical evidence that will help us understand what trials can and cannot accomplish for victims;[65] and Fiona Ross points out, about truth commissions, that "few studies have yet focused on the social ramifications of testimony."[66]

There are now studies—using data from South Africa, Sierra Leone, Rwanda, the former Yugoslavia—suggesting that testifying in institutional settings can be healing for some.[67] But there is as much evidence that testifying can reawaken trauma or a sense of injustice rather than helping victims find closure. Stover asserts that

> human rights activists often valorize the "therapeutic value" of war crimes trials for victims and witnesses. They argue that victims who are able to recount horrific events in a context of acknowledgement and support will often find closure and be able to move on with their lives. The findings of this study (and corroborating data from our parallel studies . . .), however, suggest that such claims so far as war crimes trials are concerned reflect more wishful thinking than fact. The few participants who experienced cathartic feelings immediately or soon after testifying before the ICTY found that the glow quickly faded once they returned home to their shattered villages and towns. This was especially true for witnesses who faced uncertainties in their lives.[68]

Stover's observations about what testifying did for witnesses in the ICTY cases is reflected in Ross's analysis of the experience of women testifying before the South African TRC. Ross argues that, though the TRC was publicized as "giving voice to the voiceless," in doing so it assumed a connection between "having voice" and "being heard" that does not hold in all contexts.[69] Her work shows that "the effect of testimonies generated through the truth commission, media, academics and others is far broader and perhaps more complex than naïve assumptions about testimony's healing effects suggest."[70] Along those lines, Debra Kaminer and her co-authors found that there was no significant difference in the rates of depression, PTSD, or other anxiety disorders among those who gave public testimony, closed testimony, or no testimony before the TRC in South Africa.[71] In other words, having testified did not make a difference in recovery (in at least some of its aspects), though having a forgiving attitude did. A study by Karen Brounéus showed that, in Rwanda, *gacaca* witnesses were not healed by the experience: "Survivors who have witnessed in the *gacaca* have significantly higher levels of depression (20 percent higher relative risk) and PTSD (40 percent higher relative risk) than survivors who have not witnessed."[72] Judith Herman argues that "the wishes and needs of victims are often diametrically opposed to the requirements of legal proceedings," relying on her years of experience working with survivors of sexual violence.[73] And O'Connell, gathering together the spotty and mostly anecdotal evidence about how court cases affect victims, recommends "less emphasis on judicial proceedings as mechanisms for promoting healing, more attention by courts to victims' psychological needs in those human rights cases that do go forward, and additional research to deepen our understanding of victims' reactions to trials."[74] It simply is not safe to say that testifying before a court—local or international—or truth commission leads to healing or catharsis for victims.[75]

All of this points to the need to be careful about what counts as evidence when we author arguments about what institutions do and do not accomplish for survivors. Many articles rely on anecdotal evidence to make conclusions that we simply can't verify. I'll follow the chain of evidence used in a few different articles to make a point about how hopeful assertions that trials and truth commissions help survivors emerge. Before I do that I want to note that, writing about very new institutions and procedures, the authors whose work I describe here would find very little evidence other than anecdotal on which to rely. It's not that the evidence was out there and they failed to look for it. What's more, anecdotal evidence can offer fertile ground for theorizing possibilities and outcomes in a field like this where outcomes and possibilities truly matter. It is too soon to know with full confidence whether any of these institutions benefit those who testify in the long run. So, without passing blame, I simply want to discuss *how* it becomes possible to conclude that testifying is good for survivors.

Sarkin, in the context of arguing that in transitioning societies more than a legal decision may be necessary before justice is seen to be done, states that "allowing victims to testify about what occurred can have a very positive cathartic effect."[76] It's a very quick point he makes while developing a larger argument about how international institutions might best incorporate retributive *and* restorative processes. In support of the claim that testifying can be cathartic he cites an article by William Burke-White that argues for the creation and greater use of regional rather than international courts, because (Burke-White argues) "achieving the goals of restorative justice requires a close connection between the adjudicating court and the society affected by international crimes."[77] Burke-White thinks that the physical separation of some international courts (like the ICTY) from the communities they serve makes it harder for those courts to have a real impact in terms of building confidence that past injustices will be punished and will not be repeated. In making this argument, he writes (and this is the page Sarkin cites),

> To provide a concrete example, the first case of rape as a crime against humanity in international law—the Kunarac case before the ICTY— had an enormous cathartic potential to restore the people of Foča, the town in southern Bosnia in which the events occurred. Yet, even as thirty-eight women detained in rape-camps told their stories to the ICTY, the people of Foča were isolated from the events of the trial and largely unable to personally benefit from the proceedings.[78]

That is surely an important concern of international tribunals and, though it would take some time and study to know for certain whether the Kunarac case or the ICTY more generally will have a positive impact on the Foča region, Burke-White is not alone in wondering whether courts located far from the scene of the crime do justice as effectively as a more local effort would. (Similar concerns emerged about locating the ICTR in Arusha, Tanzania, and the ICC in The Hague.) But it is not clear how Burke-White's observation that the Kunarac case had cathartic *potential* for Foča supports Sarkin's contention that "allowing victims to testify about what occurred can have a very positive cathartic effect." Surely it can have a positive or cathartic effect. But it also may fail to do so, and may even inflict further harm rather than helping.

Writing about the Extraordinary Chambers in the Courts of Cambodia (ECCC, also known as the Khmer Rouge tribunal), David Sokol maintains that "the experience of speaking openly and questioning the accused on any topic can greatly facilitate the healing process for victims" and cites a comment made by one civil party to a case as evidence.[79] He adds that the court's move to reduce victim participation is "likely to negatively impact the national healing process,"[80] citing as support a scholarly article by Tessa Capeloto that argues that "providing victims a role in the process gives them a 'sense of empowerment' and 'may bring them a step closer to healing and rehabilitation.' "[81] Capeloto cites analysis by Susana SáCouto as support for this point.[82] SáCouto argues that victims derive benefit from greater participation in legal trials and offers as evidence a scholarly article by Jonathan Doak describing several surveys that "have found that, where domestic criminal law allows victims to 'participate' in proceedings, such as in Germany and Poland, those who have exercised this right expressed greater satisfaction with the criminal justice process than those who chose not to."[83] So: Sokol says Cambodia needs to keep victim participation vibrant because Capeloto says that will empower and may heal victims because SáCouto says that victims benefit from participation because Doak cites surveys about domestic practices of victim participation in Poland and Germany. SáCouto—whose article begins by stating that not enough has been done to study the wider role victims might play in bringing perpetrators to justice—does a good job balancing concern for victims with safeguarding defendants' rights. She shows why victim participation matters while also describing the very real obstacles faced by the ICC in its own plans to allow victims greater participation in trials. SáCouto also acknowledges, in a footnote, that the idea that testifying before a criminal tribunal helps victims regain their sense of power is "not without controversy," and she cites some articles arguing that the process is neither healing nor rehabilitative for victims.[84]

The article by Jonathan Doak cited by SáCouto and Capeloto is about victims' rights in domestic trials in Britain. The surveys undertaken in Germany and Poland that Doak describes cover victims who made use of "subsidiary prosecution." Subsidiary prosecution offers victims who make use of it the right to be present at all stages of a trial, to put questions to witnesses, and to provide evidence or make a statement beyond what the prosecution would do. It resembles the Cambodian court's *parties civiles* role and so it makes sense that SáCouto would use it to support her argument. SáCouto's main objective, however, is to show how victims might help bring perpetrators to justice, which is a different question from whether or not doing so is a positive or healing experience for them.

Again, I chase these articles down the rabbit hole of academic citation practices not to find fault with any of the articles—indeed all of them have valuable contributions to make to the larger debates in which they are engaged—but to show how evidence is working in this emerging field, in turn to draw attention to a lack of substantial proof for the contention that participating in a court case is healing or cathartic for victims who appear before international or hybrid tribunals.[85] Sokol's article (where this extended citation chase began), while offering a helpful background to the heritage of civil party proceedings in Cambodian legal institutions, descended as they are from the French legal tradition, and using that backdrop to show how limiting the scope of victim participation may be harmful to the court's mission to do justice, also falls into a broad pattern of offering hope as evidence.

The hope in these articles is based on a series of good hypotheses. For those who have been living in a regime defined by hidden truth or secret crime, both testifying to abuse and learning the truth of what happened can be life affirming. In addition, in some psychiatric treatments for trauma, one goal of therapy is to help survivors build a narrative of what happened so that the story can become part of a larger life story rather than that life's determining event. Speaking and being heard where before there was silence—whether because the story was too painful for the victim to tell or there was no community willing to listen—can be a powerful experience. It would thus certainly make sense if testifying in trials or truth commissions were healing or cathartic for survivors (with the caveat that, as Herman points out, "if one set out by design to devise a system for provoking intrusive post-traumatic symptoms, one could not do better than a court of law"[86]). The one victim Sokol cites supports this belief. Mrs. Chum Neou "told participants how she used to cry every time she talked about her experience with the Khmer Rouge period. However, after participating in the trial with help from the psychological support organization, TPO, she is now able to speak in public without crying."[87]

So, the hope in the articles we've examined in this section is based on a series of good hypotheses. But those hypotheses in turn seem to spring from an unquestioned faith in legalism's preferred solution to human abandonment: establishing formal equality in rule of law proceedings. As I've begun to argue and hope to show in what remains of the book, that is not a bad goal, but it is also unlikely to get a person or polity all the way to recovery. As an assumption about selves and worlds it may even cause further harm. We should be careful about what counts as evidence or truth whenever we try to determine what ought to be done about re-dressing past harm.

None of this is meant to suggest that empirical proof is somehow more weighty than theory or hope. It would be just as devastatingly wrong to submit to the tyranny of data as it would to ignore emerging evidence (in data and other forms) that what many hoped or thought was true is more complicated than anyone projected. After all, anyone who brings hope to justice already knows that it faces formidable obstacles and yet is still a necessity. As I noted at the beginning of this section, when we are work-ing with new institutions designed to deal in new ways with old or new crimes, we simply won't—for many years—have empirical evidence to back our claims. It pays to observe how new procedures and institutions affect people over time. But even when we have time and a good set of data, we may be misled in our interpretation of what it means. And even when we interpret carefully and thoughtfully the facts we have, the facts collectable in data form may not tell us the whole story. In a recent com-mentary on current use of "big data," Kenneth Cukier and Viktor Mayer-Schönberger observe that

> Google runs everything according to data. That strategy has led to much of its success. But it also trips up the company from time to time. Its cofounders, Larry Page and Sergey Brin, long insisted on knowing all job candidates' SAT scores and their grade point averages when they graduated from college. In their thinking, the first number mea-sured potential and the second measured achievement. Accomplished managers in their 40s were hounded for the scores, to their outright bafflement. The company even continued to demand the numbers long after its internal studies showed no correlation between the scores and job performance.[88]

The authors point out that if Google executives followed this logic to its conclusion, they wouldn't hire someone like Mark Zuckerberg or Steve

Jobs since neither received college degrees. And they would also fail to see how, no matter how useful data is at helping us to see the world as it is, some features of the human condition will never be fully captured in a data set.

Pumla Gobodo-Madikizela makes a similar point when, after discussing two kinds of questions about remorse—whether we can verify that someone who expresses remorse actually is remorseful and whether authentic remorse is even possible in the wake of unthinkable violence—she observes that it just is true that sometimes "when perpetrators do in fact express regret or guilt or contrition, however it may be ascertained, what seems to lie ... 'beyond the purview of apology' can in fact be transformed from an unforgivable deed into a forgivable one" in that people can admit that what is done cannot be undone and still move forward.[89] In other words, the work done to quantify how forgiveness and remorse work in personal and political situations is important since it may help us understand something about ourselves, others, and our possible joint futures. But, she adds, "philosophical questions can and should give way and be subsumed to human questions, for in the end we are a society of people and not of ideas, a fragile web of interdependent humans, not of stances."[90] Though I would be careful drawing a line between societies of people and societies of ideas (since clearly every social grouping is made up of both, the ideas come from people, and people in turn become who they are in part through their ideas), I take her main point to be that no amount of careful research will be able to capture or predict with complete success how human relationships will transpire. So, by all means, let's continue to project better futures. But also, let's not assume we know conclusively how institutions help people before we've heard people speak.

HOPE AND FACT

I've just spent some pages making the argument that while we need to pay better attention to empirical evidence, analyses based solely on empirical evidence are likely not up to the task we face when we respond to grievous harm. Why would I do that? When we are faced with recurring world-destroying violations for which no existing response is adequate, often the greater part of what we have will be theory, hope, and the responsibility to use those well in designing better responses. Philosophical approaches give us tools with which to project worlds better than what we have at present. But philosophy should also teach us to watch for evidence that what hope designed may be complicated by the realities of daily living and the inevitable human shortcomings of the initial projections. So I am not authoring an argument against idealist projection of better futures—it would be irresponsible to do so, and also self-defeating since this book is, when viewed from some angles, an idealist projection of better futures. Rather, I am pointing out that, in what is a fairly new field of endeavor, anecdote and hope sometimes conspire to create expectations that may not be borne out by the reality of lives or proceedings. Giving close attention to what institutions can and cannot accomplish helps all involved develop reasonable expectations. And when people involved—as participants, designers, activists, scholars, and a host of other roles—in an institution as important as an international criminal trial or a truth commission have reasonable rather than misleading expectations about outcomes, outcomes are more likely to be happy.[91] So, among other things, recent and future studies will help those who project, design, administer, judge, and write about transitional institutions and their alternatives to make judgments about how best to treat victims who participate.

Sometimes what is learned from such a process of reflection is as simple as figuring out how to do a better job letting everyone involved know what the process they are involved in *is*, how it works, and what its goals are. Christine Englebrecht, writing about the criminal justice system in the United States, points out that people who appear in court as witnesses are often shocked to find out that criminal offenses are considered by the state to be *against the state*, not against the persons who were most impacted by them.[92] And so they are let down when they see how little input they will have in what they rightly think of as their own case. Englebrecht recommends funding victim advocates, whose job it will be to help remedy a system where there has been too much reliance on preconceived ideas of what an average victim would want or need—ideas formed without consulting with victims and without considering the wide range of different needs and desires different victims might have. In other words, she proposes hiring someone who can listen well.

In Cambodia the domestic standard was that reparations mean money, but at the ECCC, a hybrid domestic-international court, "only collective non-financial reparation is possible," and not enough effort was put into letting participants know ahead of time that they would receive no financial compensation for their losses.[93] That led to a lot of disappointment and disillusionment with the court among the people to whom it hoped to deliver justice.

At the ICTY, Marie-Benedicte Dembour and Emily Haslam observed various indicators that witnesses had not been properly briefed on what to expect from the proceedings, which for them threw "into sharp relief the limitations of victim-witnesses' 'entitlement' to be heard."[94] That led them to wonder whether international tribunals should even *use* witnesses: "If the giving of testimony is an ordeal rather than an empowering process for the witness, one must question whether relying on witnesses is the most efficient and morally justifiable way to establish judicial facts."[95] Of course, we would want to be careful about removing those most affected by the violence from processes meant to adjudicate wrongs inflicted on them. But perhaps more care could be exercised in determining *when* witnesses get called to testify. Dembour and Haslam ask, "Why was it necessary to hear victim-witnesses to document the fall of Srebenica?"[96] What they mean is, why subject already traumatized survivors to the difficulties of testifying in a legal setting when the facts at hand could be established by other means? I would add: before answering this question with any finality, listen to the persons whose lives were most impacted by the crimes being adjudicated.

O'Connell, who, noting the lack of hard evidence for many of the arguments about the healing capacity of testifying in international criminal trials, gathers what evidence there is and combines it with the observations of mental health professionals working with survivors, argues that including victims in court proceedings is important. Inclusion matters because it may help alleviate ethical loneliness: especially if the original harms were sponsored or ignored by the government, the victim may feel that she has been abandoned by the legal system and the larger society. A successful case may help combat the loneliness of having been abandoned. But survivors of human rights abuses and other violent crime may have a wide range of posttraumatic symptoms, such as anxiety, insomnia, flashbacks, nightmares, and acute distress triggered by things that remind them of the abuse. And so O'Connell argues that courts using traumatized survivors as witnesses ought to work harder to balance the demands of due process with the needs of victims and should recognize that testifying is not necessarily a healing experience for victims. O'Connell recognizes that some victims do "find comfort and a sense of empowerment in pursuing justice through law."[97] But even those who do may also "suffer new abuses, such as reprisals or harassment through the discovery process" that may cause psychological stress or a return of trauma (301). He recommends that legal institutions "facilitate protection of witnesses and provide a range of support to them before, during and after they testify" (324). Given that common psychological effects of human rights violations include a loss of trust in the world, a sense of abandonment by humanity, and diminished confidence in one's ability to evaluate one's surroundings, O'Connell argues that, whenever possible, courts and their judges should "address victims' needs for information," reassure them that they were not responsible for the violation, and acknowledge officially the abuser's culpability. He writes, "By listening carefully, [judges] can implicitly affirm victims' understanding of what happened, helping repair their confidence in their own judgment" (343). O'Connell suggests that abandonment—what I'm calling ethical loneliness—should be countered by court officials with practices of careful listening and positive revision. Depending on the case and the facts, such practices may or may not be compatible with the larger goal of fairness contained in the idea of procedural due process. But it would be a good step forward if we stopped believing that truth and legal justice had healing powers in some simple sense for survivors of violence and abuse. That step forward would help us recognize more clearly the different things truth and legal justice do accomplish. And it would help us determine what else is necessary— beyond truth and beyond legal justice—for reconciliation or recovery from violence.

The demand to listen better may sound simple, but it is not. As chapter 3 shows, even institutions designed for hearing are designed to hear some things more than others. Sara Kendall and Sarah Nouwen add a new wrinkle with their analysis of the ICC's rhetoric of victimhood.[98] If one attends carefully to how the ICC describes its work and its goals, it becomes clear that both lawyers and the court itself claim to represent victims. The court, however, turns the plurality of diverse victims into an abstract category, "The Victim," in whose interest many different representatives can claim to be acting even if those representatives have never met any real victims and are mostly just doing their jobs as officials of a legal system. Kendall and Nouwen argue that the court may hope to act on behalf of victims but lacks the institutional capacity to understand them as real persons with specific political or cultural ideas about past, present, and future, as well as views about what justice ought to be.

Of course, the ICC's rules allow victims to participate not only as witnesses but also as victim participants—parties to the case who can contribute to the case even if they are not called as witnesses by the defense or prosecution. That innovation (based on continental/inquisitorial traditions of *parties civiles*) responds to criticism of past tribunals (notably the ICTR and ICTY) that they did not do enough to address the concerns of a wide array of victims. We might call that a step forward, offering more ways in which legal stories might get told. It is part of why so much hope is tied to the ICC. But the ICC is a young institution and victim participation was not rigorously defined by its statutes, instead leaving what it will mean to rulings in cases. It is too soon to say whether victim participation will do anything meaningful for a wider array of victims, but already one can see the many limits to what it can do. Victims who aren't witnesses can present their concerns (if the court qualifies them as victims), but they can present their concerns only through representatives; those representatives may represent a very large number of victims; the victims represented by a representative may not all have the same interests; if victims are parties to a case that doesn't end up being brought to court, those victims get no chance to be heard; if a defendant is acquitted, there will be no reparations; if there are reparations, they will likely be dispensed in community-based ways rather than to individuals; and so on. Furthermore, in order to qualify to be heard, victims have to register with the court, in either English or French, in legal documents. That means that they must know how to read and write (in English or French) and that they can prove they are who they are. That is not easy for many people who live in conflict-ridden zones. These are all limitations already placed on an expansion of the category of hearing at the ICC. Of course, when a court dismisses certain concerns as legally irrelevant and pronounces certain procedures as legally valid, it is well within its rights to do so. But in doing so it will have already decided what the right questions to ask about a situation are and, to a certain extent, what the range of answers can be. In other words, it will have circumscribed in advance what can be heard.

REFRACTION

I began this chapter by calling it a tangent or a digression from the main argument of the book. It looks at international, domestic, and hybrid post-conflict trials as well as truth commissions as serious innovations aimed at responding to harm. That this chapter digresses slightly from the arc of the book's argument demonstrates that, with regard to the larger conversation about transitional justice and political reconciliation, this *book* is a tangent. Its refraction of the field is intended to let us view some familiar things differently.

I interrupt the self-assurance of the narrative about transition and reconciliation with a description of ethical loneliness not only because I think it gives us a better understanding of the kind of being a human being is but also because it may help many—survivors and those whose lives have been more fortunate—see harm and its repair in ways more productive of new possibility. It changes the subject. Much has been accomplished by the many responsive institutions that have been created in recent decades. But few would argue that the problem of social/political abandonment has been solved; many would contend that it has barely been addressed. I call the institutions I discuss here responsive for a reason: they respond to crime. They may also hope to prevent future crime—the Preamble to the Rome Statute that created the ICC even includes the claim that the institution was established "to put an end to impunity for the perpetrators of these crimes and thus contribute to prevention of such crimes."[99] It is a tenuous "thus," but not one without hope. Any fan of arguments in favor of deterrence knows how difficult it can be to try to prove how one thing caused another thing not to happen. In any case the international community could put a lot more investment into more kinds of prevention.[100] Some kinds of prevention require tools already on offer in discourses of transitional justice and political reconciliation: infrastructure, responsive development, engaging local stakeholders, investments in education and health, developing rule of law institutions, and so on. All of those things might help decrease the isolation felt by individuals and groups facing unequal treatment or recovering from injustice. But those things also might fail to add up to meaningful change if we don't take seriously the realities of how selves and worlds are formed cooperatively in ways chosen and unchosen, for better and for worse. In addition to preventing serious harm, we must learn to prevent ourselves and others from feeling innocent of all responsibility for that harm and its prevention.

The tradition of liberal rule of law legality assumes that the subject of law and of rights is autonomous and self-sufficient, capable of consenting to take on any duty he or she would bear. That narrative respects individuals and supports liberal ideas about justice but cannot explain to us why we might bear duties beyond our legitimate legal duties. And yet such duties are indelible in our current political landscape: who is responsible for the refugee, the environment, the prisoner of war, the sufferer of poverty or famine, the victim of ethnic cleansing, the one to whom I never consented to owe anything, if we stick to narrow legal grounds? Questions like that leave us in a situation where the weight of justice hangs on the distinction between consent to obligation and responsibility for what no one would choose.[101]

As I mentioned in chapter 1, there are harms—and remedies—that are rendered utterly inscrutable if we limit ourselves to thinking that a human self can experience meaningful autonomy separate from social conditions where many others recognize that self's autonomy. We may desire the formal equality and personal autonomy of the liberal political and legalist vision. But I do not think we can attain it in any lasting or meaningful way when we approach selves as if they were self-sufficient monads. In other words, it is dangerous to assume as a starting point what you want to reach as your goal.

And so this book discusses the loneliness of social abandonment, the causes of that loneliness, practices of hearing that fail to listen, ways of revising the past in the present that make the future brighter or darker for those who were abandoned, and what we might learn from all of that about the desire and potential for political forgiveness, transitional justice, and political reconciliation. We won't find a neat theory. But that's not what we should want.

MEANINGFUL HUMAN RIGHTS

What survivors of abuse and oppression want from a process of justice or healing varies as widely as do human desires in general, but some hopes are shared.[102] Survivors want their losses to be recognized and their willingness or *unwillingness* to forgive accepted as justified. In many cases, what those who testify in diverse settings desire is to be able to trust that they and the people they love will be safe. That is an utterly reasonable request that corresponds to what we might call meaningful human rights or an as yet unattained vision of equal justice. Like almost anyone else I've ever met in the history of the world, I want to be able to live safely and freely and be respected by my fellow human beings. Most people want that. Many people do not have that.

In attempting to honor such a reasonable demand of justice, of course one can set up the rule of law and enforce it, train judges to be impartial, and make the procedures and institutions open and known to all. That is a worthy goal. But it does not suffice to set up legal institutions guided by the rule of law and then inform everyone that the institutions are just, especially in a society recovering from mass violence or long-standing oppression. Reasoned argument on its own is not likely to persuade someone who has experienced persecution—especially persecution that was ignored or even authorized by law—that the rule of law will keep individuals safe from persecution, even if institutions guided by the rule of law *are* an individual's best hope of attaining equal justice. Before reconciliation is possible, ethical loneliness must be confronted, acknowledged, and in some measure assuaged.

How this reassurance might be accomplished will vary according to history and context, but that context will always transcend legalism's scope. Survivors want the harms they have undergone to be heard and the wrongness of them affirmed in a lasting way not only by perpetrators but also by the surrounding society. They seek the help of others to reassure them that they are living in a world with others, one where they will be protected when they are under threat. They seek meaningful human rights. Decades of hoping institutions could deliver that will have taught us, perhaps, that institutions cannot, on their own, make human rights meaningful. It seems to me that understanding the kind of being a human being is from within the scope of ethical loneliness, learning how to hear well, and building conditions where positive revision is possible will sooner get us meaningful human rights than will the insulated autonomy of the legalist subject.

Understanding ethical loneliness will get us closer to defining meaningful human rights or their more effective replacement in two ways. One, by helping us develop more robust understandings of what is lost by human beings who have been oppressed, abandoned by law and humanity, unprotected. And two, by making clear to us—in a way liberal legalism cannot—that if we are content to derive our duties only from conditions to which we would consent, we may as well give up on equal justice as an aspiration. No one will be reconciled, and many will be left unprotected, in a world where everyone dispatches every legitimate legal duty and nothing more.

3

Hearing

To read from a reparative position is to surrender the knowing, anxious paranoid determination that no horror, however apparently unthinkable, shall ever come to the reader *as new*.
    —Eve Sedgwick, "Paranoid Reading and Reparative Reading"

Another, less eloquent way of stating what Sedgwick says is, if you read reparatively, you open yourself to surprise, to the sometimes unwelcome sense that you do not already have at hand the tools you need for hearing and responding. Such an experience can be unsettling—and so we may understand why what Sedgwick calls paranoid reading so often predominates in critical scholarship. Paranoid reading is a kind of insurance policy against the disappointment that comes with wanting the world to be one way and finding that it is not that way. If, when you analyze the world, its people, and events, you arrive at the analysis always already knowing that what you'll find is oppression, violence, and abuse of power needing to be debunked, you won't be disappointed when that's what you find. One of Sedgwick's points is that if that's your technique, you may, in your search for the theory-structure that explains the objects of your focus, miss ambiguities haunting the world of those objects. In doing that you may also inadvertently have subscribed to a theory of communication as transparency, where what gets said means only what is said and the truth sets things aright. And if that is your belief, you may, as Sedgwick notes, fail to note that uncovering abuse does not accomplish repair on its own. Sometimes it doesn't even help.

Reparative reading opens the reader to surprise, to finding a world in a state she did not expect, for better and for worse. Persons open to being unsettled may, at certain times and in certain places, be most able to improvise new responses to harms that no preexisting remedy fully comprehends. The self with a will to repair needs to be open to being interrupted, to hearing something other than what she expected. And that matters because some loneliness is made of a failure of hearing. Such failures may happen even in institutions designed for hearing: courts, archives of testimony, truth commissions. When a speaker speaks in an institution designed for hearing, and an audience empowered to listen hears something other than what she says, it can be difficult to determine who is responsible for failed communication, especially if we get stuck thinking that responsibility equates with culpability. If we think instead of responsibility as the duty to respond or to be responsive, other possibilities may present themselves.

Human communication is fragile. Misunderstandings abound, and their causes are so plentiful that no amount of thoughtful design could avoid them all. And so, places designed for hearing are always sites of irony. The first irony: institutions aiming to adjudicate loss may impose loss of a different kind.

Risks always attend irony—even when irony is a speaker's intent. Unless you and I already possess between us a fairly wide array of shared meaning, I am probably going to have to explain to you any attempt I make at irony because of the gap that can open up between what gets said and what gets heard. If I just assume that you know what I mean, we might end up in the situation Jonathan Swift found himself in when people thought that his essay "A Modest Proposal" was a horrifying call to cannibalism rather than a biting criticism of the average rich person's indifference to poverty.

I'll begin with a banal example. I might use verbal irony to express my feeling of being at odds with the sense of what is fitting in a situation, as when I say, in a committee meeting, "This committee meeting is a very good use of my time," when what I mean to communicate is that it is not. At the college where I teach, some colleagues might take me to be making a sincere statement of my attentiveness to important points of running the college; others would hear my intended meaning, an expression of impatience with how the running of the college is going in the present moment. In this example, I intend my statement to be ironic, and its being taken as ironic by listeners depends on how those listeners understand both me and the larger situation in which we find ourselves.

The same situation might transform from verbal irony into dramatic irony if I say, "This committee meeting is a very good use of my time," and I mean it sincerely, but some observer of the overall scene has access to information I lack in making the statement, perhaps knowing that none of the issues under discussion will matter because the Board of Managers has already made a decision that is binding. As such, my statement would be ironic, but I wouldn't know that.

Those are both low-risk scenarios produced by inequalities of knowledge. In this chapter I am interested in how the tension between what is said and what gets heard manifests itself in riskier scenes, where inequalities of knowledge have harsher effects. To set the scene I'll begin with some classic irony from the Western tradition.

IT MIGHT HAPPEN ON THE WAY TO THE FORUM

The Roman poet Horace begins one of his *Satires* with these lines: "I happened to be going along the Via Sacra, thinking, as I tend to do, on some trifle—I don't remember what—and was entirely absorbed in it, when a man whom I knew only by name ran up to me and took hold of my hand, saying, 'How are you, dearest thing?'"[1] To this man Horace responds, "Pretty well, all things considered," and then he keeps walking, only to become aware that the guy is following him. So Horace, feeling annoyed, asks the man whether he can be of help but really means "Stop following me." The guy, hearing Horace's words but not their meaning, answers, "Yes!"

Horace keeps walking. Horace speeds up, he slows down, but the guy stays with him. Finally, when they pass by the Roman Forum, the man— whose name we never learn (although we know that Horace knows it)— reveals that he has a court date there and that he wants Horace to come in and advise him in his case.

Horace replies that he can't bear standing up for that long, and anyway he knows nothing about law. The man, knowing he'll be found in contempt if he doesn't appear as scheduled, nonetheless decides to stick with Horace in the hopes of being introduced to some of his influential friends. One can assume that he lacks the power, money, and influence that would add up to a successful court case, and so he pins his hopes on Horace. However, as fate or satire would have it, as they continue on their journey, they happen to encounter the plaintiff in the suit in question, who accuses Horace's unwanted new friend of being a scoundrel for not being in court and asks Horace to be a witness to his arrest. Horace agrees, mostly because he just wants to be rid of the guy.

So, one of the many ironies in the story is that a man in need wanted Horace to help him with his legal problems, and Horace does "help" him, but not in the way the man would have wanted. Instead of standing up for him in court, he acts as a witness to his arrest. The story speaks to how law, power, and communication come together, and also to who the winners and losers in that mix usually are.

HANNA F. AND THE DIFFICULTY OF HEARING

Toward the end of a ninety-minute interview done for the Fortunoff Video Archive for Holocaust Testimonies at Yale University, an interviewer asks concentration camp survivor Hanna F. how she felt when liberation finally came.[2] Her immediate response is, "That I am alone in the whole world."[3] She had nowhere to go, no loved ones left living to reunite with, she could not return to her home in Poland, and so she was "simply lost without words." One of the interviewers then asks her how she feels about being Jewish now given that she spent all of the war either pretending she was half Jewish or not Jewish at all. She says, "It took me a while till I met my husband after the war that I still had my assumed name. And afterward I went back to my old name, my own identity. To my own Jewishness. And I am Jewish all right." Then a second interviewer adds, "And very plucky. You were able to survive because you were so plucky, when you stepped back out . . ." The interviewer is referring to how Hanna got out of Auschwitz a second time. Because she had papers that proved she was Aryan, she had been selected to be sent to Germany to work. But once she was in line to board a bus, a soldier told her to get out of the line because her head was shaved—apparently camp officials didn't want hairless women returning to Germany, making the camps look bad. When that soldier looked away she got back in line. He saw her and ordered her out again. Then he left and she got back in line a third time and made it onto the bus. That makes her "plucky" in the eyes of one interviewer. But to the suggestion that she is plucky, Hanna responds, "No, dear, no dear, no . . . no, I had, no. I blocked my. . . . How should I explain to you? I know that I have to survive. Even running away, even being with people constantly, especially the second part, the second time being back in Auschwitz. That time I had determined already to survive, and you know what? It wasn't luck, it was stupidity."[4] The interviewer adds, "And a lot of guts." Hanna corrects her, saying, "No, no, no. No, but there were no guts, there were just sheer stupidity." The interviewer counters, "Well, but you stepped back in line." Hanna responds, "I just, you know . . ." And then one of the interviewers stands up, blocking the camera, and says, "I am going to take your microphone," ending the interview. It is a curious exchange, one in which failure to hear abounds. An interviewer tells Hanna that she was plucky; she hears "lucky" and responds to clarify that luck had nothing to do with it. The interviewer doesn't catch the miscommunication and so states in other words what amounts to the same thing, "You had a lot of guts." Meanwhile Hanna is trying to correct the misperception—to describe what really allowed her to survive—but that is what we do not get a chance to hear from her.

What makes this failed communication even more puzzling is that, for the entire space of time during which Hanna is attempting to correct the mistaken idea that she is plucky or lucky, we can hear the two interviewers offscreen arguing about something, temporarily not listening to Hanna. We can hear one of them say something about "why the time gets crazy"— maybe it means they are out of time, or they are concerned that Hanna's testimony does not follow a linear temporal order. They may be having a disagreement about whether the "plucky" line of questioning should have been posed in the first place. But the outcome is that we don't find out what it means to Hanna to survive through stupidity. Interviewers set up a scene for hearing and then fail to listen. An irony.

Lawrence Langer uses this scene to draw our attention to moments when interviewers encourage certain kinds of testimony and discourage others. In his rendering of the conversation, when Hanna says she survived through stupidity, "the two interviewers laugh deprecatingly, overriding her voice with their own 'explanation,' as one calls out, 'You had a lot of guts!' "[5] Having also watched the tape, I am not certain that that is what happened. It is possible that one of the interviewers is being deprecating, but more likely that she really wants to support Hanna's strength in pushing her way through situations that many did not survive. After all, it is no small thing to get out of Auschwitz alive twice. It is also clear (to me) that the second interviewer is not being deprecating but rather is trying to establish something with the other interviewer (though it isn't clear what that is, or why it had to be discussed at that moment). However, either way, the outcome is that Hanna doesn't get heard at precisely the moment when she seems to be opening up the most. It is a scene of failed hearing.

Much of Hanna's testimony is resistant or difficult. She says multiple times, when asked to describe her experiences, things like, "No, it is very hard to describe it," "It is very hard to go into every detail," "I cannot go into the details that you want to. Some of them are so gruesome. I really cannot go back so far. It hurts," or, "Must I go back to those things? I would rather not."[6] She often starts to tell a painful story, then pauses for a long while, then changes the topic, resorting back to a more controlled narrative. That may be because "lots of survivors compartmentalize the issues and retrieve the memories in disjointed fashion to protect themselves from being overwhelmed by the whole memory," as psychologist Mary Fabri observes.[7] Or she may have other reasons for not answering the questions put to her. In the video it seems clear that she tells the story she wants to tell rather than the one she is being asked for. In her telling, the story is not about being plucky. Hanna's interviewers seem to want redemptive stories about the resilience of the human spirit and the drive to live against all odds. Because that is what they want, that is also what they hear.

Langer points out that, while there may be redemptive stories to tell, many times survivors of grave abuse do not marvel at the strength of the human spirit, especially not their own. Instead they "mourn its fragility when the isolated self has no support from the surrounding milieu to validate it."[8] In other words, if we listened well to what testimonies such as Hanna's try to convey, it might interrupt our preconceptions about what testimony after violence should accomplish. We might also find ourselves face-to-face with our own responsibility as listeners who have the power to hear or fail to hear.

Of course, those who are put in the place of the hearer of testimony may have reasons for not hearing well. They may be constrained to adhere to the facts of the case or the established laws and procedures. They may have a political interest in a restorative discourse. They may be overwhelmed by how far the demand for help exceeds their capacity to offer assistance. Or they may be protecting themselves from the trauma of hearing. After all, stenographers, interpreters, and journalists working on South Africa's Truth and Reconciliation Commission (TRC) developed symptoms of post-traumatic stress disorder from listening.[9] One need not even hear the stories in person in order to undergo effects of trauma. Priscilla Hayner reports that "a number of commissions have found that the staff who are most disturbed by the harrowing tales of torture and abuse are not those taking statements directly from victims but are instead data entry staff charged with coding and entering the information into the database."[10] It might be someone's job to spend long days entering data in codes for abuses such as forcible abduction, amputation, beating of head against wall, pulling out teeth, removal of fingernails, being buried alive, being burned with chemicals, head submerged in water, being forced to watch the torture of others, genital mutilation, gang rape, burning of body parts, disembowelment, and so on. Exposure, even in the abstraction of codes, to the breadth, depth, and volume of the terrible things human beings have done to other human beings may take its toll.

Dori Laub lists six ways in which those who listen to traumatic testimony try to insulate themselves from hearing what it says: (1) mental paralysis, brought on by a fear of merging with the atrocities; (2) outrage and anger, unwittingly directed at the victim; (3) withdrawal and numbness; (4) a flood of awe and fear—the impulse to endow the survivor with sanctity and thereby keep her at a distance, to avoid the intimacy involved in knowing; (5) foreclosure through facts, circumventing human experience through an obsession with details, or by only hearing what you already know; and, finally, (6) hyperemotionality, where the testifier is drowned in the listener's defensive affectivity.[11]

So, listeners have a responsibility to hear well. But they may have conscious or unconscious resistances to hearing well. The problem is likely even more complicated than that, however. Why do so many of us want to hear the narrative of resilience rather than the story of destruction? Psychologist Ronnie Janoff-Bulman has argued, using studies and her own clinical work as evidence, that human beings have a need to assume that the world is benevolent and that responsible actions can lead to good outcomes. That is another way of saying that human beings want to be able to take existence for granted, and so they work very hard—sometimes to the point of denial of reality—to make of the world a place where they might do that. Even though it seems to inhabit the opposite end of a spectrum, the will to believe in the world's benevolence is related to what Sedgwick calls paranoid reading in that it, willfully or not, structures experience of the world for predictability. Dan Bar-On has shown in his studies of the descendants of Holocaust perpetrators and survivors a will to distance the self from a difficult truth. In one case a man who had finally asked his father about his job as a train conductor in Germany during World War II learned, after his father's initial denial, that his father had watched a large group of prisoners shot to death on a train platform. A year later when Bar-On reinterviewed the man, he "did not remember his father's disclosure, or that he had in turn repeated the story to Bar-On."[12] Judith Herman, in commenting on this case, describes Bar-On's metaphor of a "double wall erected to prevent acknowledgement of the memory of crime. The fathers did not want to tell; the children did not want to know."[13] That is part of how we shield ourselves from painful knowledge. It is also how we perpetuate the pain of those who lack the capacity to erect such mental shelter. James Baldwin puts it well in *The Fire Next Time*: "This is the crime of which I accuse my country and my countrymen, and for which I nor time nor history will ever forgive them, that they have destroyed and are destroying hundreds of thousands of lives and do not know and do not want to know it."[14] Like Jean Améry, Baldwin recognizes that conditions for apology or reconciliation are not met and, beyond that, that few even recognize their absence.

Herman observes that the human tendency to want a benevolent world can distort the perceptions of bystanders—people who live in a violent or unjust world (this world) but whose daily lives still allow them to think otherwise. She writes,

> Like the son of the man who drove the trains in wartime, we have been reluctant to know about the crimes we live with every day. We have sought information only when prodded to do so, and once we have acquired the information we have been eager to forget it again as soon as possible. We can see the phenomenon of active forgetting in operation as it pertains to crimes against humanity carried out on the most massive scale of organized genocide. It operates with the same force in the case of those unwitnessed crimes carried out in the privacy of families.[15]

We may fail to hear because we are indifferent to what has happened, because cultural difference makes a story difficult to understand, or because it is painful to absorb the truth of violent events. We may also fail to hear because we don't want to be confronted with something we didn't foresee, or because there is no common frame for the experience being described. No matter how heroic or apt the choice of words and narrative convention of a survivor's testimony may be, someone who has never been tortured may not be able to understand what it means for a tortured person to live on with the physical and emotional scars of that abuse. And if being tortured breaks selves, perhaps it is not all bad that we cannot imaginatively put ourselves in the place of the person being tortured. Our resistance may be a good adaptation of a psyche that somehow knows how much knowledge it can live with. But if ethical loneliness consists in being abandoned by humanity and then not being heard, then the will to believe in the world's benevolence—the drive to take existence for granted—contributes to that loneliness whenever it fails to hear the stories survivors tell of misfortune and injustice. Hanna wanted to tell a story made up of equal parts resilience and destruction. We need to hear both parts. Wanting to hear only the story of resilience shares with paranoid reading's certainty that the world will offer up horrors a determination not to be taken unaware by any revelation: nothing will surprise either approach.

Janoff-Bulman observes that when a human being undergoes a trauma inflicted by another human being, "the world is suddenly a malevolent one, not simply because something bad has happened to the victim but because the world of people is seriously tainted. Trust in others is seriously disturbed."[16] Such violation damages a person's sense of her own self's boundaries and may destroy her trust in the world. Ruth Kluger adds, "For the sensation of torture doesn't leave its victim alone—never, not to the end of life. It isn't the pain *per se*, it's how it was inflicted. . . . What matters is not just what we endure, but also what kind of misery it is, where it comes from. The worst is the kind that is imposed by others with malicious intent. That's the kind from which no one recovers."[17] Recall Améry's discussion of how the loss of his sovereignty came to him as an experience of abandonment: "With the first blow from a policeman's fist, against which there can be no defense and which no helping hand will ward off, a part of our life ends and it can never again be revived."[18]

Recovery from such harm can be difficult at least in part because the shattering of the initial view of the world as kind and caring cannot be undone. Those who work to recover from human-caused trauma often face a difficult choice between letting go of old assumptions about how the world works—in particular that it is benevolent and that selves are sovereign—and living with the frightening prospect of building a new world in which one must give up the old security and admit one's vulnerability to harm.[19] Howard Zehr, a founder of the restorative justice movement, argues that victimization violates "our vision of ourselves as autonomous individuals in a meaningful world."[20] Susan Brison, who writes that trauma "not only shatters one's fundamental assumptions about the world and one's safety in it, but it also severs the sustaining connection between the self and the rest of humanity," knows this from experience.[21]

If any of us are lucky enough to have remained intact and unviolated, we don't want to hear that no matter what we do we might end up destroyed, that the fabric holding together the world that we experience as relatively safe is very fragile. We don't want to know that, and so we may find it difficult to hear a story where that is the message. That is one complication in how we hear.

There is a further, related complication. A great many of us probably inherit our sense of our own responsibilities from ideas about the autonomous self who is responsible only for actions freely undertaken—in other words, the idea that we bear responsibility only for things we've done and intended. Surely there are sites of human judgment where that is precisely how we should think about culpability. Sometimes individually responsible persons, freely acting and fully intending to cause harm, do bad things to other persons. And we find them blameworthy for that, and that's fine.

But does *that* story about responsibility correspond in any way to the harm undergone by Hanna? Even if we could find the person responsible for the years of abuse and dehumanization she endured—if, say, we could put Hitler or a camp official on trial—would finding him guilty do justice to the way a whole world of meaning had to be orchestrated around hatred and indifference in order to allow what befell Hanna to happen? Not just Hitler, not just the Nazis, not just everyday Germans but the whole world, standing by, saying nothing, doing nothing, many of them hating some people for what rather than who they are, and allowing the ghettoization, deportation, and finally extermination of the people they had abandoned. Recovery from that kind of harm doesn't come from a finding of individual criminal responsibility—which is not to say that such a finding of guilt wouldn't be just or welcome or contribute to a larger program of recovery (as we saw in chapter 2).

The two complications are related because denying you can be destroyed and believing you're responsible only for acts you intend to commit are both outcomes of an incomplete view of human sovereignty, a view that thinks self-sufficiency is possible independent of social support. But, as we learned in chapter 1, sovereignty depends.

Seven years after her initial testimony Hanna returned to the Fortunoff archive and was interviewed by Dana Kline and Lawrence Langer. In that second interview we learn a bit about what it might mean to her to survive by means of stupidity. She reveals that throughout the war she kept wanting to believe that someone she loved would survive, and she calls that stupidity. When Langer asks her directly what she meant by "surviving through stupidity," she explains that she had no fear. She would just do what she had to do. So stupidity seems to mean, for her, a kind of unreflective resistance to what was impossible about the situation in Auschwitz. My sense that this is the case gets partial confirmation from her statement late in the second interview: "You see, there was no brains. I had no fear. . . . Stupidity. I just made up my mind I have to go by and that's all."[22] The interviewers ask her, "Do you think if you had been smart you would have been afraid?" She responds, "Scared. I was not scared at all for anything over anybody. Once I put my right foot forward I was determined. I was pushing. I was going." Interviewers follow up with, "What do you think made you able to do that? Most people would have been scared." Her answer, "Determination." They follow with, "What gave you that determination? Something you did for yourself, your upbringing?" And then she reiterates her hope that someone else from her family would survive while also enacting her strategy of starting to say something difficult, pausing, and turning instead to something manageable: "I suppose the upbringing helped too. I was hoping that somebody will survive. That [pause and huge sigh] I never went home from work without a few potatoes. It wasn't stealing, it was organizing."[23] She tells a story about how, during the war, the verb "to organize" always pointed to theft.[24]

This second tape, rather than ending abruptly in confusion, ends with Langer thanking Hanna for her story, and Hanna responding, "You're welcome. Maybe I'll feel a bit better too. I unloaded a bit." That ending might leave a viewer feeling good, as if something cathartic had just occurred and maybe the speaker had derived some benefit from speaking and being heard. That may even be what happened. It starts to undo how terrible it feels to watch the first interview's ending. But one can't listen to two interviews held seven years apart during which a survivor of grave harm narrates exactly the same stories in very similar ways and not be moved by what it would mean to have *those* be the stories that underlie the self's sense of its own history.[25] If testimony works, it is not because someone gets to tell a story once, exorcise it, and then move on from past harm.

If hearing is meaningful, it has to be embedded in an openness where what is said might be heard even if it threatens to break the order of the known world for those who listen. Think about Hanna "surviving through stupidity." Stupidity is her code for hoping that someone she loved would survive. Imagine inhabiting that bleak view as your only fragment of hope and then surviving, finding it unrewarded. Anyone who labels Hanna's survival strategy "plucky" misses a deep source of harm that no amount of time, love, or justice could fully repair.

Nothing will fully repair such loss, but some approaches will do better than others at helping to rebuild worlds. The person whose world and self have been destroyed will need to rebuild a sense of self, of her own sovereignty in the world. That is where theories of the value of personal sovereignty, liberty, and autonomy come in handy. But the how and the why of that need for autonomy and what it takes to rebuild a self can't be fully explicated if we begin by assuming that any person's sovereignty is insulated from the surrounding world. No one is sovereign from the ground up. Selves can be destroyed because selves are also built, and built cooperatively, by human relationships of various kinds—rational, affective, intentional, unwitting, chosen, and unchosen. Even if selves were more self-sufficient than this intersubjective definition would have us believe, it would still be the case that before a self could rebuild her own sovereignty, she would need to feel safe. That, in turn, requires a surrounding world where safety is possible, though that is also what is destroyed by violence. A world, a cooperatively authored thing, can't be rebuilt by a person acting alone, especially not one with a destroyed self. It is the job of the wider world to help with the rebuilding. So a person whose world and self have been destroyed may need to rebuild a sense of her own sovereignty, but responsibility for offering conditions where that is possible ought to fall very widely. That is so not only because only very wide disregard allows worlds to be destroyed but also because thinking of responsibility in terms of individual culpability may mend discrete harms but will never fix a broken world.

That is why, at the same time that a person whose world has been destroyed may need rebuilt sovereignty, the person whose world was left intact may need a bit of destruction of her own personal sovereignty—or a different telling of the story about it. This claim can't be universalized in any simple way because we all carry with us varying amounts of damage and different levels of belief in our own autonomy. But I don't think it's too dangerous to say that a huge number of people could do with some destruction of their idea of the self's autonomy. Just a bit more awareness that the self's sovereignty is a fiction or a partial truth, and that the fiction can be as useful as it can be harmful.

YVONNE KHUTWANE

Fiona Ross describes the case of Yvonne Khutwane, who in July 1996 "testified about a variety of forms of violation. In the print media, her testimony was condensed to her experiences of sexual violation. Reported as a 'story' of rape, that framing was taken on and repeated in the Commission's 1998 report, and in a talk given at a conference on Transitional Justice at Yale University by Commissioner Wendy Orr."[26] Ross shows how material from Wendy Orr's talk was then reproduced in a scholarly book by Martha Minow (the widely read *Between Vengeance and Forgiveness*) and then also became part of the basis on which the effects on women of proceedings like the commission were analyzed (for instance, in Priscilla Hayner's well-known book on truth commissions, *Unspeakable Truths*).[27] Ross's telling of Khutwane's story does a good job showing just how far out of the control of the speaker a TRC testimony can spiral. Many people reading this chapter will have read Minow's and Hayner's books, and perhaps a few will have read the transcript of Khutwane's testimony. It doesn't render anyone blameworthy for having encountered Minow or Hayner first. But it does show who has more power over Khutwane's story. Upon reading a transcript of what Yvonne Khutwane said, one is reminded of how much patience and respect the TRC commissioners showed so many who testified. Khutwane wanted to tell a story of her humiliation, and she did so on her own terms, which were sometimes meandering or difficult to follow. Her story was difficult to follow (if it was) in part because Khutwane did not wish to tell the story that the commission most wanted to hear. One can read her testimony as an assertion of agency, a form of resistance to the expected narrative form, and an attempt to reclaim her self by means of her own story. Commissioner Gobodo-Madikizela helped her along and asked some questions designed to bring what harmed her to the fore, and in doing so consistently steered her back to the story of rape rather than to the wider array of harms Khutwane was attempting to narrate. Upon reading the transcript one might surmise that Gobodo-Madikizela had her reasons for doing this—rape was a common reality for women caught up in the struggles around and against apartheid, but gathering data on that abuse was difficult because of cultural taboos around speaking about sexual violence. In addition, the main objective of a TRC hearing on human rights violations was to gather information on such abuses, so commissioners would, while allowing victims to tell their own stories, consistently work to make sure that those who testified revealed the abuses that would help build the larger truth about South Africa's history and also potentially qualify victims for reparations.

Gobodo-Madikizela did succeed in getting out of Khutwane a story about rape. But the "guiding" of her testimony at times seemed to make Khutwane impatient. She would remind the commissioner that she was still telling *her* story. Since Khutwane did not mention rape in her initial written statement, and Gobodo-Madikizela gained this testimony only through persistent (but gentle) questioning, it seems likely that Khutwane had not intended to tell the story of sexual violence in as much detail as she ended up doing.[28] Ross observes, in regard to the rape charges, that Khutwane "sometimes evaded the questions posed, or answered them briefly. . . . She was not reticent in describing the other violations she had experienced. She told of being threatened, hit, beaten with the butt of a gun, strangled, suffocated, squashed. She described arson and her child's death, and her feelings of alienation from her political community."[29]

Some of the humiliation Khutwane described did include sexual violation, but the point that she comes back to repeatedly in her testimony is that she was dehumanized by young people the age of her children. They slapped her and touched her inappropriately and generally disrespected her. Since she comes from a culture that respects its elders, the violation of that respect, when added to the other losses and abuses she describes, gives us a fuller sense of what destroyed her world. In her words, "It was so painful because I couldn't stand it, because these kids were young and they were still at a very age they had all the powers to respect and honor me. They were just the same age as my children and what were they doing to me."[30] Of course she was harmed by being sexually violated. But the story she wished to tell framed what happened in terms of a broader destruction of world.[31] The TRC let her do that for the most part. The larger world of news media and academic writing then effectively reduced how Khutwane's testimony would be heard outside the TRC to a narrative of sexual violence. The hard irony here is that an institution designed for hearing may use procedures that silence some stories, and even when a resistant story gets told and, miraculously, heard, the larger world may not be willing to hear it for what it is.

Ross argues that the TRC model "assumed that what preceded the Commission's work was voicelessness and silence about the apartheid past."[32] She points out that stories of apartheid had been told for many years in diverse genres, including "stories, songs, political rhetoric, magisterial orders, court cases, newspapers, scholarly work, parliamentary debates, at funerals and rallies and so on."[33] So what the TRC offered to South Africa wasn't speech for the first time but a new structure for speaking combined with a guaranteed audience and a nonretributive but still institutionalized way of dealing with harm. Let us mark what an awe-inspiring achievement that was. Even if some of the TRC goals were at odds with one another (nation building versus individual healing), the institution was designed for the purpose of hearing, and it opened up a space where a range of stories could be heard.

But institutions have procedures, rules, and standards, or they quickly cease to be. The form TRC testimony was to take solidified very quickly. Ross describes it as follows: "From each testimony, the Commission sought to isolate a coherent chronology, a clear relation between component parts, a climax phrased in terms of the experience of a 'gross violation of human rights.'"[34] Antjie Krog and her coauthors offer a similar description: "The beginning of testimony usually consisted of some biographical detail, leading to the middle part about the circumstances and content of the violation. After clarifications, the desire and/or needs of the victim would be established, upon which the commissioner who was chairing that specific evidence would conclude the interaction."[35] A perusal of any amount of testimony before the TRC will reveal that no matter how hard a speaker tried to resist that format, in the end the format won.

Sometimes the format would win by imposing a form so gently that one would be hard-pressed to call it "imposition." Other times the presuppositions beneath the format would be revealed more forcefully, as in this exchange between a commissioner and a witness who was resistant to forgiving a perpetrator:

> Q: You do read newspapers and watch TV, not so?
> A: Yes I do read newspapers and I do watch television.
> Q: I assume that you know about this Truth and Reconciliation Commission that is going on, of which Amnesty is part thereof?
> A: Yes I heard.
> Q: Do you know that this is done by the Government to foster or to promote reconciliation in the country?
> A: Yes I do know that.
> Q: What is your attitude about this reconciliation process?
> A: I don't have any comment on that one.
> Q: Do you believe in reconciliation?
> A: Yes I do believe.[36]

It is not clear whether this exchange is meant to educate or to shame the witness, but in either case it does not succeed at listening. I'm sure the commissioners involved took seriously the nation-building goal of the TRC and hoped it would make possible a peaceful rather than a bloody transition to postapartheid South Africa. But, as others have observed, there may have been a way for the TRC to encourage forgiveness without delegitimating righteous anger.[37] Slight differences in institutional design might have allowed other truths to be emerge, and that course, if taken, might have allowed a wider array of persons to feel that their losses were heard, and that those losses had been recognized as unjust, *perhaps even unforgivable*, by institutions and the surrounding community. The just irony here would be that an institution of forgiveness may have facilitated wider forgiveness if it had allowed expressions of the refusal to forgive (which were surely justified in many cases!) to be part of the larger narrative formed by the TRC.

COLIN DE SOUZA AND SULEJMAN CRNCALO

It is not only the format of the TRC or the tendency of commissioners to encourage forgiveness and gloss over resentment that silences resistant testimony. Jan Blommaert, Mary Bock, and Kay McCormick, using sociolinguistic discourse analysis to find suffering where it is masked by forms of speech, spend a fair amount of time on the testimony of Colin de Souza before the Human Rights Violations Committee of the TRC. They worry that his testimony "does not produce his narrative of suffering in a style that flags the topic. There are few, if any, explicit expressions of emotion; de Souza doesn't cry, but tells his story in a composed, rather flat and factual way, emphasizing more the adventurous side of his experience than the devastating effects it has had on his life."[38] So they set out to interpret the story in such a way that his testimony does show how someone's life could be destroyed by the struggle against apartheid. But there is something not quite right here. Let's consider some pieces of De Souza's testimony.

> They were beating me at that stage. And at one incident they were throwing that was during the afternoon they throw in some teargas canisters in—inside the cell you know a wet cell you know, this wet with water and they closed the doors and all the windows were closed but at that time I was still clever of knowing the tricks and the tactics you know of laying down on the ground and that, the tear gas won't get me, so when they came in, they saw that I was still conscious, they were expecting somebody after a half an hour to be unconscious, so what they did is they undress me and they chained me up, you know my feet, my hands to my feet and they had a special chain you know, that were used with the prisoners that is on awaiting trial you know, that chains you know and they would chain me up by my feet and my hand and put me up against this metal gate you know, this metal and chained me up to that gate, then start beating me with the batons over my head, Van Brakel would pull my hair and you know and they was beating me till I was out.[39]

In his testimony he offers many detailed descriptions of the torture to which he was subjected. A key point for de Souza (on my reading of his testimony) is that his training prepared him for this—he knows how to react to tear gas and withstand police interrogation. On more than one occasion when a commissioner asks him a question designed to get him to talk about his suffering, he answers factually and then returns to a story of outwitting police or participating actively in the struggle against apartheid. For these and other reasons, Blommaert et al. call his testimony "a story of suffering, disguised as an event narrative."[40] De Souza also talks about how after he was released from custody some of his comrades chased him and tried to kill him because they suspected him of being a police informer:

> Jacques draw out a gun to force his way into the house like to shoot me and my father grabbed him and there was a whole twist outside and my brother-in-law he hit Jacques you know and the gun fall—fall over the balcony right down you know and they chased the group, it was a group of youths it was about sixteen of them you know. . . . The chase went right around the street and my father and my brother-in-law they arrived. At that time I had a firearm but it was for my own purpose. I took out the firearm, I put it underneath my jersey, I went outside because I check now it's too dangerous to be inside the house. And I want to move now, out of the area. As we were still standing outside to move this group of comrades and there was some gangsters also with, they came shooting around the corner, before even they take the bend the shots was firing and they were shooting and throwing bricks and my mother and my father they ran into this, and with my baby brother ran into this people downstairs house, that there surname were Brooks, they ran into this house and these people locked the door, and I and my brother-in-law Kevin Arendse was still outside, locked outside. The people inside didn't want to open the door and here these people were preparing to shoot and there was like a big fight you know and one guy he was still trying to cork [*sic*] the gun but the gun jammed you know and at that time as I was shouting open the door, the people inside opened the door and as my brother-in-law Kevin Arendse and I ran into the house, and the door closed the shots just went down and the bullets ran through the doors and through the windows and all that.[41]

Here de Souza is being attacked and shot at by people he had considered his comrades, and it is also clear that his family is in danger because of his presence. Other parts of his testimony deal with how the lives of his mother and girlfriend have been impacted by what happened to him, his difficulty finding a job, and his diagnosis by doctors, who were treating him for the long-standing effects of severe torture.[42]

A question worth asking is, what do we learn from discourse analysis here? Blommaert et al. tell us that we learn that "affect markers are not a stable and closed category, but that any feature of talk can potentially serve an affect-marking function when it is stylistically contrastive with other features."[43] Fair enough. The authors take the time to listen carefully to recordings of de Souza's testimony so they can appropriately label his speech according to pitch, stress, intonation, pause, and other indicators, and thus we may learn something about how de Souza handles his own suffering in speech form. Anyone who has both witnessed a hearing and read its transcripts knows the very important difference between the two. In September 2012, I watched Sulejman Crncalo, a Bosnian Muslim, testify before the ICTY in the case against Ratko Mladić. In the course of his testimony, he told this story:

> I'll never forget that image. It will never leave me. The street was covered in blood. There were about 30 people there—well, that's my assessment. But the part hit by the shell was covered in blood. There was a fence protecting pedestrians from the trams, and there were body parts or, rather, parts of clothing and footwear on the fence, in the streets. There were body parts. The entire fence was covered in blood. I observed all of this and there were people looking on from the side streets. They asked me, what are you doing? I said, I'm looking for my wife.[44]

The scene appears terrible when you read it, but it may seem terrible in a straightforward, somewhat "factual" way. That may have to do with the format—you know that you are reading something that is an official document, legal testimony, and it is words on a page held separate from the embodied life of the man who authored the words. But when you hear the testimony in person, and the elderly man whose wife has now been dead for twenty years is crying and reliving the trauma of the story, the experience is visceral. In the audience gallery, sparsely populated by scholars, lawyers, journalists, and "tribunal tourists," everyone is paralyzed at this moment. Very still, crying, not knowing what to do with the moment.

A neutral setting where all know their roles and easily maintain their sep-
arateness is transformed, bland space suddenly pulsing and claustropho-
bic. If this is what discourse analysis could do for the written word, I suppose that would be a good thing in that it would allow people who care
to listen to hear better.

But what do we fail to hear when we do not take de Souza at his word
that part of what sustained him is that he was well trained, that he was—
in his word—clever enough to know how to react to tear gas canisters
and being chased and detained and tortured? Blommaert et al. worry that
"it is precisely the existence of a public transcript that makes hidden transcripts invisible, obliterates resistance and shapes an image of ideological
incorporation."[45] Let me be sure to say that I think it is important that
those who read, hear, and write about testimony keep these possibilities
in mind—to look and listen for them. As Blommaert et al. state, "upon
closer inspection, we can see very different versions, rooted in very different traditions of talking and thinking about topics, and very often leading
us into a more 'subcultural' view of particular representations of reality."[46]
Institutions structured to take testimony in certain forms, settings, and languages will always make speech easier for some than others, and so those
who listen may need to learn how to attend to more than a bare transcript
of what is said. The tools of sociolinguistics are surely among the indis-
pensable tools of this endeavor. But in this case, in finding de Souza's pain
in the "hidden transcript" of how he speaks, Blommaert et al. unwittingly
obliterate his resistance to making the story only about his suffering. An
irony. Ross calls this "excavating and revealing pain in accounts that ex-
pressly set out to disguise it or to shatter normative models."[47] The authors
worry that de Souza's testimony says about him that "he was not one who
suffered, but one who struggled."[48] Though I doubt anyone who heard or
read his testimony would miss his suffering—from torture and ostracization to his continuing mental and physical health problems and the diverse effects of all that on everyone in his life—surely it matters that he
chose to tell a story of struggle rather than one only of suffering.

SILENCE

In the early 1980s in the United States, psychiatrist Stuart Grassian was
ordered by a Massachusetts court to evaluate fifteen prisoners at Walpole
penitentiary to determine whether their claims that solitary confinement

is cruel and unusual punishment and thus unconstitutional could be substantiated. While being interviewed by Grassian, one prisoner observed, "I went to a standstill psychologically once—lapse of memory. I didn't talk for 15 days. I couldn't hear clearly. You can't see—you're blind—block everything out—disoriented, awareness is very bad. Did someone say he's coming out of it? I think what I'm saying is true—not sure. I think I was drooling—a complete standstill."[49] Grassian reported that seven of the prisoners suffered perceptual distortions or hallucinations, in part because they had no way of corroborating what they thought they heard. They had been removed from the world of human relationships, where our interactions with other people help establish that we share a world in common with others where stable meanings can be created. As such the conditions in which these prisoners found themselves resemble those that destroyed the world of Jean Améry. Another prisoner reported, "I hear sounds—guards saying, 'They're going to cut [his nerve-damaged leg] off.' I'm not sure. Did they say it or is it my imagination?"[50] The prisoner lacks certainty about what he has heard, but not because he wasn't listening closely enough. Is it irony when you can listen all you want and still not hear what has happened? As Grassian observes, "If [the guards] did say [what the prisoner thought he heard], the prisoner is suffering from derealization; if they said something else, or something not directed at him, he is suffering a (paranoid) perceptual distortion; if they said nothing, he is having a hallucination."[51] But solitary confinement is structured such that no one—not even those to whom it happened—can know what happened. This is a place of utter silence. The United States has, in Colin Dayan's words, "invented a new form of death," and a number of Supreme Court rulings have only made that more difficult to see.[52] As Lisa Guenther points out, "we don't expect that our most fundamental sense of identity could come unraveled in the prolonged absence of others—but this is because we rely on the support of others at such a basic level that we can take them for granted."[53]

In her remark Guenther is talking about solitary confinement, but I think her observation has a wider meaning. Identity comes unraveled in the prolonged absence of others—and that isolation does not have to be solitary confinement.[54] What happens when a survivor tries to narrate a destruction of self and world, but what gets heard by those who listen is a redemptive story about resilience? What happens when a survivor resists reducing a complex story of disrespect to sexual violence, but what gets heard is a rape story, or when a survivor wants to tell a story about his strength, and it is converted into a story about his pain? These are forms of imposed isolation that may happen even in a crowd of people, even in a crowd of supportive people. Many of those supportive people may have failed to hear well because they are stuck in the other part of Guenther's remark: they have relied on the support of others to such an extent that they have taken it for granted. It is invisible. They don't even see that they need it or that it can be destroyed. They have taken existence for granted and so far have never allowed anything to interrupt their sense that what they experience is simply how the world is—like some kind of unchangeable essence—rather than the outcome of cooperative action that relies on others and for which they are in part responsible. That is one barrier to hearing well the testimony of those who have lost that connecting thread. Those who listen may not see that when they fail to hear, they also fail to contribute to rebuilding a world because they have failed to recognize a self who is struggling to be heard on her or his own terms.

COMMUNICATION

We might be aided here by a better, or at least a different, understanding of what communication is, what it does, how it succeeds, fails, and produces ironies, and why that matters not only to individuals seeking to convey meanings to one another but also to the politics of reconciliation, transition, and recovery.[55] I think Levinas's work can help us here, too, to get at something that is difficult in the scenes of communication we have been discussing.

For Levinas, communication is not a simple way in which I act on the world and reap the end that follows logically from its means, especially since it proceeds not only by language but also in bodily signs. We give off meanings and receive them from others all the time, whether we will it or not. A significant amount of meaning is carried and transferred in this way. In saying that, I *do not* mean that from viewing my outer appearance—my clothes and manners and modes of speaking—you might surmise something about my past and present. Of course you can do that (with varying levels of success). Instead I'm pointing to the ways in which communication is not knowledge.

Communication—verbal and nonverbal—may and often does contain a specific content, which the speaker intends a hearer to receive and understand. But communication has a prior phenomenology. Just as a sensation of heat, flavor, or odor is not primarily cognition of those things but an undergoing of a sensation, communication is, prior to its instrumental use for sending a message, a form of responsiveness to other human beings.[56] It exists because there are others, to whom we respond. That is the kind of being a human being is: exposed, responsive. It is why we can be harmed. And it is how we communicate. Some of our responses to others are reasoned and willed; many others—many of the primary ones—are not.

If irony is a space where a gap opens up between what is said and what is meant, you might say Levinas's description of human communication has irony of a certain kind built into it. Levinas reminds us that "to require that a communication be sure of being heard is to confuse communication and knowledge, to efface the difference, to fail to recognize the signifyingness of the-one-for-the-other in me."[57] What Levinas calls "signifyingness" (*signifiance*) points not only to the "meaning" of *l'un-pour-l'autre*, the-one-for-the-other, but to the idea that as beings we give off signs. We don't only "make" signs but also, perhaps, "shed" them, revealing ourselves affectively whether we wish it or not. We are for-the-other because we send and receive "messages" simply by appearing and inhabiting the world as sensing beings in proximity to other sensing beings. This may be what Kathleen Stewart intends when she writes, "Everyday life is lived on the level of surging affects, impacts suffered or barely avoided."[58] So Levinas means, among other things, that communication is not a simple transfer of meaning from point A in me to point B in another person or a larger audience. When any one of us undertakes to communicate with others, we probably desire success, precision, and certainty. But sometimes our aim will not be precise. And even when it is, we may not succeed in communicating what we intend—even when we speak in favorable conditions and from places of power. Knowledge can, at times, be certain. But communication is not knowledge.

Remember both Levinas's observation that research takes form as a question and Améry's experience of an imposed existential solitude that for him was the loneliness of utter abandonment. Even the dialogue a self may have with itself needs others; intellectual solitude is still a work of thought performed by a self *who resides in a shared world*. When a person speaks and no one listens, or those who listen fail to hear, that may undermine the sense of inhabiting a shared world for the speaker. We depend on others not only to forbear from harming us but also to respond to us and, in doing so, confirm the reality of the shared world. Without that there *is* no world. That is why Levinas writes that "communication would be impossible if it should have to begin in the ego, a free subject, to whom every other would be only a limitation that invites war, domination, precaution and information."[59] Communication begins in response and, while war and domination are indeed forms of response, they are also, like negotiated peace or social norm following, later versions, built upon a bedrock of communication not reducible to "what words mean" (which in any case is already a complicated thing). The self-sufficient subject who conceives of her autonomy as only threatened rather than also built by the presence of others would be hard-pressed to explain why communication is as fragile as it manifestly is. Affect ranges between and among us, transmitting joy, rage, indifference, and even trauma. We sense the presence of others and we respond, sometimes despite ourselves. That may interrupt even our best attempts to convey accurate messages to others, for better and for worse.

Levinas *isn't* arguing that we are passive through and through, however. After all, in his description of self-formation (discussed in chapter 1), the self undergoes a conflict between egoism and its interruption by the other fairly constantly, not (or not only) as a form of a reasoned moral inner debate but as waves of affectivity beyond the power of a self to choose or refuse. We *are* our own selves, yes. But we *do* respond to others, whether we rationally will it or not. The tensions inherent in the relation between responsiveness and self-involvement correspond to what we saw in chapter 1 about taking existence for granted. It is, for some people at some times, easy enough to take the world for granted and to experience as given a self who gets to choose how to interact with the things by which and persons by whom she is affected. We might say that theorists of autonomy are right to want to describe that self and provide conditions for its flourishing. But if we take that self as a starting point rather than a fragile accomplishment relying on many authors, we miss something important not only about who we are but also about what we owe to ourselves and others. We may fail to be interrupted by the sense that there *are* others.

Communication (like fatigue, weariness, and indolence in chapter 1) may, if we take note of how it works, interrupt our sense of the certainty of meanings and remind us that we are responsive creatures trying to build and share worlds. It does this (if we stop to notice) by drawing our attention to what we did not get to choose and to the risks none of us can escape—of misunderstanding, abandonment, and refusal of response.

Discerning truths and transmitting facts are both important aspects of world building; they help to establish a shared world and set forth standards of judgment by which we hold ourselves and others accountable. But if we think that facts and truths fill out the vessel of communication, or that when we communicate facts and truths transparent understanding always ensues, we will not be able to explain why conflicting facts and truths always emerge—unless we content ourselves with saying that wherever truths conflict, only one of them is true. In many situations—especially those of postconflict transition and reconciliation—meaningful experience will not bear out that conclusion. Indeed, every reconciliation rests on a fragile consensus—a new definition of past, present, and future—that can be won only slowly, painfully, and cooperatively and will never succeed in erasing or redefining every resistant narrative. In every transitional situation, people make hard choices about where to compromise and where to hold fast to principles of justice or recovery. Some voices get heard and others do not. Individual victims, whether or not they feel heard, will also face the inevitable disparities between what is good for the group and what is good for the self. And it won't only be calculations of rational self-interest governing how these changes come into being. People will be swept along by what Stewart calls "rogue intensities": "all the lived, yet unassimilated, impacts of things, all the fragments of experience left hanging. Everything left unframed by the stories of what makes a life pulses at the edges of things. All the excesses and extra effects unwittingly propagated by plans and projects and routines of all kinds surge, experiment, meander. They pull things in their wake."[60] Beings who communicate, as we do, through various channels, many of them neither willed nor fully controllable, will need rules, reasoned discourse, and formal equality to keep things fair. But they will need a lot more than that.

A strict accounting of facts may help shed light on abuses that were hidden, and that may help set up new expectations that where lawlessness once reigned, the rule of law will now offer equal protection. That is good. But a strict accounting of facts may also—at the same time—fail to do justice to the deeply entrenched different truths a divided society has lived in. Even the soundest logic, bringing together facts and what justice requires, may fail to persuade people in the absence of conditions for successful hearing. It may also simply miss something not sayable within its terms. As Sedgwick points out, "some exposés, some demystifications, some bearings of witness do have great effectual force (though often of an unanticipated kind). Many that are just as true and convincing have none at all, however, and as long as that is so, we must admit that the efficacy and directionality of such acts reside somewhere else than in their relation to knowledge *per se.*"[61]

Yazir Henry

Mark Henry was a member of Umkhonto we Sizwe (MK), the armed wing of the African National Congress (ANC) in South Africa during its struggles against apartheid.[62] Yazir Henry is the name he chooses now, "because Mark was a name that I could no longer live with."[63] He changed it in 1991, saying at the time that he was doing so for religious reasons, though in his testimony before South Africa's TRC he admits "it was much more than that. Mark was a name that brought me ostracization, it brought me shame and it brought me great danger."[64] He changed his name for reasons similar to those that led Hans Maier to become Jean Améry (or Paul Antschel to become Paul Celan). It marked a break with a past that was unlivable in the present. Changing a name may modify the self's relation to its history, assert an agency with regard to it, become a way of making a past that should have been otherwise more manageable. It is a form of revision.

Why did the name Mark Henry bring ostracization, shame, and danger? After joining the movement at age fifteen and rising through the ranks of the MK, undergoing training in Mozambique, Zambia, Angola, and the Soviet Union, Henry infiltrated back into South Africa, where, after being apprehended, he was tortured and forced to reveal the location where a comrade, Anton Fransch, was hiding. That friend was then killed. Henry lacked the "moral luck" Améry had—that Améry never possessed the information that he admits he surely would have given up under torture. There is much information that Henry did not give up, but what he did admit caused the death of a fellow fighter.

When he was finally released after months of captivity, torture, and abuse by the South African Security Forces, his comrades suspected him of being an *askari*, someone recruited by the South African Security Forces to work against the ANC. Nothing he said would change their minds, so he was ostracized, his life permanently in danger. That is ethical loneliness—abuse and dehumanization followed by the surrounding world's refusal to listen. In his testimony, describing what happened to him *after* he was released from captivity, Henry says,

> I began to disintegrate. I lost weight, at one point I weighed 40 kgs [88 lbs], even less. My self-confidence, self-esteem and dignity was eroded even further. My ability to concentrate and remember was seriously impaired. It became impossible to sleep, I was and still am constantly haunted by nightmares. I remember looking into the mirror and seeing somebody whom I didn't know. I could not accept that some of my comrades whom I had trusted could believe that I had become an *askari* and an enemy.[65]

What harmed him was not only his own betrayal of his comrade or the torture and abuse by the Security Forces. Abandonment by his community and by the movement to which he had dedicated his life weighed as heavily and made it impossible for him to move forward. He could not rebuild a world without the help of others. And so he lived for years in a prison of his own guilt, too ashamed to speak of what had happened to him and unable to resume living a normal life. He wanted the TRC to give him a space where he could testify not only to the truth of his betrayal but also to his own victimization: that at the age of nineteen he was put in the impossible position of choosing between the lives of his mother and four-year-old nephew and the life of his friend. In the transcript of his testimony one can witness him doing his best to balance taking responsibility for that death with giving voice to what was invisible about his own case—that he had been treated unjustly, too.

Henry's testimony, in some of its aspects, recalls the loss and disorientation expressed by the prisoners in solitary confinement at Walpole and by Améry in the concentration camp—isolation and dehumanization cause a disintegration of self. And it points to a wider responsibility for justice in multiple ways. The continuing challenges to Henry's mental and physical recovery came not only from feeling threatened but also from being abandoned. In his testimony he says, "It has been hard living and not existing. I am alive but my existence continues to be ignored."[66] One of the things he wanted the TRC to provide was a space where the lines between victim and perpetrator were less distinct.[67]

Henry testified before the TRC about abuses he underwent, not about crimes he committed, though of course the betrayal of his comrade entered into his testimony, since it was an integral part of the story of what befell him. What Henry sought from the TRC was release from his guilt and support from his community—human understanding of the impossible choice forced on him. Instead his blame for a role in a political struggle well beyond his control was formalized: his name appeared in the *TRC Final Report* in conjunction with the case of his dead friend, making his guilt official rather than helping to lift its weight. An irony. In his words, "My testimony appears under the name of someone who has been killed and I can never be freed from this version of the past. Instead of clearing my name, it is as if I am forever written into this death. No attempt has been made in the Final Report to look carefully at the reasons I went to testify."[68] He understands *intellectually* why this would happen, given the number of persons who appeared before the TRC, but knowing that doesn't compensate him for his loss: "In the context of so many testimonies I am able to make sense of this—in the context of my own personal life it is just painful."[69]

So, despite the more capacious space for storytelling offered by the TRC, the institution's strict delineation of victim and perpetrator as separate categories rendered something important about Yazir Henry's condition unintelligible. Those categories are part of why his testimony, like Yvonne Khutwane's, took on a life of its own: Antjie Krog told an edited version of it in her book *Country of My Skull*, naming the chapter in which it appears "The Narrative of Betrayal Has to Be Reinvented Every Time";[70] and various newspapers took up the story and molded it to the narrative form of crime and political forgiveness.[71] As a result, his testimony put him in more danger. As he reports a few years after his testimony, "In the two and a half years since occupying that space, I have survived one attempt on my life and I have been accosted and humiliated several times in public for reasons relating to my entering the space provided by the TRC."[72]

The TRC recognized Henry, gave him space to speak, recorded his story, and commissioners offered him supportive words. But the TRC also failed him.

However, we might ask, how far can we take the point about the risks of communication? On one level, we may want to call what happened to Yazir Henry, Colin de Souza, Yvonne Khutwane, or Hanna a simple truth, that no one is entirely in charge of her own life story, and thus when you tell your story in a public forum, it may take on meanings that you never intended because that is just how stories and public fora work.[73] But how this truth affects us may vary according to power positions.[74] We're back with Horace in front of the Roman Forum, treating a man who desires our help as a nuisance rather than reading his predicament as a commentary on the fragility of communication, our responsibility to respond, and the potential differences of power and influence between us.

THE SHIELDS (SILENCE, PART 2)

The skeletal remains of Native Americans were not considered human remains until 1990—according to U.S. law. Before that, they were considered scientific specimens, and it was perfectly "legal" to rob Native American graves or to store bones, skulls, and sacred objects in drawers and boxes in archives. Then, in 1990, NAGPRA (the Native American Graves Protection and Repatriation Act) was passed, reclassifying native remains as human and also giving Native Americans a place in the conversation about what to do with remains housed in federally funded museums.[75]

As a piece of legislation, NAGPRA is both forward looking and backward looking. It requires that, for remains and cultural objects already found as of 1990, museums that receive federal funds must make lists available of the remains and associated funerary and sacred objects in their collections, and, if a tribe or lineal descendant related to the remains or cultural objects requests a return of the items, the objects must be repatriated. For remains and objects found after 1990—either intentionally or inadvertently—NAGPRA "prioritizes claims of ownership."[76] First priority goes to a person or tribe able to demonstrate lineal descent from the remains in question. When funerary or other sacred objects are found and they are not clearly associated with any particular bodily remains (meaning that direct identification of lineal descendants is impossible), first priority for granting ownership of the objects goes to the tribe on whose land the objects are found, with second priority going to a Native American tribe "which has the closest cultural affiliation."[77] Third priority awards the remains and objects to the tribe judged to be the aboriginal inhabitants of the land on which the objects were found, unless another tribe can show that it has a "stronger cultural relationship" with the items.[78] These rules at times have the unintended consequence of pitting tribes against one another in disputed claims.

An interesting thing about NAGPRA is that, when it comes to establishing lineage or "ownership" (a problematic term for many of these items, as we'll see), oral history counts as evidence equally alongside scientific evidence such as linguistic, historical, archaeological, and genetic materials. That is one way in which NAGPRA is sensitive to the different ways in which cultural memory gets stored and transmitted.[79] The legislation lists "geographical, kinship, biological, archaeological, anthropological, linguistic, folkloric, oral traditional, historical, or other relevant information or expert opinion" as legitimate sources of evidence, and the standard of proof to be applied is that of "a preponderance of the evidence."[80] That is a promising step forward for the U.S. government, whose representatives were, in the past, "often blunt in their rejection of oral histories as reliable sources."[81]

But even a piece of legislation designed, like NAGPRA, to redress past harms in ways sensitive to the incommensurate forms of meaning making in U.S. legalism and Native American cultures may produce situations where judgments aimed at granting tribal requests fail to hear what tribal representatives say. The case of three shields found by the Pectol family in 1926 and then repatriated in the early part of the present century is such an instance.

The shields, found in a cave in Utah in the early twentieth century and then displayed in the Visitor's Center of Capitol Reef National Park in Utah for many decades, were of Native American origin. But experts could not agree on the precise source of the shields: estimated dates of origin varied from A.D. 1 to 1650, and various stories about the linkage of the art on the shields to diverse tribal traditions emerged. Carbon dating helped narrow the range of temporal uncertainty, though those results also varied—from 1420 to 1640. Both the "uniqueness of the shields in the anthropological record" and limited knowledge about the groups living in the Four Corners region of the United States in 1500 made scientific certainty impossible.[82] Anthropology can abide gray area wherever there is not adequate evidence to construct a full history; but law wants a decision. And so the shields—and the tribes claiming them—got caught in that site where Native American semisovereignty comes up against both the jurisdiction and the form of law imposed by U.S. legal institutions. Because anthropologists and archaeologists could not come to a consensus on which tribe(s) should "own" the shields, the tribes interested in the shields had to make arguments in support of their claims. They had to construct legal stories.

The two main groups vying for the shields were the Navajo Nation and a joint filing from the Ute Indian Tribe of the Uintah and Ouray Agency, the Paiute Tribe of Utah, and the Kaibab Band of Paiute Indians (I'll call this the Ute/Paiute claim, after Threedy).[83] The Navajo tribe had a tribal storyteller, John Holiday, who was able to offer in testimony a persuasive narrative about the shields. And, because of NAGPRA's wider standards of proof, when a respected Navajo elder offered a plausible oral history of the shields, it counted as legitimate evidence rather than being discounted as hearsay (as it likely would have been in a more traditional court setting).[84] Holiday's basic story, as characterized by Threedy, was as follows:

> The shields were made by a man called Many Goats White Hair, nine generations ago. The shields were sacred ceremonial objects. When the Navajos were being rounded up by war parties, the shields were in the care of two men, Man Called Rope and Little Bitter Water Person. Man Called Rope was John Holiday's grandfather. Concerned for the shields' safety, the two men decided to hide the shields in the area we call the Mountain With No Name [Henry Mountains] and Mountain With White Face [Boulder Mountain]. The location of the hidden shields was then lost.[85]

As Threedy puts it, the narrative has scene, agent, act, agency, and purpose, so it feels like a story. And the connections between the elements work fairly well.

The Ute/Paiute tribes did not produce a story. Instead they composed what looks at first glance to be a more straightforward legal argument, maintaining that the shields were recovered from traditional Ute territory, that there was evidence that Utes had used buffalo-hide shields for hunting, and that the shields' designs were "not inconsistent with Ute traditions."[86] From what we know about NAGPRA, that is a reasonable set of claims clearly meant to satisfy some of the priority rules for deciding how to repatriate sacred objects not associated with particular remains. Navajo land is not very close to where the shields were found, whereas that territory *is* traditionally Ute territory. However, Holiday's story included plausible information on why the shields would be found where they were: a site far from an invasion by U.S. Army war parties was chosen, to keep the shields safe.[87]

Lee Ann Kreutzer, the archaeologist judging the case, after considering testimony from the tribes and the reports of various anthropologists and archaeologists, awarded the shields to the Navajo, writing of the Ute/Paiute claim:[88] "The [Ute/Paiute] tribes have constructed a plausible, but not persuasive or even adequate, claim of original Ute/Paiute control of the shields. . . . This claim is seriously lacking in credibility. In fairness to other claimants and the general public, the National Park Service cannot simply accept a tribe's unexplained, unelaborated, and unjustified request for repatriation."[89] Initially that seems a good standard of judgment. Much of law does transpire as a series of well-constructed stories, and the most consistent and plausible stories tend to win cases. But there is also an irony here: the Navajo win with the "hearsay" of oral history while the Ute/Paiute claim is found less persuasive in part because it limits its narrative to positivist legal form. That view of the two cases also hides something, however. What Kreutzer misses in the Ute/Paiute claim is not what it says or fails to say but where it chooses to remain silent. As Marianne Constable puts it, writing about a different set of Native American cases, "what is unspeakable here is not only that which cannot be spoken, but also that which in its speaking is destructive in that it cannot properly be heard."[90]

After the decision was made to award the shields to the Navajo, the Skull Valley Goshute Tribe submitted a report that shed further light on what *wasn't* heard in the Ute/Paiute claim. In a report on that supplemental information, Kreutzer writes,

> Mr. Brewster's discussion of Punown religious thought clarified for me what Southern Paiute consultants tried to communicate to me earlier in the process. Most would confide no information whatsoever, except that the shields should be repatriated to the Utes and Paiutes; they responded negatively when asked for information that could be weighed against the Navajo claim. For instance, one consultant replied that her people are not Navajos and unlike them do not share any information about their religion. Another consultant, however, told me directly that the shields were not Paiute, Ute, or Navajo . . . , and needed to be reburied. Whereas I originally thought he was conceding that the shields are not culturally affiliated . . . I now understand

that he was trying to tell me, without divulging confidential details of his religious belief, that objects belonging to the sacred realm cannot legitimately be claimed by any particular tribe or individual.[91]

Part of what the archaeologist could not hear is that there are things that cannot be said. She also did not seem to hear that there are things that cannot be owned. Though she is supportive of the validity of oral history as a source, she is also invested (perhaps without knowing this) in the discourse of Western legalism, where silence cannot be its own phenomenon but always rather stands for something that simply has not yet been spoken.[92] Kreutzer (who surely cared deeply about her responsibility to judge well) thought she heard consultants making ownership claims without offering proof, when what those consultants were trying to say was that sacred objects cannot be owned, and that the reasons for this cannot be spoken. Is that irony? Constable argues that Native American silences are acts that raise the possibility "of 'ways' that cannot be spoken in the terminology of U.S. law and the social study of language. Native silences . . . remind us that not all law need tell its addressees what to do through utterances."[93] There are forms of law and ways of human being-together that cannot be produced as the content of propositional speech. It is almost impossible for a U.S. court (or, perhaps, a Western ear) to hear that.

The ear of Western legalism is going to want to hear evidence here, proof that there can be a form of law that does not and cannot take the form of a proposition or a rule and explanation of how something like that could offer a fair standard for judgment. That demand is going to place on the person who wants to make a claim that falls outside propositional law an unfair demand to articulate her claims in an alien form for an institution incapable of comprehending the world in which her claim makes sense. But if the person from that "other world" lacks power to evade Western legalism's jurisdiction, she's going to have to make some sort of argument in legalism's terms. There may be no proof to offer here if those are the conditions—and that is part of what lost the case for the Ute/Paiute tribes.[94]

Kreutzer thought she heard a claim unsupported by evidence. A Ute/Paiute representative simply asserted that "the shields were not Paiute, Ute, or Navajo . . . , and needed to be reburied" without offering reasons. For legalism a good argument is a claim supported by reasons, and law judges claims based on the making of such arguments. But, as the later report from the Goshute tribe revealed, when the Utes and Paiutes said that the shields "were not Paiute, Ute, or Navajo," they meant that they were sacred objects that cannot be owned. That is a reason. The Goshute report also revealed that the shields were "a permanent, on-going prayer offering, and that disinterment interrupted that on-going ceremony."[95] That is why the Utes and Paiutes wanted the shields returned and reburied rather than displayed. As Kreutzer puts it in her later report, "Even though the consultants might be convinced that the shields and offering were created by a direct ancestor, they refuse to objectify or diminish the shields' spiritual significance by claiming them on that basis."[96] The two tribe groups made different decisions about what could be said. The Navajos told a story about hiding and forgetting; the Utes and Paiutes interpreted the case to involve religious practices that cannot be told as a story.

As of August 2005, the shields are "owned" by the Navajo Nation, "stored in a vault in the tribal museum at Window Rock and are available for traditional healers' use."[97] My analysis of this case makes no judgment—because it is not qualified to do so—on whether that outcome is the right one. I do not think that a respected Navajo storyteller and elder is wrong or dishonest in the construction of his narrative—I am in agreement with Threedy here. But there is also no reason to doubt the case constructed by the Ute/Paiute tribes. And we should remember that archaeologists were unable to determine the origin in time or space of the shields with any scientific certainty. That is why some commenters on the case—other tribes, scientists interested in the shields' provenance—find it troubling to think that the shields are now locked away, accessible only to Navajo traditional healers.[98] This may be a case that could not have had a happy ending for all involved—indeed, that is a weakness of law, that it tends to impose a yes/no judgment even where a "preponderance of evidence" might have gone either way. NAGPRA surely made bold steps forward when it both addressed a history of injustice and put some of the power to right that history in the hands of those on whom the harms have been imposed. But the case of the Pectol shields leaves me wondering whether other traditions of judgment—for instance, the slow-paced consensus processes favored by many tribes—might have offered a better final result.[99] In other words, there are other forms of judgment. Indeed, from the widest angle, the loss in this case is that of the opportunity to recognize that there are other forms of judgment and meaning making.

In saying that I don't want to pass over too lightly that it was oral history that won this case. That *is* a different standard of judgment. Kreutzer, reflecting on the case in 2008, points out that "many critics accept writings as stand-alone evidence, but regard oral tradition as a hypothesis to be tested against documentation, as mere rumor, or even as entirely irrelevant. These critics, in fact, are advocating the very thing they think they protest: elevating the practices, beliefs, and world view of one culture above those of another."[100] So this is a step forward in the relationship between U.S. law and Native American tribes. Shields that the Navajo believe are tied to protection of their people were returned to the Navajo on the basis of oral history. Robert McPherson and John Fahey describe how John Holiday "sang and prayed over the shields" as they were driven to their new home in the Navajo Nation, saying that "the songs were to revive [the shields] and tell them 'You're home.' . . . It felt like a good thing to bring them back."[101] That sounds like a just and happy outcome if we look only at the Navajo case. But it is hard to feel certain that the best decision was made when only one side of the argument was truly heard.

Bradley Bryan points out that, when we subject North American aboriginal traditions to the standards of Western history and legality, it isn't only that we fail to understand something vital about the traditions we subject to that form of judgment. We also "invite indigenous litigants to understand their own testimony in a straightforward utilitarian manner. . . . Such an invitation not only alters the indigenous understanding of the relation of Aboriginal peoples to their lands—but also invites a reconceptualization of what 'their own' history is."[102] We see in the strategies employed by the Navajo and the Ute/Paiutes two different ways of taking up that unfair invitation.

But why does Western legality so consistently fail to listen for its own failures? What if, in some broader way, instead of labeling oral history a kind of history practiced by other peoples, we tried to understand what it means to store tradition in that way, to "grant the possibility of a way of life that is grounded in a completely other way of grasping the passage of time and the renewal of discrete possibilities, and to recognize its power to manifest."[103] For tribes whose traditions rely at least in part on such forms, oral history isn't an account of past events. It is itself the event.[104] Western legality is not able to see that, and even the most creative Western mind may only be able to begin to imagine what it would mean to order a world according to a history that is "not simply a reporting of events."[105] However, even if we think history is just a reporting of events, we are also constantly living the way the meaning of those events transforms over time and does not always stay in the past. Could we not—perhaps with help from other traditions—learn to tell and to hear different stories? I submit that we could. We *should* do that, because it is what justice demands. But even if we want to limit ourselves to thinking in legalistic terms of instrumental value, given the manifest difficulty peoples governed by Western legalism have coming to terms with their own unjust pasts, we may stand to learn something from considering other ways of relating to the past.

And what if we also learned to listen for silence? Unspeakability functions in multiple ways. It is how people who believe that all knowledge is propositional name what doesn't fit in that view; it protects secret or sacred truths known only to members or initiates of a group from damage by the outside world; and, after a long history of expropriation and betrayal, it helps safeguard valuable sites and beliefs from further destruction by colonizing violence (and so also expresses a lack of trust in the possibility that even well-meaning white people will make just decisions).

This has been a story about a dispute over some shields, and so it might strike us as less urgent than some of the other stories I've related. But let's not forget that this all happens against a backdrop of a long history of genocide and unjust treatment, originating in a past and extending into the present moment. It bears repeating that Native American skeletal remains were not classified as *human* until 1990. It does matter how these cases get judged.

At the beginning of this chapter I mentioned the distinction Eve Sedgwick makes between reparative and paranoid reading. Reparative readers acknowledge that they may not have already at hand the tools to understand what they will encounter. Paranoid readers expect to find a world full of oppression and injustice, and so nothing ever takes these readers by surprise—they are fully certain that they know how to read what they find. But paranoid readers also tend to think their job is done when they *uncover* oppression or injustice. I suggested that mere *revelation* of past or present harm is insufficient; further, that in some cases it may not even help. As we near the end of this chapter, we should note that even when uncovering injustice or abuse *does* help, it is only a weak beginning. Stories will be crafted out of what gets revealed, and it will matter who gets to tell those stories, where they are told, who decides what ought to be done about what happened, and whether those who listen assume that hearing and understanding stories about what happened is an uncomplicated task. It is too easy to say, of a story that seems to make no sense, that it is the fault of the teller and accordingly the responsibility of the teller to do a better job at telling. The case of the Pectol shields demonstrates one way in which that assumption meets its limit. Imagine a judgment that takes seriously the Ute/Paiute claim about unspeakability and thus crafts a story about the limits to its own knowledge. What kind of justice might that moment of reparative reading make possible?

HEARING AS RESPONSIBILITY

Primo Levi writes that "our language lacks words to express this offense, the demolition of a man."[106] Susan Brison, reading Levi, adds, "It is debatable, however, whether that is the case, or whether the problem is simply others' refusal to hear survivors' stories, which makes it difficult for survivors to tell them even to themselves."[107] Once we try earnestly to look into the gulf that separates the fortunate from the harmed in terms of ability to take existence for granted, it is easier to take Levi at his word: harm's impact on a body and mind goes beyond the neat certainties of knowledge, as Améry and Brison also have shown us. When we add to that the problem of the unspeakable—ways of being that cannot be spoken without being destroyed—we may take Brison's point but think it is made too quickly.

Still, Brison's point is about intersubjectivity, that we are formed not as windowless monads—unproblematically autonomous—but in connection, in our relations with others: "This aspect of remaking a self in the aftermath of trauma highlights the dependency of the self on others and helps to explain why it is so difficult for survivors to recover when others are unwilling to listen to what they endured."[108] If we have stories to tell and no one listens, we may be robbed of those stories. Throughout this chapter we have seen multiple sites of resistance to such loss. Hanna changes the subject whenever she doesn't want to discuss what interviewers want to hear and thus she tells the story she wishes to tell rather than the one she is being asked for; Colin de Souza chooses to narrate a story about his bravery rather than one about his suffering even though the format of the TRC dictated a focus on his losses; Yvonne Khutwane insists that her story is about wide-scale disrespect rather than the narrower crime of rape; and Yazir Henry writes and publishes his own history of his TRC testimony once he realizes that he has lost control over what the official record would produce.[109] Trauma is involved here, of course, but if we reduce what doesn't get said in these stories to the remnants of trauma, we also fail to hear something of what *is* said. In turn, Native American traditions of unspeakability seem to stand for (among other things) a refusal of further loss rather than loss itself and so point us to other ways of thinking about silence and cultural meaning. It isn't that the stories are being denied, but that only certain conditions render them knowable. That point may not be entirely at odds with Brison's. She quotes Paul Fussell, a combatant in World War I:

> One of the cruxes of war . . . is the collision between events and the language available—or thought appropriate—to describe them. . . . Logically, there is no reason why the English language could not perfectly well render the actuality of . . . warfare: it is rich in terms like *blood, terror, agony, madness, shit, cruelty, murder, sell-out* and *hoax*, as well as phrases like *legs blown off, intestines gushing out over his hands, screaming all night, bleeding to death from the rectum*, and the like. . . . The problem was less one of "language" than of gentility and optimism. . . . What listener wants to be torn and shaken when he doesn't have to be? We have made unspeakable mean indescribable: it really means *nasty*.[110]

That observation is still situated squarely in the Western tradition where silence doesn't speak and language can expand to fill every gap. Other traditions, as well as knowledge of what trauma can do, ought to leaven the hopefulness of that belief with a sense of what cannot be said. Brison's point is that, as resistant to language as violent abuse is, there is also much that can be communicated. But communication is interpersonal. A narrative can be successfully communicated only if it is also heard—by an audience willing to be interrupted. Fussell describes one kind of lack of audience. Brison argues that "as a society, we live with the unbearable by pressuring those who have been traumatized to forget and by rejecting the testimonies of those who are forced by fate to remember."[111] That pressure and rejection might be overt, or might be hidden. Those who exert them may not even recognize that they are doing so. In his testimony for the Fortunoff Video Archive for Holocaust Testimonies, Stanley M. describes his experience of trying to tell his story. Interviewers ask whether he has discussed his experiences with his daughter, and he lists all the things he underwent that she would not believe: people who have not been abused do not believe that people survive being starved, frozen, and beaten for years. He talks about trying to share his story with young people who ask him about it:

What can I say? Sit with a young person, woman or man, and explain her what it is to be hungry, hated and hunted and not having hope? It is very difficult. Their reaction is very, very, you know, curious one. Curious for my part. Because . . . if you start to build up the climate of brutality what men can do to men, how prejudice can lead to disaster and hatred, at one point they inject argument and say we are better generation and things like that will not happen because we are better. This puts you in a very difficult position because you cannot argue with that and try to prove, no, you are just as bad as me, because that would be immoral from my point of view. So the dialogue ends and I say yes, you are better and I hope you stay that way.[112]

What Stanley describes here is a complex failure of hearing made up of his own understandable cynicism, the difficulty of conveying true horror to people who have lived safe lives, and the failure of those people to listen, truly, to what narratives of horror try to convey.[113]

POSTMEMORY

Though we need to be careful in how we approach educating people about violence and the wider responsibility for it that all of us bear—because sometimes even hearing about the evils human beings commit upon one another inflicts a kind of trauma on a listener—we do need to find ways of learning to hear. We need to do this not only because we cannot rebuild destroyed worlds or help survivors recover if we do not listen but also because trauma can be passed down through generations in the form of stories and behaviors. Susan Brison records this account:

Yael Tamir, an Israeli philosopher, told me a story illustrating cultural memory, in which she and her husband, neither of whom had been victims of the Holocaust, literally jumped at the sound of a German voice shouting instructions at a train station in Switzerland. The experience triggered such vivid "memories" of the deportation that they grabbed their suitcases and fled the station.[114]

Trauma doesn't stay in the past, and it doesn't always reside only in the body of the initial victim. If selves are formed in a cooperative if unchosen feedback loop between self and other, self and world, then in any society recovering from widespread infliction of trauma, it won't be only the survivors who are contending with the aftereffects of violence. Even people who aren't listening may be absorbing the negative effects (and affects) of a violent legacy. Adults may "teach" children and other adults how to inhabit trauma because of how affect is transmitted between persons. "Postmemory" is a term used by Marianne Hirsch to describe "the relationship that the generation after those who witnessed cultural or collective trauma bears to the experiences of those who came before, experiences that they 'remember' only by means of stories, images, and behaviors among which they grew up. But these experiences were transmitted to them so deeply as to *seem* to constitute memories in their own right."[115] Postmemory doesn't affect only those whose parents were subjected to genocidal regimes or long-standing abuse and oppression. Brison points out that "girls in our society are raised with so many cautionary tales about rape that, even if we are not assaulted in childhood, we enter womanhood freighted with postmemories of sexual violence. . . . Postmemories of rape are not primarily inherited from one's parents, but, rather, absorbed from the culture."[116] Statistics make this point well: an adult American woman has a one in eight chance of being raped and a 50 percent chance of being assaulted by an intimate partner.[117] Adolescent girls have a one in five chance of being raped or battered by someone they date.[118] Postmemory points backward toward a harm already undergone. But it also sets up a present moment wherein the future is unsteady. Anyone who watches television or film will have seen so many depictions of rape or its aftermath that they can't fail to have made an impression even on those whose lives have felt safe. Even where rape is successfully depicted as an inexcusable crime and a harm, it is also shown to be an ever-present threat. In other words, even when nothing has happened, present-day social conditions are far from offering a reasonable guarantee of female safety. Sometimes it seems as if no one is listening to that truth. And yet it also seems that too many of us have heard it, for better and for worse. Kathleen Stewart, writing about how affect colors everyday life, puts her finger on how affect's transmission may be ignored or experienced as "how the world is" rather than as a series of forces ranging between persons:

> The notion of a totalized system, of which everything is always already somehow a part, is not helpful (to say the least) in the effort to approach a weighted and reeling present. This is not to say that the forces these systems try to name are not real and literally pressing. On the contrary, I am trying to bring them into view as a scene of immanent forces, rather than leave them looking like dead effects imposed on an innocent world.[119]

The omnipresence of rape has intersubjective cultural force. But its force is inevitable only if we do nothing about it.

THE USES OF IRONY

Human resilience makes a more satisfying story than does a permanently damaged self. Gross human rights abuses are easier to punish than are the diffuse practices of disrespect that also dismantle a person's sense of safety in the world. It may feel safer and more productive to embrace forgiveness rather than resentment. It is usually easier to support a narrative that rewards set expectations about how stories and evidence work than it is to find oneself made uncertain by unfamiliar ways of thinking. And tales of suffering may compel sympathy or create nation-building narratives more successfully than do stories about continuing anger or pride in one's violent resistance. Add to all of that the differing cultures, languages, levels of education and familiarity with testimonial forms, and we simply cannot avoid the fact that some stories will always be easier to hear than others. How might those of us who care to listen learn to hear better?

One could hear my earlier assertion that some of us could use a bit of destruction of our sense of the self's own sovereignty as provocative. But it doesn't have to be. Anyone hoping to understand what justice or recovery is in the wake of world-destroying violence will also have to get a sense of what it means that worlds and selves can be destroyed. She will have to listen, to be responsive. She'll have to *experience herself as responsive* rather than or in addition to autonomously self-sufficient. In listening, she should be ready to hear things that don't accord with her expectations, things she doesn't want to hear, even things that threaten to destroy her idea of how the world works. She will have to be disarmed.

As I mentioned earlier, when those who can listen choose not to, and when those who do listen fail to hear well, it imposes a loneliness on a survivor, a second harm in addition to the original violation.[120] Of course, one could take a very practical stance and say that one simply can't listen to everyone, and that missing a resistant narrative here or there isn't going to stop a nation from transitioning to democracy or keep communities from learning to live alongside one another. That's not entirely untrue. But approaching testimony with a preconceived idea of what it should accomplish might make the breadth or depth of resistance to that settled idea of what should be achieved illegible. When you encourage forgiveness and gloss over resentment, when you want only the facts of the case, when you want to hear only about gross human rights violations, when you think that healing comes from emphasizing resilience rather than destruction, or that only propositional claims backed by reasons can testify to what builds or breaks worlds, you will have determined in advance that certain stories may not be heard. And then, even if you listen, you will not have a sense of a whole universe of harms that will be there whether or not they are heard, forming a backdrop to all efforts to move forward. This matters—not only for those who don't get heard. And it gives us a sense of just how broadly responsibility for recovery, transition, and reconciliation must fall. In order for any large and complex recovery to succeed, a wide array of persons must contribute actively to building a world where it is actually reasonable for a survivor to trust that, though she was once abandoned by humanity, that will not happen again. That will involve building institutions, yes, but more is needed than that. A large number and broad range of persons will have to learn to tell themselves different stories about who they are and how they come to owe things to others. Brison writes that forming narratives "facilitates the ability to go on by opening up possibilities for the future through retelling stories of the past. It does this not by reestablishing the illusions of coherence of the past, control over the present, and predictability of the future, but by making it possible to carry on without these illusions."[121] More of us should be more aware of the fragility of human safety—that we are all always at risk of misunderstanding, abandonment, and refusal of response—and be willing to work with others to build a world with a more equitable distribution of safety from within that vulnerable site.

We've seen that institutions aimed at facilitating transition, recovery, or reconciliation often have, despite their best intentions, outcomes that may redound upon those least able to survive them, who are also the same persons the institutions are meant to help. An irony. What made the satire by Horace funny? The answer knowledge gives us is the discordance between what the butt of the joke wanted and what he got. The same joke might not look so funny if we often found ourselves inhabiting the position of the butt of jokes that tend to express relations of unequally distributed power and knowledge. As such, we should attend to sites of irony, figure out how they work, and remedy the source of their disjunction wherever that disjunction stands for an injustice we'd rather not laugh about.

Of course, I've said the risks are unavoidable—built into the kind of communication human beings must undertake. We're all butts part of the time, for better and for worse. And some ironies are not harmful. It is ironic when an institution designed for hearing fails to listen. But it is also ironic that an institution aimed at forgiveness that also allows refusal of forgiveness might make forgiveness or reconciliation more likely for some. The first irony is unjust. The second opens up new possibilities of just hearing.

4

Revision

In 1945 Jean Améry felt vindicated because the world was collectively horrified at what had befallen him. In 1965 he felt as if the magnitude of the loss imposed on him had not been truly marked by the German people. He felt that way for many reasons: lack of accountability for those who participated in his destruction, the impatient attitudes of younger generations of Germans tired of hearing about the crimes of their fathers, and even the silence of his fellow camp survivors.[1] Améry's experience, the histories of nations like South Africa and Argentina, and probably each of our own lives will show that the meaning of the past in the present changes over time. In other words, a human being is the kind of being for whom revision is possible. But this is not a simple story about the power of the human will. Changes in how we experience the past in the present moment are impacted by institutions, politics, social practices and attitudes, and the ranging of affect between persons and groups. Transitional justice, truth commissions, political reconciliation, and forgiveness, all these forms of response to violence might be called revisionary practices: they work, in a present moment, to revise memory or experience of a past, with the hope of opening up a future not fully determined by past harms.[2] For anyone whose past should have been otherwise—who needs to rebuild a self and a world after being abandoned by humanity—some revisions are positive, making the present more livable than it otherwise would be. Other revisions are negative, failing to release the present moment from past harm, blocking access to the future. Positive and negative revisions can be facilitated in various ways in diverse settings: social groupings, families and friends, chance encounters, political and legal actions, and so on—all play a role in defining what is possible. In Améry's case, it pays to note that many of those responsible for his continuing inability to move forward are not what the law calls perpetrators—younger Germans, fellow camp survivors—a fact that both points us to a wider responsibility for the success of reconciliation and complicates Améry's refusal to forgive.

In 1964, when the Auschwitz trials began in Frankfurt, Améry was asked to write an essay on the plight of the intellectual in Auschwitz for presentation by the South German Broadcasting Company. He called it "At the Mind's Limits." It led him to author a series of essays in which he produced "a phenomenological description of the existence of the victim."[3] In "Resentments," he laid out principled reasons for his unwillingness to forgive or move on absent a greater acknowledgement of the infamy of Germany's past by the German people. His defense of resentment helps us better understand his ethical loneliness. It voices a skepticism about the role of forgiveness in the aftermath of violence while also laying out an alternative path for restorative justice. It doesn't rule out forgiveness; indeed, it may help us better understand what conditions make forgiveness or other conciliatory processes possible, and what conditions make the success of such efforts less likely. But it also does not rely on forgiveness as a solution; Améry's refusal points in a different direction toward the future.

RESENTMENT

Anger and resentment are just responses. They express what we tend to feel when we face a moral harm. We think: that should not have happened. In other words, we undergo a will to revision. Jeffrie Murphy argues that "the primary value defended by the passion of resentment is *self-respect*, that proper self-respect is essentially tied to the passion of resentment, and that a person who does not resent moral injuries done to him . . . is almost necessarily a person lacking in self-respect."[4] Of course, Nietzsche famously wrote, "To be incapable of taking one's enemies, one's accidents, even one's misdeeds seriously for very long—that is the sign of strong, full natures in whom there is an excess of the power to form, to mold, to recuperate and forget"[5]—he would counsel us to practice forgetting rather than forgiveness or resentment. Indeed, for Nietzsche, *that* is what self-respect would look like. Nonetheless, for those of us less free of the influence of others, Adam Smith suggests that what enrages us about a wrongdoer's act is his "absurd self-love, by which he seems to imagine, that the other people may be sacrificed at any time, to his conveniency or his humour."[6] Along those lines, Margaret Urban Walker defines resentment as "a kind of accusing anger at something done" and argues that "it is not the fact of harm and suffering in itself but the sense of wrongfulness of that harm or suffering that is embodied in these kinds of anger."[7] Smith and Walker both locate resentment in the space between persons—it is a response to harm that seeks acknowledgment and amends. Charles Griswold adds, "Vengeful resentment may seek to communicate a moral principle that all reasonable people would acknowledge, and whose acknowledgement is required if one is to form part of the moral community."[8] These thinkers all contend that if we fail to see what is appropriate about resentment, we may also fail to contribute to building a shared world where justice (or even fairness) is a value. There are, of course, times when resentment and revenge are unreasonable, out of proportion or simply ill used by those who take them up. However, "even when badly expressed, resentment and revenge engage their owner in a morally tinged exchange with the community."[9] Walker adds, "Resentment both expresses a wrong and calls out to others for recognition and a reparative response"—it is dialogic.[10]

That it is dialogic lends new significance to the idea that resentment asserts the self's dignity in the face of unjust treatment. Rather than simple response, it seeks what Walker calls "normative confirmation" when she writes, "When we express our resentment to others, we invite confirmation from others that we have competently judged a normative violation and that others share our interest in affirming the norms we hold" (93). Resentment thus presumes—or in some cases hopes to insist on the formation of—"shared moral rules, norms, or boundaries that define some actions as morally unacceptable" (92). It seeks "security of membership in a community of normative judgment" (146). For Walker, a violation of norms threatens not only the life, safety, or well-being of an individual but also the very existence of norms and, by extension, human community. Pamela Heironymi writes that "resentment protests a past action that persists as a present threat," adding to the sense of the thinkers collected here that resentment seeks both response and safety.[11] All of this reflects what we learn from Améry's description of what he lost when he was tortured and interned in concentration camps: he lost not only his sense of his own autonomy but also the expectation that others would respect its boundaries. Resentment seeks response—acknowledgment of the dignity of the person harmed—and safety: assurance that the harm will not recur. It is a reasonable reaction, voicing just demands.

But let's not call resentment—or norms—an unqualified good. After all, there are other ways to safeguard community, people often resent in silly, harmless, or unjust ways, and norms can be as stultifying as they can be just. If resentment is an "accusing anger at something done" (as Walker suggests it is), nonetheless sometimes we might find ourselves resenting things that have no power to observe norms, like air travel delayed by snow or a drawer full of disorderly Tupperware. Or we might resent something like another person's success, even when it is well deserved. Resentment is not always just. But nor is it always immediately clear that resentment we don't share is wrongheaded. In some cases what seems unreasonable on first glance may be a mode of address seeking response about emerging rather than established norms—and it may deserve a listen. Walker points out that words like "uppity" and "arrogant" are sometimes used (resentfully, even) to describe persons who are perceived to be claiming power they ought not have—people who are trying to challenge existing norms (with their resentment, possibly) by making new claims of justice.[12] Resentment thus marks a site where one person might rouse another out of the "codified abstraction" (as Améry puts it) of her daily life and into deeper engagement with our shared responsibility for the worlds we author cooperatively with others. What matters about resentment— and why those around it ought to take note of it even where it may not seem to fit—is that it is about a perceived threat to norms and expresses a sense a self has of having been unjustly treated. It expects in response a confirmation that certain shared norms exist, that they apply equally to all, and that all have a stake in protecting said norms. Granting that response helps to establish what norms are shared. That is no small component of world building.

Still, resentment carries a lot of baggage, even when it is just. Nietzsche accused it of being a morality of the weak and a way of hindering the human capacity for creativity from opening a better future. As Améry puts it, "it nails every one of us onto the cross of his ruined past."[13] Psychologists diagnose it as problematic, with its threat ranging in degree from bad for one's health to a symptom of trauma. (To which Améry responds that it sets for him "the task of defining anew our warped state, namely as a form of the human condition that morally as well as historically is of a higher order than that of healthy straightness."[14]) We must keep these criticisms in mind as we consider resentment as a revisionary practice.

REVISIONARY PRACTICE

"Willing backwards" is Nietzsche's name for learning to live with what troubles us most about the past: that there is no changing it. Nietzsche's Zarathustra proclaims, "The now and the past on earth—alas, my friends, that is what I find most unendurable; and I should not know how to live if I were not also a seer of that which must come."[15] Perhaps we are all haunted by pasts we wish were otherwise, though the fecundity of possible futures may at times save us from entrapment in those pasts. The aim is to imagine better futures and then bring them into being. We can recognize that as a goal shared with revisionary practices such as transitional justice and political reconciliation. But it is no easy task to overcome a past. Zarathustra tells us that he is a seer, willer, and creator, and a bridge to the future but also a "cripple" at that bridge. He would like to redeem the past, to "recreate all 'it was' into a 'thus I willed it' " (139), but the creative will fairly constantly meets the limits to its powers when it finds itself wishing for the impossible: to change the past. For Nietzsche, that is the birth of revenge, the will to strike back against what can't be changed: "This alone is what revenge is: the will's ill will against time and its 'it was' " (140). Time effectively destroys the will to power of anyone bent on revenge, because the will's energy exhausts itself in attempts to change what cannot be changed. Those who think and act only out of revenge end up conceiving of willing as punishment rather than a creative power—because that is what the will is for them. Whole theologies are born out of that resignation. But Zarathustra calls that a fable and instead teaches that "the will is a creator. All 'it was' is a fragment, a riddle, a dreadful accident—until the creative will says to it, 'But thus I willed it.' " (141). One can say, of an unchosen past, that one now wills it to be what it was and is—one accepts the world and the finality of all past moments for what they are. That frees the will from being "a cripple at the bridge" and opens up new futures. Zarathustra counsels the will to "unlearn the spirit of revenge" and reconcile itself with time or, better, aim at "something higher than any reconciliation" (141). It is no easy feat (indeed it may be impossible for some), but one who achieves it will have learned how to live with the past.

Willing backwards is, for Nietzsche, a species of *amor fati*. It does not pretend to change the fact that what happened happened but rather embraces the fatality of the past. When I will backwards, what I wish were otherwise about the past *is not otherwise*. But my way of thinking about it has changed, *is otherwise*. Willing backwards is revision.

Heather Love has argued that "a central paradox of any transformative criticism is that its dreams for the future are founded on a history of suffering, stigma, and violence," founded on everything we might wish were otherwise.[16] Given that truth, one might hope to overcome a difficult past, just leave it behind, "to let, as Marx wrote, the dead bury the dead."[17] But as Love also points out, "it is the damaging aspects of the past that tend to stay with us, and the desire to forget may itself be a symptom of haunting."[18] Love's point both shows that Nietzsche is right to name the past unchangeable and takes us farther into the difficulty of letting it go. Refusing to forget, hanging on to the past, not letting go of one's resentment—those may all indicate a failure to move on. But, as we learn from Améry and others, they may equally be signs of a self's will to repair, clinging to harm that has not been redressed, demanding conditions where positive revision is possible. We've seen that conditions that allow an easy relation to the present moment, one where a self might take its own existence for granted, are unequally portioned out across time, space, and political, social, and economic realities. Resentment may be a political tool most likely to be used by those who, because of inequalities of various kinds, have a hard time finding an audience willing to hear their grievances well—and that may complicate what Nietzsche believed. My hope is that clarifying the positive role resentment may play in recovery will help us see more clearly something that is at stake in a discourse of reconciliation after mass violence or oppression. That is, the restoration in each individual of the self's capacity to take on the present moment freely—and to make positive revisions of an unjust past. Reconciliation, as revision, seeks a way out of ethical loneliness.

For Meir Dan-Cohen, writing about practices of mercy, forgiveness, and repentance, revisionary practices redraw the boundary of a wrongdoer's self, leaving the offense outside, absolving the wrongdoer of responsibility, and rendering negative attitudes toward the wrongdoer no longer appropriate.[19] They let the past go. Dan-Cohen is interested in wrongdoers because he wants to focus on the "normative significance of the wrongdoer's identity" rather than on the "victim's psychological limitations" (130). He chooses that focus because, he tells us, most accounts of pardon, mercy, forgiveness, and the like oscillate back and forth between normative and psychological approaches, often without admitting they are doing so. By choosing a strictly normative approach he hopes to avoid that messiness. In support of his claim, he points out that state boundaries can be redrawn without changing the identity of a state. When boundaries move and, for instance, a pollutant is now in another state, it is no longer the responsibility of the original state to handle that pollutant. We may want to retort that a shift like that could never dissolve responsibility for actions undertaken by states that cause environmental damage. Dan-Cohen's response would be that "a state's border is nothing but the reflection of such normative arrangements" (126). In other words, since boundaries are normative arrangements, a change in boundaries just is brought about by the practice of boundary shifting rather than by any reasons for activating the practice. By engaging in the practice, those involved exercise their normative powers of redefinition. That, according to Dan-Cohen, gives us a "conception of change strong enough to support and explain the cessation of negative attitudes toward the offender without being so strong as to disrupt identity" (124). It means I can will backwards without ceasing to be who I am. So, if Texas were no longer part of the United States, then it would make no sense to blame the United States for the textbooks Texas produces. The shift of boundaries hasn't changed the identity of the United States or what's wrong with the textbooks. Dan-Cohen says we can think of selves in a similar way. Human beings can invent processes that redefine the boundaries of things and, since selves are not autonomous monads but rather are formed in part by meanings authored collectively in a shared world, we are capable of awarding new boundaries to selves, too. If I destroyed your garden and then made amends in some way, maybe you won't think of me only as "that garden destroyer."[20] You and I will have redrawn my self's boundary, leaving that offense outside. If, together, we can manage that, it will be because selves, norms, and worlds are cooperatively authored things. That is one way that revision is possible.

Of course, one might have the power, normatively speaking, to change the boundaries of a territory, or to award amnesty to an offender who fulfills the requirements set forth by law for that award. But it takes more than a normative arrangement for borders and amnesties to feel real. Dan-Cohen calls these "complicating factors" that don't touch the relevant fact—that we do succeed, at times, in making legitimate changes in normative relationships or, in the case of mercy, pardon, and the like, "changes in the significance we attach to past events."[21] It matters here, however, that there is no formal or normative way to force other people to agree with a border change, whether temporal or spatial. Absent widespread support for a change, no institution's power of enforcement can make someone feel membership in a different community or cease to feel a sense of belonging with a group that now dwells on the far side of an abstract border, nor can it force people to let the past go or embrace amnestied offenders as members of a community. Every normative power of redefinition may be contested. And resistance to that redefinition may be powerful. If Love is right that it is "the damaging aspects of the past that tend to stay with us," then things are going to be messier than Dan-Cohen argues. Of course, Dan-Cohen is likely thinking about offenses of a slighter nature than genocide, torture, and crimes against humanity. It may (or may not!) be easier to imagine redrawing boundaries around petty thieves, embezzlers, or garden destroyers. As Améry, Brison, Kluger, and others have pointed out, there is something about a harm in which both parties lose their humanity—one by acting, the other by undergoing—that is not so easy to get beyond. Those offenses destroy selves and worlds. Perhaps what they do is make it difficult to understand where to *put* a rezoned boundary. Before undertaking a normative shift, first one would need to build a norm or reconfirm an undermined norm—one would need to build a world. As such, willing backwards or redrawing boundaries will require more than the will of one person or institution.

Dan-Cohen admits as much when he writes that, with some crimes, "the enormity of evil may defy our capacity to overcome resentment," though he considers that to be a "regrettable external limitation" rather than an attribute of certain bad acts (130). About that he may be right: we cannot know in advance all the forms of mercy or forgiveness—all the forms of revision—of which we will be capable given the right circumstances. That is simply a feature of harm. It forces you to work with what you've been handed. It is also a mark of the kind of self each of us is, affected by others whether we wish it or not, sometimes in unpredictable ways. It seems to me, however, that calling investments in resentment or forgiveness—whether they be presented in logical or affective terms— "external limitations" fails to understand the very form of the self on which his argument relies. If we really are, as Dan-Cohen argues, "the product of the web of meanings we spin around various objects and events, most importantly the human body and its career," that will mean that we can redraw boundaries, but it will also mean that we are prey to meanings we may not get to choose—and we are prey to them because we are formed as much by our reasoned choices as we are by our implication in myriad scenes of affective significance over which we lack perfect control (128). Dan-Cohen adds that "considerations of identity preclude revision when the wrongdoing looms so large within the offender's self that removing the wrongdoing would not result in a viable or recognizable version of a self" (130–31). Maybe the United States could remove Texas and be off the hook for bad textbooks. But it won't be possible to dispel the world's idea of U.S. guilt for Guantanamo, even if it's not officially on U.S. soil. Some boundaries are harder to redraw than others. That might be because justice partakes of more than a set of normative arrangements. Nonetheless, Dan-Cohen's bracketing of affect helps us understand— perhaps ironically—that resentment can be, rather than an "unreasonable" emotion to be kept out of law and politics, an appropriate response to harm. Thus any request that resentment be overcome—any hope of revisionary practice—must also provide conditions that make a decision to forgive, pardon, move on, or reconcile reasonable.

THE ETHICS OF RESENTMENT

Améry's inability to recover fully from what had been done to him—even twenty years after his release from the camps—surfaces as a defense of his continuing resentment, which he describes in these terms: "The time-sense of the person trapped in resentment is twisted around, disordered, if you wish, for it desires two impossible things: regression into the past and nullification of what happened."[22] Resentment demands revision. Améry suggests that a person who forgives rather than resents, under the conditions existing in Europe in the decades following World War II, can do so only if he "submerges his individuality in society and is able to comprehend himself only as a function of the social" (71). Instead of voicing resentment at having been treated in ways that no one should be treated, the forgiver "calmly allows what happened to remain what it was" (71). In such conditions, forgiveness does not succeed as a revisionary practice. It simply acquiesces to the passing of time.

Améry argues that if you forgive without the proper conditions for forgiving, you participate in a "natural" process—the idea that time heals all wounds. This natural or biological time sense gets analogized into a social one when human beings elect to "forgive and forget" harms or "move on" simply because of the passing of time.[23] But that process is not moral. Améry writes,

> Precisely for this reason it is not only extramoral, but also *anti*moral in character. Man has the right and privilege to declare himself to be in disagreement with every natural occurrence, including the biological healing that time brings about. What happened, happened. This sentence is just as true as it is hostile to morals and intellect.[24]

Yes, the past is past and there is no changing it. But Améry insists that there is no *moral* sense to that. Human judgment must reckon with how to deal with the past. His point runs parallel to Dan-Cohen's observation that we can redraw not only the spatial but also the temporal boundaries around an offense. Human beings have the capacity to mark the past as past or as not yet past. Améry argues that we can even resist time's passing, as sometimes we must, for ethical reasons.

Consider this statement by a woman named Kalu, commenting on the goals of the South African Truth and Reconciliation Commission (TRC):

> What really makes me angry about the TRC and Tutu is that they are putting pressure on me to forgive. . . . I don't know if I will ever be able to forgive. I carry this ball of anger within me and I don't know where to begin dealing with it. The oppression was bad, but what is much worse, what makes me even angrier is that they are trying to dictate my forgiveness.[25]

Kalu, who has spent a lifetime being oppressed by a racist system, is, at the very moment she is being told she is now equal, having one of the only powers she has with regard to her losses under apartheid—the power to choose to forgive or not to forgive—taken from her by the format of the TRC. "I don't know if I will ever be able to forgive" amounts to a declaration in the present moment that the past cannot be past—because of the conditions of the present moment. As Thomas Brudholm puts it, "her anger seems at root a moral response to a perceived wrong."[26] The TRC sought stories of forgiveness because of widespread assumptions that forgiveness would build a new nation from a divided society. Kalu and many others sought to tell a different story. It is important to note that that does not mean that they aimed to be divisive. The presumption that only forgiveness accomplishes unity throws resentment's form of restorative discourse into the shadows. A different form of hearing might have opened up wider possibilities. That is one part of the meaning of Kalu's anger. Améry's ethical claim presages Kalu's when he writes, "The moral power to resist contains the protest, the revolt against reality, which is rational only so long as it is moral. The moral person demands annulment of time."[27]

Another example from the South African TRC: Charity Kondile—whose testimony we encountered in chapter 1—refused to speak face-to-face with Dirk Coetzee at his amnesty hearing, though Coetzee admitted that he had barbecued her son Sizwe over an open fire after killing him. She had a representative present this statement to the commission in her stead: "You have said that you would like to meet Mrs. Kondile and look her in the eye. It is an honor she feels you do not deserve. And that if you were really remorseful, you wouldn't apply for amnesty, but in fact stand trial for what you did."[28] We can't know why Mrs. Kondile made this choice, but we can guess that she saw no profit in facing a man who tortured and mutilated her son. By refusing to face him she also decreased the risk that her presence at the hearing would be understood, against her will, as embodying a willingness to participate in a ritual of forgiveness. In an interview Mrs. Kondile gave later, she makes clear what she wishes to communicate: "It is easy for Mandela and Tutu to forgive . . . they lead vindicated lives. In my life, nothing, not a single thing, has changed since my son was burnt by barbarians . . . nothing. Therefore I cannot forgive."[29] To put this in Améry's terms, forgiving would ask her to sacrifice her individuality to a social scheme that has not fully addressed the harms imposed on her. We might say that Mrs. Kondile communicates more by not speaking to Coetzee than she would have if she had faced him. She also makes clear that current political and institutional conditions do not make reconciliation possible for her.

Kalu and Mrs. Kondile both recognize that an institutional goal threatens to subsume the meaning of their stories, and so they act to resist being part of an orderly narrative. As I remarked earlier, resentment may be a tool more likely to be taken up by those lacking the institutional or social power to make themselves heard. Kalu and Mrs. Kondile resist forgiveness at least in part in order to demonstrate that only some conditions allow the past to be past. Similarly, Améry's perception of the West Germany of the 1960s is that the world forgives and forgets, the generation of the perpetrators ages comfortably, and the new generation resents the moral weight of the past. He condemns this not because he finds the new generation guilty but because it shows that the past has not yet been dealt with adequately. So what would satisfy him? Something like: along with Goethe, cite Himmler as cultural inheritance. For Améry, were there more of a sense of the bad inheritance along with the good in 1960s West Germany, that more honest tale could represent, morally, "the German revolution that did not take place."[30] If that were accomplished, integrating the Nazi past into Germany's narrative of self, then both sides, victim and perpetrator, would be "joined in the desire that time be turned back and, with it, that history become moral."[31]

That is the heart of his ethical claim. Rather than wanting a present moment in which everyone lets the past be, Améry demands a present moment in which everyone wants a time machine. Everyone, all victims and all perpetrators, should be joined in wishing the past were otherwise, asserting that what happened should not have happened.

RESSENTIMENT

A glowering and mustachioed elephant lurks in the back corners of the room, and it is time for us to address him directly. Is what Améry describes here what Nietzsche named ressentiment? When you want the past to be other than it was, you tie yourself to something that you are powerless to change. In doing so, you undermine your own future. Améry was not unaware of the dangers, nor of the Nietzschean diagnosis attending them. The essay "Resentments" appears in a book Améry called *Jenseits von Schuld und Sühne* (*Beyond Guilt and Atonement*), a title clearly meant to evoke Nietzsche's *Jenseits von Gut und Böse* (*Beyond Good and Evil*).[32] Améry also quotes a passage on ressentiment from Nietzsche's *Genealogy of Morals* in the essay, in order to demonstrate that he knows the ground on which he is treading.[33] There is no denying that Améry wants the past to be otherwise. But is he Nietzsche's man of ressentiment?

Nietzsche writes, "For every sufferer instinctively seeks a cause for his suffering; more exactly, an agent; still more specifically, a *guilty* agent who is susceptible to suffering—in short, some living thing upon which he can, on some pretext or other, vent his affects, actually or in effigy."[34] That is surely what Améry longs to do to Herr Leutnant Praust, who tortured him at Fort Breendonk in Belgium.[35] And it is what he wishes on SS-man Wajs, who beat him with a shovel whenever he didn't work fast enough.[36] Wajs did eventually pay for his crimes with his life, and Améry goes so far as to say that, when Wajs faced the firing squad, "he experienced the moral truth of his crimes. At that moment, he was with me—and I was no longer alone with the shovel handle. I would like to believe that at the instant of his execution he wanted exactly as much as I to turn back time, to undo what had been done. When they led him to the place of execution, the antiman had once again become a fellow man" (70). That certainly sounds like revenge. But more than revenge Améry wants those who harmed him to share in his desire that what happened should never have happened—he needs to see evidence of a widespread will to revision. If he does want payback, he wants it not (or not only) out of a will to harm others but in order to regain a moral equivalence stolen from him by abuse. At first glance Wajs at the firing squad accomplishes that; he joins Améry in wishing the past were otherwise. But Wajs at the firing squad is successful revenge only if we isolate Wajs from the conditions that formed him and gave him power. We should not, and Améry could not do that.

Améry explains that if everything that had befallen him had happened only between Wajs and Améry, the punishment and death of Wajs would have let Améry achieve a sense of peace with the past. But instead "an entire inverted pyramid of SS men, SS helpers, officials, Kapos, and medal-bedecked generals" weighed on Améry (71). The crimes to which he was subjected were not those we might easily describe in the terms of criminal law with its concept of individual responsibility. That is why Améry begins the essay on resentment by insisting that he isn't concerned about whether or not statutes of limitation are extended for Nazi crimes—that kind of justice isn't going to change how he experiences his relation to others in his daily life. Améry continues,

> Wajs from Antwerp was only one of a multitude. The inverted pyramid is still driving me with its point into the ground. Thus the special kind of resentments of which neither Nietzsche nor Max Scheler was able to have any notion. Thus my scant inclination to be conciliatory—more precisely, my conviction that loudly proclaimed readiness for reconciliation by Nazi victims can only be either insanity and indifference to life or the masochistic conversion of a suppressed genuine demand for revenge. (71)

Here Améry wields Nietzsche against those who might wish to use Nietzsche against Améry. It isn't that he is the man of ressentiment, covering over his lack of power by turning his instincts against life toward others who have power, or inward against himself. Instead, Améry suggests, the wish for reconciliation does that. Améry's resentment, then, is his way of saying Yes to life rather than remaining indifferent to it or suppressing a "genuine demand for revenge." He is not the impotent being whose "inability for revenge is called unwillingness to revenge, perhaps even forgiveness."[37] Instead he refuses to forgive wherever forgiveness means forgetting, or wherever reasonable conditions for forgiveness have yet to be met.

Nietzsche, after describing for us how every sufferer seeks a cause for his suffering, continues,

> for the venting of his affects represents the greatest attempt on the part of the suffering to win relief, anaesthesia. . . . This alone, I surmise, constitutes the actual physiological cause of *ressentiment*, vengefulness and the like: a desire to deaden pain by means of affects. This cause is usually sought, quite wrongly in my view, in a defensive retaliation, a mere reactive protective measure, a "reflex movement" set off by sudden injury or peril, such as even a beheaded frog still makes to shake off a corrosive acid. (3:15)

So, for Nietzsche, the cause of ressentiment is a desire to deaden pain by replacing it with a powerful affective response. The cause is *not* what most people seem to think it is—defensive retaliation, a mere striking back out of instinct. And that matters. Nietzsche continues,

But the difference is fundamental: in the one case, the desire is to pre-vent any further injury, in the other it is to deaden, by means of a more violent emotion of any kind, a tormenting, secret pain that is becoming unendurable, and to drive it out of consciousness at least for the moment: for that one requires an affect, as savage an affect as possible, and, in order to excite that, any pretext at all.   (3:15)

Ressentiment's goal is to deaden a secret pain, while retaliation aims to prevent more injury. If the solution Améry proposes for the problem of his resentment is a widespread embrace by all of Germany—perhaps even all the world—of complicity in the Holocaust, it is not (or not only) to deaden his pain but to return to a life worth living. He wants to prevent further injury. Améry needs *safety* from Germans contemporary with him, and he wants to regain the human status taken from him by abuse. He holds out for a guarantee that, though the world once abandoned him to death, such a thing will not be allowed to happen again. Given what he survived that is an utterly reasonable demand, one that ought to be heard. For Améry, resentment is not anesthesia but retaliation, his bid for the kind of security that allows a person to be a person, to take existence for granted. Resentment is his path out of ethical loneliness.

It wouldn't be enough to punish Wajs and Praust—they were cogs in a machine. They surely do bear criminal responsibility. But a finding of in-dividual criminal responsibility does not fix a world broken by a regime made up not only of Nazis but also of millions of collaborators and by-standers. If Améry's resentment casts a wide net, it is not because his re-sentment is aimed at any old "living thing at which it can . . . vent his affects" but because he knows too well that what harmed him was a sys-tem as much as it was any singular human being.[38] Because of the nature of the abuses to which Améry and so many others were subjected—that they were long-standing, visited upon him not because of anything he did but because of *what*, rather than who, he was, ignored by bystanders and the whole world, and thus world destroying—Améry recognizes that sim-ply finding someone to blame will never accomplish what he most de-sires: the ability to forget, in Nietzsche's sense. Améry is not Nietzsche's man of ressentiment in any straightforward way, and if he resists the kind of forgiveness that equals forgetting, it is because that won't help him ac-complish the more meaningful forgetting that a different justice might make possible.

FORGETTING

Nietzsche reminds us that "forgetting is no mere *vis inertiae* as the superficial imagine; it is rather an active and in the strictest sense positive faculty of repression."[39] Forgetting amounts to being able to focus on the present moment or aspirations for a future rather than on the past's harms. It is the ability to take on the present moment freely. Or it is the freedom to take existence for granted. Améry would love to be able to live a daily life undetermined by his memory of the Nazi past. To do this, he would need to feel safe. To feel that, he would need to be able to voice his resentment to an audience willing and able to hear, and do so in a world where the abuse and torture he underwent are widely and actively confirmed as harms that never should have happened. Only that wider context would grant him the sense of safety in the present moment that makes meaningful reconciliation—with time or with others—possible. As Nietzsche puts it,

> To close the doors and windows of consciousness for a time; . . . a little quietness, a little *tabula rasa* of the consciousness, to make room for new things, above all for the nobler functions and functionaries, for regulation, foresight, premeditation . . . —that is the purpose of active forgetfulness, which is like a doorkeeper, a preserver of psychic order, repose and etiquette: so that it will be immediately obvious how there could be no happiness, no cheerfulness, no hope, no pride, no present, without forgetfulness.[40]

Let's be clear: no one subjected to physical or psychological abuse by other human beings forgets what happened. When an interviewer for the Fortunoff Video Archive for Holocaust Testimonies asks Stanley M. about how his days and nights are "now" (in 1980), he begins by saying, "Things don't bother me. I think, you know, that man is very well equipped with mechanism that can forget."[41] He describes how excelling in his professional life gives him pleasure. But then he adds that sometimes things come to his mind very suddenly and upset him. He says that he can control those things, but then describes a scene that doesn't seem subject to control: "I can go to bed and lie and think and maybe sometimes wake and scream. . . . So it's very difficult."[42] We should be careful when we talk about "forgetting" whenever we are dealing with traumatic violence. But part of the work of recovery is to accomplish what both Nietzsche and Stanley M. call forgetting: a preservation of psychic order that makes room for new things.

Susan Brison, posttrauma, worked, like Améry, to dwell in a present moment undetermined by past harms. Améry never felt that he was truly heard, leaving him with an unabated bitterness:

> I know: even the most benevolent will finally have to become as im-patient with us as that young correspondent cited earlier, who is "sick and tired of it." There I am with my resentments, in Frankfurt, Stutt-gart, Cologne and Munich. If you wish, I bear my grudge for reasons of personal salvation. Certainly. On the other hand, it is also for the good of the German people. But no one wants to relieve me of it, ex-cept the organs of public opinion-making, which buy it. What dehu-manized me has become a commodity, which I offer for sale.[43]

Brison, on the other hand, though she did experience the silence that sur-rounds violence when various of her friends and family failed to acknowl-edge the original violation or its continuing impact on her life, did feel heard. A successful court case found the man who attacked her guilty and sent him to prison. She joined a support group and published essays on her recovery. People listened. Being heard offered her the freedom to take up a revisionary practice—which means that she could not accom-plish revision on her own. Like subject formation, communication, and resentment, revision is not accomplished by a solitary subject.

Brison writes that building a narrative of the trauma is important in that it allows what happened to be part of the larger story of one's life without taking over and ruling that life's meaning. But she adds that build-ing a stable narrative may, "if taken too far, hinder recovery, by tethering the survivor to one rigid version of the past."[44] Once established and held in safety, the trauma narrative, like the human subject, may require for its freedom a present moment in which something new is possible. Brison continues, arguing that a set narrative

> may be at odds with telling to live, which I now see as a kind of let-ting go, playing with the past in order not to be held back as one springs away from it. After gaining enough control over the story to be able to tell it, perhaps one has to give it up, in order to retell it,

without having to "get it right," without fear of betraying it, to be able to rewrite the past in different ways, leading up to an infinite variety of unforeseeable futures. (103)

What Brison describes here sounds like Nietzsche's "*tabula rasa* of the consciousness, to make room for new things." Brison doesn't explicitly call this an intersubjective process (though a persistent message of her book is that "the self exists fundamentally in relation to others" [102]). After all, a lot of work of recovery is individual. But her account of the loneliness of not being heard and the strength she gained from support groups and friends makes clear that the conditions of the surrounding world will make all the difference to a person trying to create a livable present moment in the wake of past harm. In Brison's account, the past, once digested, may be able to take on multiple forms, to change over time. That is reconciliation with time—concerned less with perpetrators and retribution than it is with how to live after violence. It is a revisionary practice, as necessary to the present moment as what Nietzsche calls forgetting.

INTERRUPTION

Améry's perception of the West Germany of the 1960s is that the world forgives and forgets, the generation of the perpetrators ages comfortably, and the new generation resents the moral weight of the past: they write letters to German newspapers about how they are sick and tired of hearing that their fathers killed six million Jews.[45] For Améry this means that time is being allowed to pass in the wrong way. And so he uses resentment to make a point about time. He says that what he wants would be accomplished if "two groups of people, the overpowered and those who overpowered them, would be joined in the desire that time be turned back and, with it, that history become moral."[46] That is the core of Améry's ethical claim, and it requires a reversal of time. Everyone—victims, perpetrators, bystanders, and beneficiaries—should be joined in wishing the past were otherwise, asserting that what happened should not have happened. This is less a form of ressentiment than it is a revisionary practice.

The aim of such a practice is not (or not only) to punish those responsible for imposing grievous harm on others but to mark how we are all implicated in a responsibility for the worlds we inhabit. It takes more than liberty, personal autonomy, formal equality, or cessation of hostility to rebuild a destroyed world. If, in the wake of the destruction of self and world occasioned by egregious trespass of norms on which everyone ought to be able to rely, no remedy is offered, ethical loneliness continues unabated. Walker attaches to this condition a second-order fear:

> It is bad to be injured or affronted, so to be under threat of, even in fear of, further injury or affront because what protected you from it is destroyed, ineffective, or in doubt. It is worse to see no way to reestablish the security the norm was supposed to provide, for now you are afraid that you are going to have to be afraid, to live in fear, without assurance or protection of a community of shared boundaries that one's fellows are willing to assert and enforce both with you and for you.[47]

It is difficult to "take on the present moment freely" or believe that the past is past if present conditions do not restore the safety and trust on which our shared humanity relies. Heather Love insists "on the importance of clinging to ruined identities and to histories of injury" because that, to her, also means "refusing to write off the most vulnerable, the least presentable, and all the dead."[48] Améry engages in a similar practice when, in refusing to let the past be past, he continually interrupts the way time has of smoothing things over. After all, time has a tendency to smooth things over mostly for people who live comfortably and have not been grievously harmed. In the description of ethical loneliness in chapter 1, Levinas's work helped us see that our own bodily fatigue and indolence draw our attention—if we look—to how we are situated in a world not of our own making and that, as selves, we are always in need of the support of others if we are to remain safe. In a similar way, resentment—our own and others'—might interrupt us when we fall too easily into set ways and thus fail to note the who and the how of the stories that can't be heard when time just passes and things continue on "as they always have."

FORGIVENESS

Améry resists forgiving absent conditions where such a practice might be meaningful, but forgiveness is not a simple thing. So we should take a detour into its complexities before we decide where it fits in the range of revisionary practices.

The worry about ressentiment, the problem of a will undermined by time's inexorability—we might even call it a structural concern—is at the heart of Hannah Arendt's use of the concept of "forgiveness" as a political tool in *The Human Condition*. She writes, "Without being forgiven, released from the consequences of what we have done, our capacity to act would, as it were, be confined to one single deed from which we could never recover; we would remain the victims of its consequences forever, not unlike the sorcerer's apprentice who lacked the magic formula to break the spell."[49] As beings who err, without forgiveness we would never get free of our mistakes. Forgiveness is a tremendous accomplishment for someone who can manage it. Plenty of studies have shown that refusal or inability to forgive "carries an increased risk of psychiatric morbidity" or is otherwise bad for one's health.[50] Being able to let go of past harms, whether for one's self, for the sake of the one who caused harm, or for a community or a larger project of state building, can be tremendously freeing. Forgiveness, then, can be a meaningful form of revision.

Forgiveness may also create new sites of power: the party who was once at the mercy of the offender now has the power to offer or refuse mercy, so the story goes. Aaron Lazare calls this power given to offended parties—to engage in or refuse social relationship, to forgive or not to forgive—"a compensation for the power we took from them in the offense."[51] Forgiveness might also rebuild, or build for the first time, a form of equality necessary to social relationships. Griswold says of forgiveness that "each party holds the other in its power, in this sense: the offender depends on the victim in order to be forgiven, and the victim depends on the offender in order to forgive," so that forgiveness functions as a reminder to all involved of their vulnerability as humans who must live together.[52] That seems to be part of what is at stake in the following statement made by Cynthia Ngewu before the South African TRC when she was asked if she could forgive the man who killed her son: "This thing called reconciliation . . . if I am understanding it correctly . . . if it means this perpetrator, this man who has killed Christopher Piet, if it means he becomes human again, this man, so that I, so that all of us, get our humanity back . . . then I agree, then I support it all."[53] Forgiveness may help each of us recognize others as equals involved in the cooperative work of building a world. As Arendt puts it, "*what* is done is forgiven for the sake of *who* did it."[54]

But there is reason to balance enthusiasm for the power of forgiveness with knowledge of its limits and its multiple uses. Avishai Margalit wants us to be sure we hold on to some of our independence in the process of forgiving. For him, forgiveness is "a conscious decision to change one's attitude and to overcome anger and vengefulness."[55] Forgetting might get more work done for us, but since forgetting is an omission rather than a decision, we have less control over whether it will happen. Nonetheless, if we actively decide to forgive, that might, over time, help us manage a bit of forgetting: "The decision to forgive makes one stop brooding on the past wrong, stop telling it to other people, with the end result of forgetting it or forgetting that it once mattered to you greatly."[56] In cases of grievous harm it is likely easier said than done and may also depend on whether others are willing to support forgiving as a practice or a value.[57] Deciding to forgive may not get me all the way to feeling or acting in forgiving ways, especially if those around me, whether for or against me, still harbor hostilities. That is true not only on the level of decision making but also on the level of affect transmission. Forgiveness is a form of communication, and communication is, as Levinas reminds us, not a simple transfer of meaning from point A in me to point B in an interlocutor. It transpires at least in part by means of bodily signs that are not the product of rational will. But Margalit wants to preserve a space for the self's own practice of forgiveness, so for him the complication isn't communication's relation to affect in a shared world but rather affect's dialogue with a self's reasoned decision making. So he argues that "*forgiveness* denotes both a process and an achievement, just as the word *work* denotes both the process of working and the work that is accomplished."[58] In other words, Margalit turns difficult forgiveness into a second-order desire.

A first-order desire is simply what a person wants: I want to eat ice cream and drink bourbon and be healthy. A second-order desire is a thought about what you "want to want," a determination of the will you'd like to have. I want to want to be healthy. So I work to have my second-order desire for health overrule my desires for ice cream and bourbon as much of the time as is necessary for me to achieve healthiness. According to Harry Frankfurt, if a person, having reflected on the kind of will she wants to have, succeeds in living up to those desires (turning her second-order desire into a successful second-order volition), we can say she has free will even if her actions are constrained by outside factors—in this way free will is compatible with determinism.[59]

Margalit points out that for anyone faced with a difficult past and a wish to move on, there are likely to be conflicting first-order desires: I want to move on but I also want to continue resenting what happened. There is only so much I can do, rationally, to get rid of resentment: "Only the decision to begin this process is voluntary: the end-result of complete forgiveness is not voluntary any more than forgetting is, and so it cannot be guaranteed."[60] Walker adds, "Someone who otherwise wants to release himself and his offender from the sequels to a wrong may be able to do so conclusively in a determined and practical way without ceasing to experience many difficult feelings at the memory of a wrong."[61] I can't make myself forgive or forget (just as, as Levinas points out, I don't get to *decide* to be weary and never have complete control over what I communicate to others), and I have incomplete power over my feelings about harms I've undergone, but I may nonetheless form a second-order desire to forgive and work to put that into practice. If I succeed, I may even, over time, not only express forgiveness but also actually feel it. This is a practice of the self, done for the sake of the self. Margalit is not much concerned with perpetrators. He is more interested in how to release the self from its entrapment in past harm. (This is strikingly similar to what Nietzsche would call "willing backwards," though Margalit never acknowledges Nietzsche in his writing.) That is important, as we would not want victims of grave harm to be held hostage to a practice that, if it relies on remorseful perpetrators, might never come to pass. What Margalit does not acknowledge is that with grave offenses it may not be possible to accomplish this on one's own. (This is another way in which Margalit's account resembles Nietzsche's.)

However, Arendt (like Griswold, Lazare, and many others) sees forgiveness as strictly a dialogic process:

> The fact that the same *who*, revealed in action and speech, remains also the subject of forgiving is the deepest reason why nobody can forgive himself; here, as in action and speech generally, we are dependent upon others, to whom we appear in a distinctness which we ourselves are unable to perceive. Closed within ourselves, we would never be able to forgive ourselves any failing or transgression because we would lack the experience of the person for the sake of whom one can forgive.[62]

Forgiveness is *for others*, and we miss something about what it is, Arendt suggests, if we isolate it from its necessary relationality.[63] Maybe what we need in a case of grave harm, like Améry's, is a space somewhere between independent forgiveness and forgiveness as solely for others, where forgiveness is not held hostage to the remorse of perpetrators but is still acknowledged to be a component of world building and thus a shared or intersubjective activity.

There is a possibility we have not yet considered: that forgiveness might also come from a site of weakness or *lack* of power. Pumla Gobodo-Madikizela describes a scene at South Africa's TRC where a mother was asked on live television to forgive Winnie Mandela—who was responsible for the death of her son—though Mandela had shown neither remorse nor responsibility for her crimes in her testimony:

> Nine years after Stompie Seipei's body was discovered, Madikizela-Mandela, once the embodiment of suffering, resistance, survival and all the images associated with the fight against apartheid, was questioned as a perpetrator on the stage of the TRC. . . . At the end of the public hearing, during which Madikizela-Mandela essentially denied any knowledge of what had been happening in her own backyard, and offered no meaningful apology, she approached Stompie Seipei's mother while the TV cameras rolled. With a triumphant smile and open arms, she embraced her. I watched the moment of contact between the two women: the mother's humble smile and return of the gesture, and Madikizela-Mandela's triumphant smile, enacting her imposing power through her embrace. Two smiles: one a symbol of power, the other a symbol of impotence.[64]

After watching for nine days as Madikizela-Mandela failed to apologize or admit responsibility, Seipei's mother was given a choice between embracing Madikizela-Mandela or spurning on live television someone who had once been a symbol of the fight against apartheid. Gobodo-Madikizela observes that, especially in a long unjust society where promised changes are not yet made, "some of the victims who encounter perpetrators cannot make that psychological leap and recognize that the tables have turned, that now the power is theirs to demand what is rightfully due to them."[65] We can't know for certain whether Stompie Seipei's mother felt this way. But Gobodo-Madikizela's impression of the encounter shows how forgiveness might offer to a victim the power to grant or refuse mercy, but unequal social conditions might make the possibility of refusal more difficult for some than others.[66]

So forgiveness might emerge from a site of power, a place of new or renewed equality, or it might be undertaken for the self rather than for others. It might also spring from powerlessness. Like resentment, it is not an unqualified good. A disposition to forgive might as soon reveal a generous spirit or healed psyche as it does a damaged self unable to demand that violations of the self be redressed. In turn, an insistent resentment might show us a victim's vengeful obstinacy, or it might correspond to justified refusal to forgive in a social situation where reasonable conditions for recovery have not been met.[67]

RECONCILING WITH TIME

Améry resists forgiving because that would equal an amnesiac forgetting, which is both impossible and unjust. He writes that his resentment "is my personal protest against the antimoral natural process of healing that time brings about, and by which I make the genuinely humane and absurd demand that time be turned back."[68] But Nietzsche and Margalit would say, for similar reasons, let the past go—because if you don't, you will have given up control over your own fate. Nietzsche says "let it go" by willing backwards, changing "it was" into "thus I willed it." Margalit advises "letting go" by making forgiveness a rationally asserted second-order desire that overrules the understandable first-order desire to resent relentlessly. Neither Nietzsche nor Margalit are much concerned with perpetrators. Their aim is to reconcile the self with time.

So reconciliation has at least two senses. One can wish to reconcile with human beings who have wronged or been wronged—the goal of this kind of reconciliation can range from civil cohabitation to forming a new basis for community. But one can also wish to reconcile oneself with time, or the world as it is—for the sake of the self's own recovery, or for a better future—leaving those who wronged you out of your thoughts and plans. Either way, the hope is that reconciliation creates a present and a future that are not entirely determined by past harms.

Améry struggles to reconcile himself with time, but in doing so he finds that he cannot divorce that struggle from the role played by the perpetrators of his abandonment. For Améry, reconciliation with time, or with the world as it is, is possible only under certain conditions. And he cannot achieve those conditions on his own. (At first glance it seems that this is what Nietzsche did not foresee. But another engagement with Nietzsche's work, one that dives deep into his view of the will as pathos, might argue otherwise.)

And so Améry clings to his resentments. He requires a time machine. And yet no one can change what happened. What happened in the past *is not otherwise*. Perhaps no one can know that more thoroughly than someone who has been forever marked by torture and internment. But that is what I take to be his point: the irreparable past can resonate in the present moment in vastly different ways, and only some of those ways offer to those whose humanity was destroyed—but who still live on—a sense that, instead of being forced into ethical loneliness, a dehumanizing existential solitude without escape, they now inhabit a world, a human community, where they will be safe. They will be offered help when it is needed. They are persons capable of taking on the present moment freely.

Améry suggests that a present moment in which all Germans "owned" Hitler would create, symbolically, a past moment in which the Germans rose up and revolted against Hitler, ending the war themselves—a revision, a reversal of time. Sure, it never happened that the Germans rose up against Hitler. But what is a revisionary practice if not a way of changing how the past is lived in the present? If Hitler were accepted as a cultural inheritance by 1960s Germany, and the majority of Germans openly wished that what happened had never happened, then Améry's resentment would, as he puts it, be subjectively pacified and become objectively unnecessary.[69] Perhaps only at that point could a person take Margalit's or Nietzsche's advice and, for the sake of the self's own health and future, learn to will backwards, "forget," or form a second-order desire to forgive or move on rather than to continue resenting.

Walker, writing about moral repair in general, says the following about ending resentment:

> Where there is opportunity and ability to get transgressors back within bounds, or to impose some corrective action on them, or at the very least to summon support from others for a clear repudiation of what transgressors have done, resentment may be relieved as threat is di-

minished. It is something at least if the rules and boundaries are reit-
erated. . . . It is best of all if those who have broken the rules can actually be brought to reaffirm their subscription to them.[70]

That describes a best-case scenario of what Améry demands. When everyone joins together in wishing the past were otherwise, it effects a revision of an injurious past and grants to those most harmed by that past
the liberty in the present moment to imagine a future not determined by
past harm.

SITES OF REVISION

One goal after conflict or a history of violence should be providing conditions where positive revision is possible. There are some pasts that no
amount of *individual* backwards willing will convert into a livable present. Améry couldn't move forward because the crimes to which he had
been subjected had not been adequately acknowledged by the German
people and the wider world. For him the harm was not only that he was
tortured, detained, beaten, and starved. It was also that what happened
to him could not have happened without the cooperation of a large number of people, many of whom would never describe themselves as guilty
of a crime. Absent widespread acknowledgment of that, there can be no
safety, and so it is reasonable for him to continue resenting.

It may be easy to think that none of "us" could be "bad Germans." But
scratch the surface of most reasonably comfortable lives and you'll find
something uncomfortable. Accountants help wealthy individuals find tax
loopholes to decrease their contribution to a larger social scheme. The
clothes we buy are likely made by slave labor or something strikingly
similar to it.[71] The food we eat is likely harvested by underpaid workers
without citizenship or protection.[72] Much of modern life in the Western
world is so distanced from knowledge of what makes that way of life possible that those whose modes of wealth cause worldwide misery do not
feel implicated in that misery. Powerful nations pay corrupt elites in underdeveloped nations for natural resources at rates that benefit everyone
except the people living in those underdeveloped nations. Powerful Western states no longer practice colonialism, slavery, or genocide, but their
economic, political, and military dominance facilitates enslavement and

genocide elsewhere.[73] As Thomas Pogge puts it, all this is possible without anyone involved taking leave of the operating moral norms. It is all legal.[74]

What Améry craved more than criminal sanction of the behavior of the most guilty was a broad responsiveness to—knowledge and acknowledgment of—what befell him and so many others. He wanted the wider world to accept a responsibility set free from legal culpability. Especially for those who have been abandoned by humanity and survived, that kind of responsibility may at times matter more than the individual criminal kind. All of this points to a site of repair outside the victim-perpetrator continuum. Repair may be focused on rebuilding the agency of victims, designing institutions that support fragile communities, offering diverse forms of help: economic, medical, psychosocial, educational, and so on. But if reconciliation, transition, or peaceful cohabitation is to last, victims and perpetrators cannot be the only sites of transformation. Those lucky enough to have remained relatively safe and secure will need to perform revisionary practices on themselves so that they will be able to see that they are implicated both in the destruction of worlds and in a responsibility to rebuild those worlds.

Derek Summerfield, writing in the *British Medical Journal* about the effects of war, points out that observers too often think that the main site of revision after violence is the psyche of the victim: "Victims of war are often expected to be vengeful because of their 'traumatization' or 'brutalization' and to promote new 'cycles of violence.' The emotional reactions of people affected by war are perceived as harmful to themselves and dangerous to others; this leads to a belief that the reactions of victims should be modified."[75] Summerfield does not dispute all the studies that show that lack of forgiveness can be personally and politically devastating, nor does he neglect the very real traumas with which many survivors struggle. His point is, rather, that Western approaches to therapy usually intend to change not just a person's behavior but also her mind. That may be part of what is needed. But if we back up and look at the larger setting, we might also ask, what is it about the mind of a person who feels justified resentment at being unjustly violated that needs to be changed? Along those lines, here is an exchange between someone testifying about human rights abuses at the South African TRC and a commissioner:

Commissioner: Now, when you say, ever since this incident took place and you have this problematic relationship with white people, did you ever try to get a treatment or some counseling with regard to that?

Mr. Morake: No, I've never thought of getting any treatment because I feel that where they are, they are the ones who should be getting the treatment.[76]

One is reminded here of James Baldwin's worry, in the context of race relations in the United States, that black people hoping for an apology for slavery from white people might divert attention from both blacks and whites focusing on the pathological state of the white psyche. His impulse is "to dismiss white people as the slightly mad victims of their own brainwashing"—since black Americans have never been able to believe the stories white Americans seem to tell themselves about who they are and how they came to be that way: "that their ancestors were all freedom-loving heroes, that they were born in the greatest country the world has ever seen . . . that Americans have always dealt honorably with Mexicans and Indians and all other neighbors and inferiors," and so on.[77] As Elizabeth Spelman reads it, "If whites are too sick to be sorry, to know what sorry could mean, they need to get well before being able to offer an apology and know what they would be saying."[78] Similarly, among a diversity of positions on the value of apology and forgiveness for political healing, participants in a survey of the attitudes of Aboriginal Australians tended to see "the value of apology more in terms of the need for white people to have a better knowledge and understanding of the issues than for black people to experience emotional support and healing," especially if that healing meant transformation of the affective states of Aboriginal but not white Australians.[79]

It isn't that survivors of violence and abandonment don't need psychological help—they very well may—but that assuming that survivors are the sole site of transformation misses something. Summerfield's conclusion is that "'recovery' is not a discrete process: it happens in people's lives rather than in their psychologies. It is practical and unspectacular, and it is grounded in the resumption of the ordinary rhythms of everyday life—the familiar, the sociocultural, religious and economic activities that make the world intelligible."[80] Summerfield probably takes it too far when he says that healing from the trauma of human rights abuses happens in people's lives rather than in their psychologies. Surely it is both. But if recovery "is grounded in the resumption of the ordinary rhythms of everyday life," and everyday life can't be achieved by a person acting alone, then responsibility rests in a much broader set of locations than the minds of victims and perpetrators. It matters what stories we tell ourselves about who owes what to whom and for what reasons. We are all responsible for building worlds where a life's ordinary rhythms might resume or originate. Why? Because how else will it get done? Conditions where positive rather than negative revision is possible will likely be created only by a plurality of persons who don't rely only on law to declare where responsibility lies. No one can rebuild a broken world on her own. It is that kind of reconstruction that we are called upon to participate in when we try to adjudicate the aftermath of violence—as legal practitioners, as victims or perpetrators, as bystanders, as theorists of law or politics, or simply as people who care about justice and recognize that we are all implicated in its successes and its failures. We need to think more carefully about scenes of recovery and transition, to guard against taking up an unreflective legalism. Only then might we extricate ourselves from the false dilemma of thinking that, in the wake of the kind of harm caused not only by acts of violence but also by widespread complicity in or indifference to that violence, people are only either innocent or legally guilty. There is so much responsibility between those two poles. And I'm not sure very many people reside anywhere near the one labeled "innocent."

When we revise the self of the one who allows legalism alone to define the terms of responsibility, that revision contributes to possibilities of rebuilding worlds for what they are: cooperatively authored, shared, always in process, and, for that reason, fragile. If safety is ever guaranteed, it is the outcome of a world built to honor a commitment to safety. It may not be safe for a recovering individual to rebuild her trust in a society that has not adequately condemned the wrongs that caused her abandonment, or in which bystanders and beneficiaries do not acknowledge their responsibility for a past that should have been otherwise. Positive revision is unlikely under such conditions. But worlds built widely and well make hopeful revisions possible. The intersubjective aspect of world building should return us to what Améry hoped to achieve by describing the reasons for his continuing resentment and remind us of the social dimension of what Eve Sedgwick called reparative reading:

"Because the reader has room to realize that the future may be different from the present, it is also possible for her to entertain such profoundly painful, profoundly relieving, ethically crucial possibilities as that the past, in turn, could have happened differently from the way it actually did."[81]

5

Desert

If thou didst ever hold me in thy heart,
Absent thee from felicity awhile,
And in this harsh world draw thy breath in pain,
To tell my story.

—William Shakespeare, *Hamlet*

Many systems of justice, historically and at present, have acknowledged the value of the desire for revenge. But, as Teresa Godwin Phelps points out, *feeling* something is not the same as *doing* something, and so even those who would caution against revenge might benefit from asking what it means that so many people desire it in the wake of serious wrong-doing.[1] Many people *feel* vengeful. But does having that feeling mean acting on it? And, more important, does having that feeling and acting on it mean committing further violence? I think the answer to both questions is no. Desiring revenge and acting on that desire may lead to violence but does not have to. Feeling resentment and acting on that resentment might block the way to a reconciled future, but it might not. It might even open an alternative way to that future.

What if we took what resentment demands seriously and asked what might be done to fix it, to render resentment, as Améry wanted, both "subjectively pacified" and "objectively unnecessary"?[2] Phelps gives us a compact genealogy of how revenge disappears from official accounts of justice—beginning as a virtue and an honor owed to friends and kin, slowly converted into a formalized retribution owned only by the state (because, the reasoning goes, personal revenge is savagery), which then gets replaced by utilitarian calculations of social utility (because, the reasoning goes, retribution is also savage, or at least "not useful"). When revenge is virtue and honor, it is meted out personally between those affected, both victim (or the victim's champions) and perpetrator equally involved. When revenge becomes state retribution it pits state against perpetrator, placing the need to rebalance state order higher than the right a victim once had to claim satisfaction for loss undergone. When state retribution becomes calculations about deterrence and incapacitation, not only do victims disappear but individual perpetrators matter less as well. State power remains. Of course, few would look at the current state of imprisonment in the United States, for instance, and call it a social good—though some might make an ill-conceived argument that only prisons "solve" the problem of crime. At this time in the United States, we seem to view response to crime retributively, imprisoning record numbers of offenders and treating them as if they were irredeemable. There is certainly not enough space left in this book to take on that issue, but let's at least admit that it is retribution in its lowest form, punishing for the sake of punishment (which is basically revenge) rather than out of a Kantian respect for the free will of an individual who chose the wrong path (which is the classic Western take on why retribution would matter). The desire for revenge does not disappear, no matter how a culture works to extinguish it. As Margaret Walker points out in *Moral Repair*, whether it will surface in ugly forms or in potentially reparative forms will depend on what social conditions, ideas, and affects, created by many interacting forces, prevail in a given time and place.[3]

A continuing resentment or desire for vengeance might lead to violence. But it might also lead to political activism, commitment to social organizing, solidarity between and among abandoned persons and populations, creation of groups bent on getting new truths heard and assuaging ethical loneliness, and any of a host of other positive developments. A desire for vengeance that doesn't lead to violence might also end in despair or resignation. That despair might be converted back into violence in certain conditions. The existence or nonexistence of social support for positive revisions of past harm will make a difference in the outcome. After all, anger doesn't always lead to a desire for revenge.

I bring up retribution at this moment because, in the wake of grave wrongdoing, one of the important questions to ask is what the different parties involved are owed. In our intuitions and calculations about justice, we are all interested in just deserts on some level. I think that is true even if we take seriously (as I do) Linda Ross Meyer's point that debt might not be the best metaphor for how to address wrongdoing. She writes,

> We tend to think of crime in pseudo-monetary terms as a "debt." Debts, of course, have to be paid, and criminal debts have to be paid in years. However if, using a different metaphor, we think of crime as a breach of trust between real people, then what seems right to do about it changes. The ideal fix for a breach is a reunification and an attempt to restore trust, not a "payment." Reunification can come about in many ways, but at some point it requires a willingness of community members to trust and to take risks. The language of mercy reflects the lack of surety and lack of reciprocity inherent in taking that risk.[4]

Meyer's work has much to teach us about response to harm and corresponds with my purpose in drawing attention to alternative definitions of retribution. As Meyer points out, in order for mercy to work, there has to be trust. Part of what recognizing ethical loneliness as a problem does is draw our attention to the importance of the surrounding world: some conditions will allow loneliness to be assuaged, some will not. Some make trust possible, others render it simply too dangerous. For most of us, willingness to risk trusting others requires background conditions of relative safety. In this chapter I revisit the heritage of retribution, with its attention to recognition of harm and the need for redress, to see what strengths and weaknesses it might bring to a scene of recovery.

"Retribution": it comes from the Latin verb *retribuere*, "to give back," "restore," or "repay." It means "to *tribuere* again," where *tribuere* means "to distribute, bestow, or confer," "grant, allow, or devote." So calls for retribution always reflect a sense that something has been unjustly taken and that a balance must be put right. One must redo, offer again, something that should have remained intact. Clearly, in many circumstances the punishment of perpetrators will not be sufficient to accomplish such a goal. That is why retribution needn't appear as an antonym of repair: in some cases its best goal will be to bestow, confer, grant, allow, or devote something deserved to one who deserves it. It repays those harmed for their harm. Or, where what has happened cannot be undone, it offers compensation for loss. Requital according to merits or deserts; something given or inflicted in such requital; distribution of rewards and punishment; something justly deserved; recompense; something given or demanded in repayment: all these possible definitions may sound less restorative than Meyer's suggested "reunification," but after divisive conflict, it is unlikely that reconciliation or reunification will be possible if reasonably equal conditions have not also been restored. Part of what all parties *deserve* in the wake of grievous violence is the creation of those conditions. That sets the scene for a possible reunification.

In any legal case there will be desert on both sides—an offender may deserve punishment and a victim may deserve reparation. The surrounding community may also deserve some sort of recompense for the destruction of its peace. But current institutional legality doesn't tend to include a consideration of desert in terms of reparation, and so retribution gets flattened into a concern with punishment rather than inhabiting its richer resonances as a way of putting right a balance that was disturbed by wrongful conduct. That more abundant definition of retribution may even be considered a form of repair: it aims to give to each what is her own. Revenge, like resentment, finds its basis in measured justice as much as it does in excess, and people whom law does not serve may find their way to a different justice. But modern legal thinking has so absorbed the fear of powers other than the state's that retribution has come to be thought of as, on the one hand, solely the duty of a "sovereign" rather than a power held by individuals to right a wrong and, on the other, as focused on perpetrators rather than meting out to all parties (perpetrators, victims, surrounding community) what they are owed. That set of ideas dominates at present, but, though states may be able to vitiate the sense most individuals have of their powers of response (including retaliation), they will never be able to crush that sense entirely. That is one of the ways in which human beings really are what liberal political theory calls autonomous—we give the law to ourselves (though our success in doing so may also rely on social conditions and the social imaginary of a given group—what is considered possible or just or fitting, and what affective charges attend different choices of response).

That the definition of desert has been compressed for us is perhaps why we are uncomfortable (if we are—that is Phelps's reading of the play), in

Ariel Dorfman's play *Death and the Maiden*, when the vengeful Paulina asks, "But what about my good?"[5] As Jeffrie Murphy puts it,

> In the present age, most of us do not feel comfortable talking about the criminal law [in terms of anger], for we are inclined to think that civilized people are not given to hatred and to an anger so intense that it generates a desire for revenge. . . . We prefer to talk high-mindedly of our reluctantly advocating punishment of criminals perhaps because social utility or justice demands it and tend to think it is only primitives who would actually *hate* criminals and want them to suffer to appease an anger or outrage that is felt toward them.[6]

Paulina's husband "talks high-mindedly" and invokes social utility when he tries to convince her that letting the past go is what is best for the greatest number. But Paulina is not able to do that—perhaps because she carries an excess of anger, perhaps because reparative conditions have not been offered to her. Though she is a fictional character in an unspecified South American state, she is a torture survivor whose testimony will not be heard because the state's official truth proceedings cover only the disappeared. The predicament itself is not purely fictional.

One thing is clear: we will not know why she cannot let go of her anger if we refuse to hear her express it. Institutions aimed at rebuilding law, nation, and civil relationships after violence may be animated by an understandable desire to quell anger and encourage conciliation. But I doubt, in the history of anger, that very much of it has been quelled by silencing its expression. One ought to be careful about how much space it is given, and what those spaces look like. Not only governing institutions concerned to protect their central authority but also ordinary people tend to fear talk of revenge because unchecked violent revenge does destroy lives. Ancient Greece transitioned from clan-based revenge killing to centralized legal punishment not only because those in power wanted better control but likely also because many ordinary citizens longed to escape a way of thinking and acting where "even small disputes could require families and clans to enter into blood feuds that continued indefinitely in a state of vendetta, thereby weakening the clan by the loss of most men of fighting age," ending only when something like mutual extinction was achieved.[7] This was a problem not only for ancient Greece. It is also alive in Kosovo, in gang culture everywhere, and it sometimes resurfaces after conflict ends when peaceful mechanisms for transition falter—Israel and Palestine come to mind here, of course—always with devastating impact, making reconciliation or peaceful cohabitation difficult or impossible. Revenge is not at all an unqualified good.

But anger and resentment are not only negative affects. They may be a powerful demonstration of a person's righteous indignation at being treated badly and so may be an important *positive* expression of a relationship to the past, present, and future that is both reasoned and affective. And they may call for different things. Phelps points out that in Shakespeare's *Hamlet*, the ghost of Hamlet's father tells him, "If thou didst ever thy dear father love— . . ./Revenge his foul and most unnatural murder."[8] He asks for the kind of revenge we think of when we hear the word "blood." Most of the play is taken up with precisely that kind of retaliation. But later on, having lived the toxicity of revenge, a dying Hamlet asks something different of Horatio: "If thou didst ever hold me in thy heart,/Absent thee from felicity awhile,/And in this harsh world draw thy breath in pain,/To tell my story."[9] For Hamlet justice will be done if the truth is known. Phelps reads it this way: "Hamlet does not ask Horatio for revenge; he asks him to tell the story."[10] Of course, it may be easier for Hamlet not to request blood for blood when all the killing has been done already. Let's just note that Hamlet and his father both do and do not want the same thing. Dad wants vengeance, son wants remembrance, and those are both ways of acknowledging and memorializing loss. But those two possibilities represent different choices made about the past and exact different tolls on the present and future. And they reveal different conceptions a self may have of itself. Hamlet's father is the autonomous "I" whose idea of retribution is only about what is owed to him. Hamlet is closer to the cooperatively authored self who knows his story matters but that it is also one part of a much larger story that will continue on after him and to which he owes a thoughtful contribution. So perhaps during the course of the play he subjects his own self to a revisionary practice. Perhaps not.

Part of the reason why truth commissions, international tribunals, and institutions of transitional justice exist is that sometimes a central authority—that institution that would replace the need for private revenge with a guaranteed end to impunity for crimes—either does not exist or cannot or will not play its assigned role.[11] A government or legal institution might lack power against an entrenched military or warring factions; there may not be enough police officers, lawyers, or judges to respond to crimes, or the ones who do respond may be corrupt; a government may be ruled by a majority that wishes to let the past be past rather than dealing with its injustice; an imbalance of power may determine whose stories get heard. In all these cases retribution is ruled out, but no effective response takes its place. (In Hamlet's case, King Claudius is unlikely to open an investigation into the death of Hamlet's father since Claudius is the killer.) The proliferation in recent decades of new or alternative institutions—ones that transcend a local context or strict legalism where adequate response is lacking—designed to respond to crimes against humanity answers at least in part to the human need to see justice done as well as the deeply felt sense that if it is not seen to be done, the past will not be past.

Rather than asking for more killing, Hamlet asks Horatio to tell his story. Is Hamlet then on the side of the truth commissions? Perhaps. Maybe Denmark would (as Horatio might put it) be less rotten if the truth of various murders and corruption were revealed and the people were given meaningful use of language to tell their own stories. Hamlet might also want legal trials, however, especially if truth commissions would mean amnesty for those whose crimes caused the rotting—he's not exactly a restorative justice kind of guy.[12] But Hamlet might also suspect that institutions would not, on their own, clear out the rot.

REPARATIVE RETRIBUTION

Institutions will not clear out the rot on their own. But what can they do? And what else needs to be done, beyond what institutions can do? Even if they have not been traumatized or abandoned, victims who testify in any institutional setting may experience a distressing loss of a sense of agency in their own case. Nils Christie points out that victims participating in criminal law cases can be double losers: "first, vis-à-vis the offender, but secondly and often in a more crippling manner by being denied rights to full participation in what might have been one of the more important ritual encounters in life. The victim has lost his case to the state."[13] What he means is that something that happened between two (or more) human beings is converted into a conflict between one of the parties and a state or international institution. Christie laments the ownership of conflict by the state because it depersonalizes social life—people are no longer linked in social networks where they might both understand others' motivations and successfully predict their behavior. Elizabeth Spelman agrees, arguing that retributive systems seem to take from the community any sense it might have that it can figure out how to deal with loss and conflict without state intervention.[14] It also may make "offenders think that the only consequences of their acts they need to think about are the punitive consequences for themselves" (56)—yet another possible outcome when personal sovereignty functions free of dependency on others in the stories we tell ourselves about our selves and others.

But there are different or more expansive ways to think about response to wrongdoing, even if we don't want to give up the retributive idea entirely. Judith Herman argues that victims want to have a "sense that the people who did the damage are made to give something back, or to try to clean up the mess that they made," and calls this a demand for a justice that is different from punishment.[15] That sense of justice seems to aim more squarely at rebuilding worlds than does state monopoly on retribution but is still at least partly retributive. It wants restoration of a lost equality.

Christie argues that conflict is not only a disturbance of order that must be remedied but also a "potential for activity, for participation."[16] In a relatively peaceful society, a greater stake in conflict and its resolution would give to victims and perpetrators alike greater "opportunities for norm-clarification" and for "continuous discussion of what represents the law of the land" (8), all of which brings to mind Walker's reminder that victims desire normative confirmation—they want to be able to trust that those around them agree that what happened to them should not have happened, should be unlawful, and should not be allowed to repeat. They want what Améry wanted. Writing in 1977, Christie reveals his work to be a precursor of the restorative ideal when he argues that if the main focus of a proceeding was not "meting out guilt but a thorough discussion of what could be done to undo the deed, then the situation might change" (9). Christie is interested in revision, what might "undo the deed." His aim is not to be "soft on crime"—because he still thinks the state should punish, even adding to that punishment a need for offenders to address concretely the harms they have done to others—but to involve those affected by crime in the solution to the problems that both cause and are caused by the crimes in question. We could call this reparative retribution. Spelman gives us a sense of why this matters to our thinking about repair when she remarks that mainstream positive law has "evolved in ways that have kept most people from developing the kinds of knowledge and skills needed to properly understand the damage that needs attending to, the creativity it takes to think about how best to do the repairs, and the abilities to carry them out."[17] Reparative retribution might play a role in moving victims, perpetrators, and bystanders to see how broadly responsibility for entrenched wrongdoing must fall. It would be a form of legalism that has a better sense of the limits to what law and legal culpability can accomplish.

A recent *New York Times Magazine* article, "Can Forgiveness Play a Role in Criminal Justice?" describes a process of mediation between the families of a killer and a slain child as both sides struggle to understand the crime and its consequences: what the outcome is for those who have lost a loved one, what the outcome should be for one who has imposed that loss, and whether bringing the two sides together has potential to help all involved rebuild the world they inhabit together.[18] The case—in which nineteen-year old Conor McBride killed his girlfriend, Ann Grosmaire—brings to the fore all the complexity of violent crime and its aftermath. The McBrides and the Grosmaires are exceptional in that they kept contact with one another and worked together to insist on using restorative justice processes instead of just letting the system take over. It happened only because a prosecutor let slip that he had wide discretion in recommending sentencing in murder cases. That made Ann's mother, Kate, change her thinking. Despite the magnitude of her own loss, she had been musing about how terrible it was that Conor would spend the rest of his life in prison. But she didn't think any other outcome was possible. Once the prosecutor opened the door to thinking otherwise, the McBrides and Grosmaires worked together to find a restorative justice expert who could change how the case was viewed. That was difficult, since restorative justice is used mostly for nonviolent crimes like robbery, forgery, or drug offenses—crimes where it is relatively simple to figure out who owes what to whom and how to repay it. There is much more controversy over whether it is appropriate to use it for crimes such as domestic violence, let alone murder. It didn't seem likely that a murder charge in Florida could be viewed through a restorative lens. Then an Episcopal priest whom the Grosmaires had sought out for counsel suggested that the pre-plea conference—a meeting between the prosecutor and the defense lawyer that anyone can attend and that remains off the record in terms of the court case—might work as the setting for a restorative justice "community conference." The prosecutor agreed to let that happen but insisted that decisions about charges and sentencing recommendations would remain his.

The conference gathered together the Grosmaires, Sujatha Baliga (their restorative justice expert), the McBrides, both lawyers, a victims' advocate, the Grosmaires' priest, and Conor. Charges were read, police reports summarized, and then various participants spoke in turn, each with no interruptions allowed. Baliga notes that what Kate Grosmaire said to Conor during the conference was "way tougher than anything a judge could say," with the prosecutor adding, "It was excruciating to listen to them talk. To look at the photo [of Ann] there. I still see her. It was as traumatic as anything I've ever listened to in my life."[19] Conor admitted that "hearing the pain in their voices and what my actions had done really opened my eyes to what I've caused."[20]

Conor told the story of what happened, and it offered a larger context for his crime, but it also failed to offer the solace Ann's parents had hoped to find. Rather than learning that it had been a terrible mistake, a finger slipping on a trigger, they heard that he had shot their daughter while she was on her knees, blocking the gun with her hand, saying, "Please don't."[21] It was also difficult for Conor's parents to hear the details of what Conor had done. Sometimes practices of hearing will produce what you didn't expect. The surprise of that will not always be welcome.

The Grosmaires elected to forgive Conor. But they didn't do it for Conor. Ann's mother Kate said,

> Because we could forgive, people can say her name. People can think about my daughter, and they don't have to think, Oh, the murdered girl. I think that when people can't forgive, they're stuck. All they can feel is the emotion surrounding that moment. I can be sad, but I don't have to stay stuck in that moment where this awful thing happened. Because if I do, I may never come out of it. Forgiveness for me was self-preservation.[22]

The Grosmaires desired reconciliation with an offender, yes, because they cared about Conor. But perhaps more than that, what they needed was reconciliation with time—a way to live with a past that should have been otherwise. Restorative justice, in this case, seems to have allowed that to happen, perhaps more than a strictly retributive proceeding would have. Baliga notes, "The Grosmaires got answers to questions that would have been difficult to impossible to get in a trial."[23]

It helped Conor as well—not only because his sentence was twenty years instead of forty but also because, as he remarks, "with the Grosmaires' forgiveness, I could accept responsibility and not be condemned."[24] Instead of being cut loose from the world of human relationships, he took responsibility for his destruction of a part of that world. Only *that* response might fully reckon with the weight of what he did. The liberal "I" can be cut loose from its ties, think incarceration is only a punishment he must bear, and thereby fail to see the world he builds in believing that, but the responsive self never fully escapes its ties to the world in which it is irredeemably implicated. Paul Tullis, the journalist who reported on the case for the *New York Times Magazine*, adds, "Forgiveness doesn't make him any less guilty, and it doesn't absolve him of what he did, but in refusing to become Conor's enemy, the Grosmaires deprived him of a certain kind of refuge—of feeling abandoned and hated—and placed reckoning for the crime squarely in his hands."[25] This is forgiveness but not acquittal. The slate is not wiped clean, but all involved find a way to make the past more livable in the present moment than it otherwise would have been.

Bringing both the victim and the offender into a discussion of what a just punishment would be is one way to achieve reconciliation, Christie argues. In doing so, he suggests a hybrid of retributive and restorative goals that bears a resemblance to what happened in Conor McBride's case (though in his case the primary victim wasn't there—because he had murdered her). Christie proposes that, once a court has established that a law has been broken, perpetrators of harms *will* be punished—the harm won't be smoothed away by a form of mediation that flattens out the very different roles victim and offender have played in wrongdoing[26]—but after that initial determination, the victim's needs will be considered. That might result in orders for further kinds of reparation, anything from fixing what was broken to offering medical or other help. The further measures might be state authored, or they might come from the offender *in addition to* any punishment the state requires. "Punishment, then, becomes that suffering which the judge found necessary to apply *in addition to* those unintended constructive sufferings that offender would go through in his restitutive actions *vis-à-vis* the victim."[27] The offender would thus, perhaps, contribute to rebuilding a world in addition to undergoing punishment for having destroyed some part of it.

Offenders may benefit under the system Christie envisions as well. He adds a wider concern for the offender's well-being, arguing that there may well be needs for social, medical, or educational action that should be met for wrongdoers. All that would be determined after sentencing, so as to keep the need for legal redress in some measure distinct from its wider social ramifications. So Christie preserves law and order while doing more to address both the conditions that produced the initial disturbance of order and the measures to be taken to repair the harm and prevent future harm—and he does it by building in a process where each side might more successfully hear the other. It is a more thorough justice. We might even call it retribution if we think retribution is meant to give to each what is her own.

COMPLEX POLITICAL PERPETRATORS

When Tullis writes that "in refusing to become Conor's enemy, the Grosmaires deprived him of a certain kind of refuge—of feeling abandoned and hated—and placed reckoning for the crime squarely in his hands," he alludes to something we've barely considered so far—that perpetrators might also undergo ethical loneliness.[28] When those who commit grave crimes are locked away and treated as if redemption is impossible, that is a form of abandonment. It is an "earned" abandonment, in that it is the outcome of bad choices, complex as the surrounding context of those choices may be.[29] It is not precisely equal to the kind of loneliness undergone by someone who was abused and abandoned without having committed grave wrongs. I am not saying that victims have to be "innocent" to count as victims, only that the loneliness of perpetrators is a distinct category.

In present-day discussions of international criminal law the category of the "complex political perpetrator" describes well how ethical loneliness might be an apt description of the life of someone who has committed unforgivable violence. For instance, what happens when a person is charged with war crimes of which he is also a victim? Many fall into this category in the era of child soldiers. Dominic Ongwen was abducted as a child, so small that he had to be carried by his abductors. He was abused and lied to, made to terrorize and kill people throughout his life, and then rose in the ranks of the Lord's Resistance Army (LRA) to become one of its more infamous killers, extremely adept at abducting and enslaving children. He is a perpetrator (in the language of legalism he is an alleged perpetrator—the distinction matters). But does that erase the very real way in which he is also a victim? The International Criminal Court (ICC) issued a warrant for Ongwen's arrest in 2005 with seven counts of individual criminal responsibility for crimes ranging from murder and enslavement to attacks on civilian populations. At the same time many other ex–child soldiers were being accepted back into their communities with cleansing rituals.[30] I doubt we'll find anyone arguing that Ongwen has done nothing wrong. But his case, like the difference between Jeffrey Benzien's amnesty, the silence of the political elite, and Eugene de Kock's prison sentence in South Africa, points to a weakness in the hope that individual criminal responsibility will teach us something meaningful about protracted conflicts with complex causes and many contributing stressors.[31] Erin Baines asks, "How should individual responsibility be addressed in the context of collective victimization? What agency is available to individuals who are raised within a setting of extreme brutality?"[32] In posing those questions Baines aims not to release Ongwen from responsibility but to complicate what we think he is responsible for and where a larger responsibility may also lie.[33] After all, who is the "I" responsible for these wrongdoings? Surely Ongwen is that "I" on some level—he is alleged to have committed a great many heinous crimes. But what made possible the conditions where the options available to him basically reduce to a choice between his own death or abuse and playing a role in the death and abuse of others?

We saw in chapter 2 that the ICC will only ever prosecute a small number of those responsible for the crimes in its jurisdiction. So Ongwen, now that he has surrendered and is in ICC custody, will face the court, but many others who committed similar crimes will not. That should matter to us but is still not the main point in this case. Ongwen also stands for a large number of abandoned people—30,000 to 60,000 children and youths abducted by the LRA alone, and the LRA is by no means the only group using abducted child soldiers—who matter to international law as victims but whose fate in international legal institutions becomes unreadable once a victim also becomes a perpetrator.

As Baines points out, by the time Ongwen was five years old, his country had gone through three coups d'état. A fourth sparked a long and bloody war during which the ruling militia raped, pillaged, and destroyed villages with impunity. He likely slept in the bush rather than at home to avoid being abducted. Structural violence would have defined his life long before he became a child soldier.[34] Once he was abducted, he would have been initiated into the LRA with tactics such as hard physical labor, frequent beatings, and being forced to kill other children (in some cases, children were forced to kill their own siblings).[35] LRA commanders regularly told children that their parents were dead, forced into elimination camps by the government—news that would make children less likely to attempt escape and more likely to want revenge on the government. Reports of those who knew Ongwen convey that he was a good soldier, and ruthless, and that he sometimes let children escape if he could but that he advanced through the ranks of the LRA because he was very good at following orders and at killing. Rising up through the ranks was probably the only means he had available to him to achieve a bit more security in terms of personal safety and access to food and comfort, the only way to have any control over his life at all. Safety is a rare commodity in a war zone. As Mariane Ferme points out about child soldiers in Sierra Leone, "remaining behind in the communities they inhabited was the dangerous option, not the safe one, and, paradoxically, joining fighting factions was the only way to remain protected as civilians."[36] Her description echoes Baines's reminder that "for Ongwen and generations like him, the state is absent, unable to extend protection or provide basic goods or services to affected populations."[37] A central authority existed, but for Ongwen's entire life, it did not play its assigned role of protecting citizens. As Baines reminds us, Ongwen "made certain choices to commit crimes against humanity—choices others did not make (by escaping, by refusing to kill, by melting into the background, by choosing death)."[38] But what kind of justice would comprehend the context in which Ongwen made the decisions he made?

Legal prosecution, as we've seen, often fails to recognize a wider context in which wrongdoing emerges, singling out individuals as responsible and then, if they are found guilty, excluding them from society. But reifying a good/evil category in a complex conflict with a long history will not help anyone understand the kind of horror the Ugandan conflict is. And, in any case, if there are at least 30,000 to 60,000 victim/perpetrators in Uganda, how will reconciliation or mere cessation of violence proceed? As Baines points out, if a large group of young men who know "nothing but the way of the gun" are excluded from other, less-violent possibilities, they will likely return to violence. Baines recommends setting up a special commission to deal with complex political perpetrators, a commission that "could identify the overlapping layers of responsibility of national and international actors for failing to protect the Ugandan population from abduction in the first place, in addition to questions about underage recruitment and war crimes committed by all parties" rather than just the LRA.[39] She suggests the commission could, on a case-by-case basis, recommend responses varying from trials to local reparations like community work on memorials or social infrastructure—rebuilding destroyed worlds. Her proposal recalls Christie's call to consider "what could be done to undo the deed" alongside what retributive law requires. Murder can't be undone, just as a violent life of abduction and forced killing can't. But some ways of responding to an unjust past make imagining a different future more possible. Whether a desire for revenge, an attempt to reform, or being haunted by a traumatic past will take ugly or reparative forms will depend on broadly intersubjective social conditions. Institutional response can make a difference here.

There will be no easy end to violence in Uganda, especially given that even when former child soldiers are allowed to rejoin their communities, they do so in conditions of chronic crisis: population displacement, internment in camps, constant vulnerability to attack, and reliance on humanitarian aid due to being severed from access to agricultural land in a country without ability (or, perhaps, will) to offer social services. These are not conditions where resentment can be "subjectively pacified" and become "objectively unnecessary," or where practices of careful hearing might offer normative confirmation, assurance of safety, and the possibility of positive revision. It is not clear what would make those conditions possible, but I doubt convicting Ongwen would do much more than put him in jail. It might, as noted in chapter 2, give some victims satisfaction or solace, and that is not nothing.[40] But punishing him for his crimes will not, on its own, help anyone understand or truly address the situation in which he participated both against his will and willfully. What institution or set of practices would be able to discern properly what someone like Ongwen deserves? Who is responsible here?

RACIALIZED ABANDONMENT

Sometimes perpetrators are also victims. Sometimes context makes a mockery of our ideas about criminal responsibility. And sometimes our assumptions about both hide our own responsibilities from us. Were it to learn to listen for its own failures, the United States might use such a process of reflection to reckon with its own systems of incarceration. Although black Americans make up roughly 13 percent of the population in the United States, they are almost 40 percent of the prison population.[41] African American men in their early thirties are seven times more likely than white men of the same age to have a prison record. Blacks charged at the federal level often receive sentences 10 percent longer than whites charged with the same crimes. Though some of this may have to do with prior record, recent studies have shown that initial choices made by prosecutors about what crimes to charge have a huge impact here, with prosecutors almost twice as likely to file charges carrying mandatory sentencing against black offenders.[42] Most people who justify using imprisonment as a way of dealing with crime argue that it allows the surrounding community to affirm its values and satisfy its retributive impulses, or that it protects the public by taking offenders off the street and deterring others from similar wrongdoing, or that it helps rehabilitate those who do not follow norms, and so both creates better citizens and helps affirm shared values. Those are not bad goals, all things being equal. But nothing is equal here. The prison system, entrenched in a considerable economy as an employer and a consumer of goods, also serves, as Derek Brookes points out, as a "politically expedient substitute for providing adequate social welfare, education, and public health to marginalized groups, such as the homeless, the mentally ill, drug-users, the illiterate, immigrants, racial minorities and the like."[43] John Pittman takes the point farther, arguing that "it is only by addressing the public representations and repressions of racialized reality that we can hope to articulate fully the functions of imprisonment today."[44] Pittman (citing Goldberg) describes a cycle of inequality, where residential segregation leads to educational segregation, which may produce inequalities in employment and income, which contributes more to residential segregation, and so on.[45] "To this must then be added the deployment of crime control policies that overwhelmingly focus on surveillance and control of populations in poor inner-city neighborhoods—which are predominantly black and Latino."[46] It isn't that young black men produce 40 percent of the crime in the United States but that their life circumstances combine with policing practices to produce an outcome for young black men that is much less likely for someone living in a neighborhood not subjected to that kind of surveillance. If that is not social abandonment, I do not know what is. Pittman continues, "From the standpoint of public policy, then, social problems are not addressed at the level of their root social conditions, but are contained in specific socially and racially defined locations based on cost-benefit calculations or the relative political clout and social power of distinct—again racially defined—social strata and populations."[47] This is where social utility fails to distinguish itself from the lowest form of retribution. Lisa Guenther, in an interview about solitary confinement, says of some of the testimony cited earlier in this book, "We cannot understand the experience of [these prisoners] apart from this context in which some acts are criminalized and others are not, some criminal acts are punished with prison time and others are not, some prisoners are isolated within prison and others are not, some groups of people are subject to intense surveillance and others are not, and so forth."[48] This is about multiple practices of isolation. Guenther continues, "Racism is a form of isolation (and exposure). Poverty is a form of isolation (and exposure). These and other forms of oppression render certain people both invisible and hypervisible, systematically removing them from the space of public encounter and engagement."[49] That is a harm left hidden as long as we focus solely on individual criminal responsibility, ignoring the isolation and deprivation that can cause crime and the structures that determine that some neighborhoods get policed more aggressively than others, where police arrest some categories of persons rather than others. Paying attention to deeper causes and wider responsibilities does not absolve those who cause harm of their legal or ethical responsibility for that harm. But it may make us think differently about what they owe and what the larger society complicit in this abandonment owes.

"THERE WAS THIS GOAT."

What is owed and who owes it? Notrose Nobomvu Konile appeared before South Africa's Truth and Reconciliation Commission (TRC) to face

one of the men accused of killing her son. During her testimony Konile—
who refused to forgive—kept insisting on the importance of a dream she
had, where "there was this goat." It didn't seem like a story about loss
and desert but, as we shall see, it was. She testified, "We went and came
back from getting our pensions. I said oh! I had a very—a very scary period, there was this—there was this goat looking up, this one next to me
said oh! having a dream like that with a goat looking up is a very bad
dream."[50] Mrs. Konile, in testifying, often interrupted her own narrative
to address comments to herself, and each interruption sounded to most
ears like a loss of momentum, an inability to stay on the point. As a story
it was hard to follow, and her testimony was mostly dismissed as confused
and incoherent. But Antjie Krog, a writer reporting on the commission
for South African radio, suspected that her testimony might matter precisely because it was different from the stories that conformed more easily to the format the TRC did its best to elicit from all testimony.[51] So Krog
and two colleagues, Nosisi Mpolweni, a Xhosa language expert, and
Kopano Ratele, a professor in the University of South Africa's Institute for
Social and Health Sciences, decided to see what would happen if they took
a closer look at the woman's story in its original language. In Mrs. Konile's
testimony they found ordinary transcription errors, interpretation mistakes, and "cultural codes and references that did not survive the interpretation process."[52] As Krog puts it, "The meta-codes that could have
transmitted her shared reality with many South Africans were greatly
hampered by the different processes her testimony had to live through
in order to become an official version. . . . The dominant discourse at
the Truth Commission had no way of 'hearing' Mrs. Konile" (46). We are
familiar by now with the perils of hearing at hearings.

However, when filtered through a more responsive process, it became
clear that self-interruption and reliance on dream narratives are modes of
oral storytelling in Mrs. Konile's Xhosa heritage. And goats are associated with ancestral rituals in that culture, such that the dream of the goat
would signal, to many Xhosa listeners, that ancestors were preparing Mrs.
Konile for her son's death. The goat would function both as comfort—a
reminder that she was connected to the wider world of her people—and
as a form of narrative foreshadowing (55). In Mrs. Konile's culture,
"dreams are used to endure suffering and to read happiness, to interpret
losses and accomplishments, to bury the dead and to raise children, as well

as to communicate with God and the neighbors" (57). Thus it was normal for Mrs. Konile to bring a dream to the TRC (though, as Krog points out, we may not be helped in understanding it by Freud or Jung).

At one point in her testimony, Mrs. Konile says, "I am suffering, because I have been forced to become an individual" (61). Rather than standing up to demand she be awarded the human dignity that attends a Western idea of autonomy, she argues that without her son she was reduced to an "I" and could no longer make sense of the world. Krog relates this to the African concept (or lived experience) of Ubuntu: "It is precisely because we cannot understand the self-in-community (I am because we are here) and the unity-of-the-world (we are all interconnected, even if we don't always know in what ways exactly) that makes a person like Mrs. Konile sound incoherent. . . . It is very difficult for the western psyche to accept that others *make* a person" (61). But if we recall Jean Améry's caution at the beginning of his writings about his own isolation—"the little word 'I' will have to appear here more often than I like, namely wherever I cannot take for granted that others have shared my personal experience"[53]— we begin to see shared experience across so many differences in culture and context. Améry and Konile do not thereby become the same; differences remain intact. But in both cases "I" is a meaningful autonomy only where it is supported by others. When it is lone because it has no such help, it likely lacks both sovereignty and a full sense of self. Of course, when Mrs. Konile says she suffers from her own individuality, she doesn't mean that she wishes she could shed the weight of existence (as Levinas described), or at least not exactly that. She seems to mean that "for some people this idea of 'me-first' does not quite hold—does not hold them together as persons and does not hold their world intact."[54] Mrs. Konile is not alone in thinking and feeling that way—her whole tradition agrees. That is why

> if Mrs. Konile, or another person, wanted to perform a ritual in which she slaughtered a goat, she could not simply get up one morning and declare, "I have had a dream and I am going to buy a goat and offer it as a sacrifice to my ancestor and invite you people." Instead, she would tell people about the dream. They would help her to decipher it. If she wanted a ritual they would have to agree and find a date suitable for all. Mrs. Konile could not simply slaughter a goat and say, "I have a dead goat; I have my ritual; come and eat." People would stay away and they would ask themselves: who is this person? (61)

In Xhosa culture, being an individual does not on its own offer existential solitude or the freedom of personal sovereignty. And so Mrs. Konile uses "I" as a form of complaint. She wanted to be "us," but the killing of her son reduced her to an "I." That is what she suffers from. She begins her testimony by saying, "It was my son and I, we were standing together— the two of us" (75) and ends her statement (before the questions from the commissioners begin) saying, "Life is very difficult in the township when you don't have anyone" (80). That makes a lot of sense in her Xhosa context. But I would argue that once we admit that we are formed intersubjectively and that, even in the autonomy-celebrating Western tradition, sovereignty can be sovereign only if others help build a world where sovereignty is meaningful and others respect its boundaries, it is not so difficult to understand something of the suffering imposed on a person who is "forced to become an individual." For Mrs. Konile, individuality is dehumanization. That may seem to reverse a Western concept (assuming that dehumanization is the removal of individuality), but only if we ignore the particulars. Rather than reversal, what we have here is cultural difference in description of the experience of intersubjectivity and its loss. Mrs. Konile couldn't just sacrifice a goat without the cooperation of her community because the meaning of that sacrifice can't be made by an individual. Améry couldn't achieve a reconciliation with time on his own without some acknowledgment and reparation from the diverse groups of people who contributed to accomplishing his abandonment.

Krog, raised with the West's idea of the autonomous self, struggles to understand how a self produced in the cultural context of Ubuntu (if Ubuntu means "a self is a self only through others selves" or "I am because you are") could refuse to forgive and also, in losing one person, lose an entire world. Ratele and Mpolweni try to explain to Krog what it means to think of the self as formed by others, and she ends up thinking it means that "there is no border" around the self. Ratele corrects her:

> To ask how the self is formed, about borders, are the wrong questions. You should ask, what is the self in the family? Within the networks, the maps of networks, where is the dot that is you? There is no dot without a connecting line. The self is a combination of things that are connecting. When the lines are removed there is no self. That is the troubling thing. It is as if I want to pull back, I don't want these lines connecting me. Part of me cannot run away from them, they are the me.   (204)

Just as the Western mind may have a hard time understanding what it means that Native American oral history is not simply a recording of events, it may also stumble trying to think of a self without borders. However, this conception of selfhood, though it is African, recalls Levinas's description of a self made up of self, me, ego, and other. I don't get to choose whether or how to be affected by others because others have always already called on me—prior to freedom or my own conscious thoughts about it—to be responsive. We are all "dots" connected to countless others by "lines" we have and have not chosen. Konile's son Zabonke's death was highlighted before the TRC because he died as part of the political struggle, but before she lost her son, she had also lost her husband, brother, and daughter, and since the loss of her son she had lived in dire poverty and bad health with very little social support. The TRC addressed Zabonke's death but remained blind to the larger context in which that death resonated: it could see only one line, but one line does not make sense of a life.

Kopano Ratele adds that even if white people think they just happen to know what their values are (or that they got them without being connected with others), that is due to a lack of self-questioning, to a lack of attention to how a self even comes to question itself. In other words, it is because of the stories white people tell themselves about how they get to be selves that they think of selves in terms of borders instead of connecting lines. But Ratele asks Krog, "How did the self get to these values? Where did you learn that?" (205). As Levinas might remind us, research takes form as a question. Or, as Judith Butler has argued,

> When we lose certain people, or when we are dispossessed from a place, or a community, we may simply feel that we are undergoing something temporary, that mourning will be over and some restoration of prior order will be achieved. But maybe when we undergo what we do, something about who we are is revealed, something that delineates the ties we have to others. . . . It's not as if an "I" exists independently over here and then simply loses a "you" over there, especially if the attachment to "you" is part of what composes who "I" am. If I lose you, under these conditions, then I not only mourn the loss, but I become inscrutable to myself. . . . On one level I think I have lost "you" only to discover that "I" have gone missing as well. At another level, perhaps what I have lost "in" you, that for which I

have no ready vocabulary, is a relationality that is composed neither exclusively of myself nor you, but is to be conceived as the tie by which those terms are differentiated and related.[55]

Butler is describing her own conception of what Ratele tries to explain to Krog about Ubuntu: we are all rooted in multiple, diverse contexts and relationships. We dwell in these in a vital way, and those relations make us who we are, at least in part, no matter what we have to say about personal sovereignty.

When, in the documentary *Long Night's Journey into Day*, Thapo Mbelo asks Mrs. Konile and the other mothers of the Gugulethu Seven for their forgiveness for his role in killing their sons, forgiveness is offered to him by all except Mrs. Konile, who physically turns her back on him and says she will never forget the face of one who betrayed his people.[56] Her anger is understandable but only adds to what makes her testimony difficult to hear in a setting seeking forgiveness. But, as we've seen, anger doesn't have to be divisive or unhealthy. Whether its expression will create ugly or reparative outcomes will depend at least in part on whether those who listen can hear what it is asking for.

It is likely that Mrs. Konile's life is better because of her testimony at a truth commission—even one that could not hear her. That is true for many reasons. The location of burial is very important in her culture: for as long as he had been buried elsewhere, Zabonke would appear in her dreams and tell her he was cold. She tried going to Cape Town to put a blanket over his grave, but it didn't grant his spirit or her dream life any rest. The TRC reparations process granted to her enough money to move Zabonke's body to her hometown of Indwe. She is still poor and largely alone, but she has a place to live and works in a women's co-op that she helped to found, where dresses, skirts, and beadwork are sold. So, though the TRC gave her an imperfect space to speak and modest reparations, those two things do seem, in Konile's case, to have made it possible for her life to be slightly better than it otherwise would have been had she left her trauma unprocessed, never gotten recognition for Zabonke, been left without a place to call her own, and with her son's burial place far away from his home.

So, if Mrs. Konile, who refused to forgive at an official TRC amnesty hearing, finds herself thinking after some time has passed and the material conditions of her life have improved "that it is high time that I teach myself to accept somebody's plea for forgiveness," it may be because her relation to a larger world has been repaired.[57] Repair does not return a world to a prior condition. But it compensates for loss. Mrs. Konile finally lived in a world where she could trust that she would be safe and that others would come to her aid if she needed them. To put it in terms of the description of ethical loneliness, she could take on the present moment freely, or take existence for granted. Perhaps one cannot even *make sense* of forgiveness absent these conditions; its offer would have no shared norms to which to cling. Any request to overcome resentment must offer conditions where forgiveness or some other remedy is reasonable. As such, we can recognize Mrs. Kondile's original refusal of forgiveness not as divisive or selfish but as holding out for repair of what was broken: a demand for just deserts. Even if her losses cannot be redeemed, she deserves some sort of recompense for them, something of her own. Once she got that, even in meager form, she was able to consider forgiving. In other words, she was able to embrace a revisionary process. She could not have gotten there on her own—not because of a character defect, a lack of education, or a failure to commit to nation building but because of how selves and worlds are harmed and built.

After years of cooperative work and a visit to a woman whose words had been dismissed as meaningless, three authors found that, rather than being ignorant and incoherent, Mrs. Konile was "narrating coherently within particular frameworks" and "resisting other frameworks from being imposed on her (frameworks that initially we had suspected she wasn't aware of)."[58] A very complicated set of conditions form the site where Mrs. Konile cannot be understood. Translating languages that do not share perfect fit of grammar and concept (as is the case with all languages), in a highly charged setting where pain and trauma are omnipresent, in an institution itself charged with the conflicting goals of nation building and individual healing, with a definition of both goals as attached to forgiveness— all of this made it almost impossible for hearers to understand that Mrs. Konile knew what had been done to her, why it was wrong, and that it could not be fixed by forgiveness. Even in the context of a community governed by Ubuntu, forgiveness could not restore her community or help her reconcile herself with time absent a wider form of reparation.

The joint investigation Krog undertakes with two colleagues in *There Was This Goat* is simultaneously a continuance of the work of *Country of My Skull* and its antithesis.[59] In *Goat*, rather than using a plurality of stories to give voice to the complexity of reconciliation in postapartheid South Africa (something to which some of those whose voices she used in *Skull* objected[60]), she shows what it takes to listen well to the story of someone who has been subjected to multiple layers of betrayal and isolation. The work of *There Was This Goat* is both a moving testament to the dedication of three scholars to the pursuit of a marginalized truth and a demonstration of a sad truth about numbers: the sheer amount of time and labor that went into their research establishes (whether that was wanted or not) that it would be impossible to pursue such a just and thorough truth in every case.

RESPONSIBILITY BEYOND CULPABILITY

The limits of what can be done are sobering. But we might also learn from the work of Krog, Mpolweni, and Ratele that, though there will never be a perfect set of rules for how to hear well, and it will never be possible to hear everything, what will matter in many settings is whether people who listen will, while listening well to what is said, also listen for moments when it is clear that something is not being heard. It will be important for those who listen to reflect on the limits to what they already know and how that affects what they are able to hear. Krog writes, of Mrs. Konile's initial testimony, "I suspected that her testimony was important, precisely because it was different from the others, and considered the possibility that, perhaps, you needed other tools to make sense of it."[61] In other words, she had learned to listen for her own failures. After explaining that she was reluctant to use existing studies on trauma and testimony, based as they were on experiences from World War II, to understand Mrs. Konile, she clarifies why that caution arose. She asks, "How do I use [those theories] without riding roughshod over her 'strangeness,' or without usurping her 'Otherness,' without interpolating what I, with my background, wanted to hear, without assuming that, if you work on it, whiteness could be well-informed neutrality? I felt I had to be careful."[62]

That caution about the limits of hearing didn't arise for archaeologist Lee Ann Kreutzer when she was called upon to decide whether the Pectol shields should be awarded to the Navajo or to the Ute/Paiute joint claim (discussed in chapter 3). She heard two stories: one that conformed to widespread expectations about the relationship between plot, character, and action, and another that offered legalist reasoning but also refused to claim ownership—because in Ute/Paiute religious traditions sacred objects cannot be owned, but it is also not permitted to tell stories about why that is so. It wasn't until another tribe sent an explanatory letter to her that she understood what she had failed to hear in the Ute/Paiute joint claim. Reflecting back on the case later, she observed, "It seems ironic that we are writing down oral historical and religious narrative and then employing methods derived from Greek logic to objectify, analyze and evaluate it."[63] She caught what wasn't being heard about oral history but missed the potential importance of what cannot be spoken. This case underscores the difficulties involved in hearing and judging: Kreutzer cared about judging well but simply was not able to hear what some of the claims she judged were saying.

The same is true of commissioners at truth commissions who may fail to hear unforgiving testimony because they seek a discourse of forgiveness; or of judges and lawyers who seek the facts of a case on narrow legalist grounds and thereby miss the context where what happened matters to victims; or of someone whose goal it is to collect testimony, who dearly wants to hear stories of human resilience and so fails to hear stories about a destruction that is irredeemable; or of academics or activists who look for a rape story and so hear only that even when it is embedded in a wider story about disrespect and destruction of a world; or who want to reclaim a survivor's ability to convey pain in testimony but ignore the same victim's desire to narrate what was life affirming for him about his ability to resist in addition to feeling pain; or a host of other sites where listening is the aim but hearing fails.

This is a point not only about institutions but also about people. If retribution resonates as an inclination of justice even for repair-minded persons, it is likely because desert is compelling as an impetus for practice or as an orientation to repair. It aims to mark the loss of, and compensate for, something that should have remained intact. In other words, it insists on the creation of conditions where selves who were harmed might take on the present moment freely rather than remaining stuck in a space where their continuing safety is in question; it seeks an end to ethical loneliness. A discourse of desert, when read as a search for repair rather than a bare requirement for payback, engages in creating conditions where imposed social isolation is recognized as a grave harm that requires remedy and redress. It seeks to offer conditions for building selves and worlds, and does so with an understanding that these things cannot be built by individuals who are autonomous and nothing more. It asks us to listen and take responsibility.

There is much to be done in the wake of political violence, social oppression, and so many other far-reaching harms. Alleviating ethical loneliness is not the only thing that must be done. That is why discourses about transitional justice, political reconciliation, forgiveness, amnesty, memorialization of loss, and rebuilding (or building for the first time) social infrastructure and just institutions all matter. But it has been this book's claim that ethical loneliness is also one of the things to which those who wish to redress an unjust past must attend if what is desired is justice, a hopeful future, or even a stable present moment.

Institutions can help here, and they can hinder, but either way they cannot get the job done on their own. If focusing on ethical loneliness changes the subject of discourse around political reconciliation and transitional justice, it is because it also aims to change the *subject*—the person treated or acted upon, our ideas about the kinds of selves we are. We aren't the autonomous monads we hear about when we encounter hopeful or defensive accounts of self-sufficient liberty. Understanding ourselves that way may help advance some important ideas about political freedom, but if we think that "autonomous" is *all* we are, we will likely be unable to understand how the selves and worlds of human beings can be destroyed by other human beings.

There are countless ways—lawful and unlawful—of not taking responsibility for all others or some others: desensitization to others and to violence; elitism, racism, and bigotry; acceptance of structural violence; reasoned limitation on responsibility; contracts and rules of behavior; social norms of inequality; and so on. But the self is not a monad. It is changed by circumstances, and circumstances are peopled by others. That is why "most reconciliations are fragile, partial, and in constant need of renewal."[64] Human beings live each new moment traversing time, facing other human beings—and time and other human beings change things. That is part of what Améry hoped to show by resisting time's passing. But it is this very feature of human beings, that they are vulnerable to others and to the passing of time, each of us a self changed by circumstances and not precisely identical to itself over time, that makes reconciliation possible— because subject formation is reconciliation of self with self and other.

That renders reconciliation both more fragile and more hopeful than it might otherwise be. That our selves and worlds are formed by others and may be destroyed by others puts us at the mercy of our relations, chosen and unchosen. But if we know this well enough to pay attention to the building of those ties, to what binds them and to how the threads begin to fray, then reconciliation, whether it builds community or simply manages a civil cohabitation, may take hold. There can be no onetime settlement of claims such that the future is set free from the past. We've seen the truth of that in Argentina, South Africa, the Balkans, the United States, and Israel-Palestine and will continue to see it wherever the past should have been otherwise. (Everywhere.) Something settled might be unsettled by changes, stressors, the passing of time. People may begin to develop different ideas about rules, norms, trust, and desert. Those ideas might emerge from political or legal institutions, or they might arrive in communication with others, whether by rational discourse or the way human beings give off meanings prior to speech. Kathleen Stewart shows how that remains true over time, not just in a moment of crisis or its aftermath, calling it the "politics of the ordinary":[65]

> The politics of ordinary affect can be anything from the split second when police decide to shoot someone because he's black and standing in a dark doorway and has something in his hand, to a moment when someone falls in love with someone else who's just come into view. Obviously, the differences matter. The politics of any surge depends on where it might go. What happens. How it plays itself out in whose hands.
>
> Ideologies happen. Power snaps into place. Structures grow entrenched. Identities take place. Ways of knowing become habitual at the drop of a hat. But it's ordinary affects that give things the quality of a *some*thing to inhabit and animate.[66]

That is only one reason why we should listen to what anger and resentment say as carefully as we hear calls for forgiveness and reconciliation. It will matter what the public discourses are around continued reconciliation, transition, or peace. And it will matter what widespread attitudes are toward desert: what kinds of outlets are encouraged, what other kinds are not tolerated. All of this will make a difference in what might happen, what is possible. Those are the stakes, and they are made that way by our ties to one another.

All of this will show us, if we look, why we ought to learn to find our home in a sense of responsibility separate from legal culpability. It has been my argument that, for those of us who do desire some kind of justice for all, we build these things not (or not only) out of a Hobbesian will to self-preservation but because we are prey to the affective charge of a responsibility that hits us prior to the liberty to choose otherwise. And so we create conditions (when we do) where individuals can thrive both together and separately at the same time. That is why theories of autonomy matter. But those come later. As Wallace Stevens writes (quoted in the epigraph to this book), "We reason of these things with later reason."[67]

Changing the subject means that we can't just say, "We need to be better at recognizing our responsibility for a wide array of harms." That claim assumes that what matters most is what we will in the freedom of reasoned volition. Of course that matters, and we should be better at recognizing our responsibility for a wide array of harms. But we also need to stop telling ourselves stories of self-formation where our acts and intentions get all the work done. And if we do that, it will likely change some of our acts and intentions, hopefully to tend more toward a fuller justice.

To end where we began: beyond acts and intentions, there are conditions—or moods or modes of attunement—that reveal to those who look or who listen the limits to our unreflective ideas about selves, liberty, and autonomy. We might find them in the everyday experience of weariness or fatigue, in the fragility of human communication, or in how we are formed by responses to others in ways we do not get to choose. The lucky among us might succeed in living a whole life without ever having the false sense of the self's autonomy interrupted. But listening well to the stories told by those who have not been so lucky is one way of shaking that confidence. If we listen, it might reach deep into our unquestioned ideas about personal sovereignty and reveal how dependent that "unshakeable" sense of self is on others who share it as an idea and build a world where such a self is a possible achievement. And that might reveal to those who reflect on it that no liberty is an essence; all liberty is the result of human interaction. And so we might reconsider law as a responsibility rather than a means to an abstract freedom. We will not achieve this if we rely on law, legal or political institutions, ruling parties or leaders of any kind to do all the work for us.

Hamlet asked Horatio to "absent thee from felicity awhile,/And in this harsh world draw thy breath in pain,/To tell my story." A story can't truly be told if there is no space of hearing for it. And so, if ethical loneliness is a condition caused by a kind of abandonment that can be accomplished only by multiple sites of neglect, including failure to hear, what it asks of those called to listen is that they, perhaps, absent themselves from felicity awhile, to hear a story on its own terms, and to try to hear it before assuming they know what needs to be told, how the telling will transpire, what needs to be repaired, how to repair it, and who gets to answer those questions.

Epilogue

It is as if I were constantly accompanied by another self, in unparalleled friendship, but also in a cold strangeness that life attempts to overcome.
—Emmanuel Levinas, "The Other in Proust"

A recent headline on the news satire site *The Onion* reads, "Political Cartoonist Not Sure How to Convey That Sack in Senator's Hand Is Full of Money."[1] Writing (or reading) the conclusion to a book sometimes feels like that, so I'll risk stating something about selves and time that is both obvious and yet sometimes hard to see or feel.[2]

That I am exposed to others means that I cannot so easily "move on" from past loss. My losses haunt me, and they may resurface despite myself even when I have willed to reconcile with those who have harmed me. Trauma haunts reconciliation. But that does not render this a hopeless story. This exposedness also means that time and other human beings might make it easier *or* more difficult for the past to be past. More difficult. *Or* easier. Here the passivity of the subject, rather than resonating only as a loss of autonomy, opens up a future because of how relationships between human beings transpire. I may be able to find myself sovereign and unchanged in relation to objects in the world (there's a chair: I encounter it and nothing about me changes). But the encounter with other human beings is different. My relations with others do change me, for better and for worse, and I can't say that the movement of that change necessarily accords with my desires or the reasoned choices I make.

I can't say that in part because of how time works. A chair is a chair over time, and so with chairs $A=A$. But I cannot be certain that $A=A$ with regard to my self and others in time. Let's say that across a span of moments I encounter another human being, and she affects me—maybe with kindness, maybe with cruelty. We could call the moments before and after this event $Jill_1$ and $Jill_2$. In the interval of time between $Jill_1$ and $Jill_2$, I have been affected by something other than me, and it has made an impact on what I am. Perhaps something has changed, such that I am not certain that I am precisely the same Jill who would have allowed me to say $A=A$ or $Jill=Jill$. Maybe I thought I embraced a restorative ethic of forgiveness. But when I faced your lack of remorse, something changed. Or maybe I once thought I could never live in peace alongside you. But then I came to understand something of your own loss. Or I saw that you genuinely wished you had never harmed me. Or I began to see that the conditions of your life had been such that you were never offered anything resembling kindness or a good option. Or maybe a set of government policies or community organizations lifted me out of a life of daily deprivation. Perhaps now I have begun to think I can live alongside you, whether or not I can forgive. Other human beings open up a dimension of the future that I would not achieve on my own. My point: this reading of the subject gives us a sense of why revision is possible for a human being. The narrative of the autonomous liberal subject, on its own, does not.

This reading also shows why it is possible for human beings working together to forge a path out of ethical loneliness—even when what happened in the past is unforgivable.

Notes

INTRODUCTION

1. I take the term "revisionary practice" from Meir Dan-Cohen, "Revising the Past: On the Metaphysics of Repentance, Forgiveness, and Pardon," in *Forgiveness, Mercy, and Clemency*, ed. Austin Sarat and Nasser Hussain, 117–37 (Stanford: Stanford University Press, 2007). I discuss this essay in chapter 4.

1. ETHICAL LONELINESS

1. As Karl Marx put it, "Men make their own history, but they do not make it just as they please; they do not make it under circumstances chosen by themselves, but under circumstances directly encountered, given and transmitted from the past." See *The Eighteenth Brumaire of Louis Bonaparte* (1852), in *The Marx-Engels Reader*, 2nd ed., ed. Robert C. Tucker (New York: Norton, 1972), 595.

2. Jean Améry, "At the Mind's Limits," in *At the Mind's Limits: Contemplations by a Survivor on Auschwitz and Its Realities* (Bloomington: Indiana University Press, 2009), 2.

3. I should mention that this topic is currently under discussion among historians, with studies appearing showing that in various European countries and the United States, stories were collected in the early years after World War II and people were attentive to them. I do not think the new evidence and analyses show the postwar silence to be a "myth"—because plenty of evidence remains for the silence and for the discomfort with survivor stories—but recent work does add nuance to the idea that no one spoke about these things until the Eichmann trial. See Laura Jockusch, *Collect and Record! Jewish Holocaust Documentation in Early Postwar Europe* (Oxford: Oxford University Press, 2012), and Hasia Diner, *We Remember with Reverence and Love: American Jews and the Myth of Silence after the Holocaust 1945–1962* (New York: New York University Press, 2009). Samuel Moyn summarizes the debate in a recent article in the *Times Literary Supplement*: "Silence and the Shoah," August 7, 2013, http://www.the-tls.co.uk/tls/public/article1297137.ece.

4. Ruth Kluger, *Still Alive: A Holocaust Girlhood Remembered* (New York: Feminist Press at the City University of New York, 2003), 180.

5. Anton Gill, *The Journey Back from Hell: An Oral History—Conversations with Concentration Camp Survivors* (New York: Morrow, 1988), 4, 94, cited in Jamie O'Connell, "Gambling with the Psyche: Does Prosecuting Human Rights Violators Console Their Victims?" *Harvard International Law Journal* 46, no. 2 (2005): 324.

6. Kluger, *Still Alive*, 180.

7. Jean Améry, "Torture," in *At the Mind's Limits*, 24–25.

8. O'Connell, "Gambling with the Psyche," 295, 310.

9. Améry, "Torture," 25–26.

10. This is as true of the sovereignty of nations as it is of persons. Sovereignty, in order to be what it is, requires either cooperation or domination. In either case it is defined by relationality. For an expansion of this claim, see Jill Stauffer, "Equality and Equivocation: Saving Sovereignty from Itself," *Law, Culture and the Humanities* 6, no. 2 (2010): 167–84.

11. Améry, "Torture," 28.

12. Emmanuel Levinas, *Otherwise Than Being: Or Beyond Essence*, trans. Alphonso Lingis (Pittsburgh: Duquesne University Press, 1998), 23.

13. Ibid., 24.

14. Améry, "At the Mind's Limits," 7.

15. Emmanuel Levinas, *Existence and Existents*, trans. Alphonso Lingis (Pittsburgh: Duquesne University Press, 2001), 12; Emmanuel Levinas, *De l'existence à l'existant* (Paris: Librarie Philosophique Vrin, 2004), 31.

16. Jean Améry, "Resentments," in *At the Mind's Limits*, 70.

17. In the preface to *Existence and Existents*, he writes, "These studies begun before the war were continued and written down for the most part in captivity. The stalag is evoked here not as a guarantee of profundity nor as a claim to indulgence, but as an explanation for the absence of any consideration of those philosophical works published, with so much impact, between 1940 and 1945" (xxvii).

18. Emmanuel Levinas, "The Name of a Dog, or Natural Rights," in *Difficult Freedom: Essays on Judaism*, trans. Seán Hand (Baltimore: Johns Hopkins University Press, 1990), 153.

19. Ibid.

20. Levinas, *Otherwise Than Being*.

21. Ibid. Hebrew dedication translated by Salomon Malka in *Emmanuel Levinas: His Life and Legacy*, trans. Michael Kigel and Sonja M. Embree (Pittsburgh: Duquesne University Press, 2006), 80.

22. Margaret Walker, *Moral Repair: Reconstructing Moral Relations after Wrongdoing* (Cambridge: Cambridge University Press, 2006), 84.

23. The argument of this section first appeared in abbreviated form in my article "Speaking Truth to Reconciliation: Political Transition, Recovery, and the Work of Time," *Humanity* 4, no. 1 (2013): 27–48.

24. This is as close as Rousseau gets to a "thesis statement" in *The Social Contract*: "To find a form of association which will defend and protect the person and goods of each associate with the full common force, and by means of which each, by uniting with all, nevertheless obey only himself and remain as free as before." *Rousseau: The Social Contract and Later Political Writings*, ed. Victor Gourevitch (Cambridge: Cambridge University Press, 1997), 49. The only just law is a law one freely obeys, and that is the law one gives to oneself using one's capacity for reason. It is clear here what it was about Rousseau's theory that so impressed Kant, who took it up, removed the passions that are so vital to its expression, and converted it into the categorical imperative.

25. Levinas, *Otherwise Than Being*, chapter 4, "Substitution."

26. Levinas's story about subject formation is notoriously difficult to pin down. He constructed it that way on purpose, to keep it from solidifying into a system. So my somewhat systematic summary of how it works goes against the grain of Levinas's writing, though I do think it works as a form of rough clarification. Levinas uses the terms *soi* (self), *le Moi* (ego) and *moi* (me), and, though in *Otherwise Than Being* one can most often find them in the roles I've assigned them, one will also encounter moments where his use of terms is not as strict as my own delineation. The description I offer here comes from my article "Speaking Truth to Reconciliation" and is in turn

indebted to earlier attempts I made to work out the relationships in Levinas's ideas of subjectivity: "The Rule of Law and Its Shadow: Ambivalence, Procedure, and the Justice Beyond Legality," *Law, Culture and the Humanities* 3 (2007): 225–43; "Productive Ambivalence: Levinasian Subjectivity, Justice, and the Rule of Law," in *Essays on Levinas and Law: A Mosaic*, ed. Desmond Manderson, 76–92 (Hampshire, U.K.: Palgrave Macmillan, 2009); and "The Imperfect: Levinas, Nietzsche, and the Autonomous Subject," in *Nietzsche and Levinas: "After the Death of a Certain God,"* ed. Jill Stauffer and Bettina Bergo, 33–47 (New York: Columbia University Press, 2009).

27. Levinas, *Otherwise Than Being*, 141.
28. Judith Herman, *Trauma and Recovery: The Aftermath of Violence—from Domestic Abuse to Political Terror* (New York: Basic Books, 1992), 51.
29. Levinas, *Existence*, 83; *De l'existence*, 141.
30. Levinas, *Existence*, 85.
31. This section expands an argument originally made in Stauffer, "Speaking Truth to Reconciliation."
32. Testimony of Charity Kondile, Hearing on Human Rights Violations, Truth and Reconciliation Commission (South Africa), Case EC0021/96, East London, April 17, 1996, http://www.justice.gov.za/trc/hrvtrans/hrvel1/kondile.htm.
33. Ibid.
34. Susan Brison, *Aftermath: Violence and the Remaking of a Self* (Princeton: Princeton University Press, 2002), 3.
35. Ronnie Janoff-Bulman, *Shattered Assumptions: Towards a New Psychology of Trauma* (New York: Free Press, 1992), 9. This theme returns in chapter 3.
36. Brison, *Aftermath*, 64.
37. Ibid., 12.
38. Ibid., 16.
39. Améry, "Resentments," 65.
40. Walker, *Moral Repair*, 94–95.
41. David Bloomfield, Teresa Barnes, and Luc Huyse, *Reconciliation after Violent Conflict: A Handbook* (Stockholm: International IDEA, 2003), 168.
42. See Judith Shulevitz, "The Lethality of Loneliness," *New Republic*, May 13, 2013, http://www.newrepublic.com/article/113176/science-loneliness-how-isolation-can-kill-you. See also John Cacciopo and William Patrick, *Loneliness: Human Nature and the Need for Social Cooperation* (New York: Norton, 2008).
43. Shulevitz, "The Lethality of Loneliness."
44. Ibid.

45. Claire Katz points out that since "the twins shared a space, an environment, for nine months, it would seem too overdetermined to separate genes from environment" in such a case, especially since they were sharing that space *while* they were developing.

46. Margaret Walker makes a similar point in *Moral Repair* when she writes, "If the community or authority to whom the victim looks for validation and vindication ignores the victim, challenges the victim's credibility, treats the victim's complaint as of little import . . . the victim will feel abandoned and isolated. That abandonment is a 'second injury' that can be humiliating" (20). On "second injury" she cites Janoff-Bulman in *Shattered Assumptions* (147), who in turn cites Martin Symonds, "The 'Second Injury' to Victims of Violent Acts," *American Journal of Psychoanalysis* 70 (2010): 34–41.

47. Barbara Hernnstein Smith, "Afterthoughts on Narrative," in *On Narrative*, ed. W. J. T. Mitchell (Chicago: University of Chicago Press, 1981), 228. Quoted in Brison, *Aftermath*, 102.

48. Brison, *Aftermath*, 102.

49. Friedrich Nietzsche, *Daybreak: Thoughts on the Prejudices of Morality* (Cambridge: Cambridge University Press, 1997), 171.

50. Ibid.

2. Repair

1. There may, as well, be instances where repair is possible but simply not advisable. As Michel Feher puts it, "In 1945, everyone would agree, the issue was not to reconcile the Nazis with their enemies and victims but to make reconciliation with Germany incumbent on its rejection of Nazism." "Terms of Reconciliation," in *Human Rights in Political Transitions: Gettysburg to Bosnia*, ed. Carla Hesse and Robert Post (New York: Zone Books, 1999), 331. Reconciliation may also be impossible because of cultural attitudes and histories. As a United Nations High Commissioner for Refugees memorandum notes, "In Rwanda . . . the attitude of the government in the years that followed the genocide was to insist on the need for justice. The word 'reconciliation' was taboo for those who had survived the genocide, and was never publicly used. . . . In Kosovo, the very word 'reconciliation' is so charged for the Albanian community, that it is simply not used." Quoted in David Bloomfield, Teresa Barnes, and Luc Huyse, eds., *Reconciliation after Violent Conflict: A Handbook* (Stockholm: International IDEA, 2003), 25.

2. Elizabeth Spelman, *Repair: The Impulse to Restore in a Fragile World* (Boston: Beacon Press, 2002), 9–25.

3. Ibid., 74.

4. Juan E. Méndez, "In Defense of Transitional Justice," in *Transitional Justice and the Rule of Law in New Democracies*, ed. A. James McAdams, 1–26 (Notre Dame: University of Notre Dame Press, 1997). That is by now dogma about what transitional practices should achieve: "narrowing the range of permissible lies," as the IDEA's *Reconciliation after Violent Conflict* puts it (141). Antjie Krog credits South Africa's TRC (rather than court cases) with achieving that: "It is asking too much that everyone should believe the Truth Commission's version of the truth. Or that people should be set free by this truth, should be healed and reconciled. But perhaps these narratives alone are enough to justify the existence of the Truth Commission. Because of these narratives, people no longer can indulge in their separate dynasties of denial." *Country of My Skull: Guilt, Sorrow, and the Limits of Forgiveness in the New South Africa* (New York: Random House, 2007), 113.

5. Méndez, "In Defense," 4.

6. Muhamed Sacirbey, "International Criminal Tribunal Born as Bastard?" *Huffington Post*, May 30, 2013, http://www.huffingtonpost.com/ambassa dor-muhamed-sacirbey/international-criminal-tribunals_b_3344169.html.

7. Debra Kaminer et al., "The Truth and Reconciliation Commission in South Africa: Relation to Psychiatric Status and Forgiveness Among Survivors of Human Rights Abuses," *British Journal of Psychiatry* 178 (2001): 375.

8. See, e.g., Carlos H. Acuña and Catalina Smulovitz, "Guarding the Guardians in Argentina: Some Lessons About the Risks and Benefits of Empowering the Courts," in *Transitional Justice and the Rule of Law in New Democracies*, ed. A. James McAdams, 93–122 (Notre Dame: University of Notre Dame Press, 1997). I discuss some of the complexities of the Argentina case later in the chapter.

9. Quoted in Jamie O'Connell, "Gambling with the Psyche: Does Prosecuting Human Rights Violators Console Their Victims?" *Harvard International Law Journal* 46, no. 2 (2005): 318.

10. Ibid.

11. Mariane C. Ferme, "'Archetypes of Humanitarian Discourse': Child Soldiers, Forced Marriage, and the Framing of Communities in Post-Conflict Sierra Leone," *Humanity* 4, no. 1 (2013): 50, citing Sally Engle Merry, "Transnational Human Rights and Local Activism: Mapping the Middle," *American Anthropologist* 108, no. 1 (2006): 39.

12. In Rwanda, by some accounts, there were only nineteen lawyers left in the country after the genocide, and public works buildings were in ruins. Domestic courts were overtasked, to say the least. The International Criminal Tribunal for Rwanda (ICTR) was situated in Arusha, Tanzania, staffed by foreigners, worked at a glacial pace, and prosecuted relatively few defendants. So a local practice of judging called *gacaca* began hearing cases—with

mixed results given that the form was never meant to judge crimes as weighty as genocide. See, for instance, Alison Des Forges, *Leave None to Tell the Story: Genocide in Rwanda* (New York: Human Rights Watch, 1999).

13. "Lustration" is one term for a practice of mass disqualification of persons associated with abuses from a former regime, used mostly in Germany and Eastern Europe after World War II. In some cases, that might leave a transitioning democracy in a situation similar to that of Rwanda postgenocide: lacking enough qualified persons to act as lawyers and judges.

14. For instance, in Uganda, Acholi victims of the Lord's Resistance Army do not want the rebels to be indicted by a domestic or international court not only because they think that will make the fighting last longer but also because they have their own rituals of reconciliation for incorporating returned soldiers back into the community: "In their view, traditional justice does not imply impunity but holds perpetrators and their clans responsible for their crimes and helps prevent future crimes by restoring relationships between victims and perpetrators." Erin K. Baines, "The Haunting of Alice: Local Approaches to Justice and Reconciliation in Northern Uganda," *International Journal of Transitional Justice* 1, no. 1 (2007): 102. There are problems with using the traditional *mato oput* ceremony to handle crimes it was not designed to judge, but that doesn't mean the approach is of lesser worth than the International Criminal Court's Western legalism. Erin Baines shows just how complex—and resistant to universalizing ideas—this narrative is.

15. See, for instance, Donna E. Arzt, "Views on the Ground: The Local Perception of International Criminal Tribunals in the Former Yugoslavia and Sierra Leone," *Annals of the American Academy of Political and Social Science* 603, no. 1 (2006): 226–39.

16. Arzt, "Views on the Ground." See also Marlise Simons, "Plea Deals Being Used to Clear Balkan War Tribunal's Docket," *New York Times*, November 18, 2003.

17. Simons, "Plea Deals."

18. Lepa Mladjenovic, "The ICTY: The Validation of the Experiences of Survivors," in *International War Crimes Trials: Making a Difference?* ed. Steven R. Ratner and James L. Bischoff, 59–65 (Austin: University of Texas Press, 2004) quoted in Arzt, "Views on the Ground," 235. Arzt quotes Mladjenovic on the conditions of Plavšić's detention. Plavšić was charged with two counts of genocide, five counts of crimes against humanity, and one count of violating the laws or customs of war. She pleaded guilty to one count of crimes against humanity in exchange for having the other charges dropped and so was sentenced to eleven years in prison instead of the twenty to twenty-five she would otherwise have received if found guilty. In 2005 she admitted that her confession had been a lie fabricated in order to escape the

genocide charges. She insists she would have been found innocent if she could have found witnesses willing to testify on her behalf. She was released from prison in October 2009 after having served two-thirds of her sentence. See Daniel Goldenberg, "Plavsic Retracts War-Crimes Confession," *The Local* (Sweden), January 26, 2009, http://www.bosnia.org.uk/news/news_body.cfm?newsid=2544, and "Bosnian-Serb 'Iron Lady' Released," *BBC News*, October 27, 2009, http://news.bbc.co.uk/2/hi/europe/8327714.stm.

19. Arzt, "Views on the Ground," 235.
20. Brammertz is paraphrased from my notes at the conference "Law and the Practice of the International Criminal Court: Achievements, Impact and Challenges," September 26–27, 2012, Peace Palace, The Hague.
21. Teresa Godwin Phelps, *Shattered Voices: Language, Violence, and the Work of Truth Commissions* (Philadelphia: University of Pennsylvania Press, 2011), 63.
22. O'Connell, "Gambling with the Psyche," 305.
23. James A. Goldston, "When Grave Crimes Elude Justice," op-ed, *New York Times*, May 29, 2103, http://www.nytimes.com/2013/05/30/opinion/global/when-grave-crimes-elude-justice.html?_r=1&.
24. Jeremy Sarkin, "Enhancing the Legitimacy, Status, and Role of the International Criminal Court Globally by Using Transitional Justice and Restorative Justice Strategies," *Interdisciplinary Journal of Human Rights Law* 6, no. 1 (2012): 97.
25. Kamari Maxine Clarke, *Fictions of Justice: The International Criminal Court and the Challenge of Legal Pluralism in Sub-Saharan Africa* (Cambridge: Cambridge University Press, 2009), 17.
26. Rapp is paraphrased from my notes at the conference "Law and the Practice of the International Criminal Court."
27. Hollis is quoted from my notes at the conference "Law and the Practice of the International Criminal Court."
28. Dirk Coetzee and Jeffrey Benzien come to mind. Dirk Coetzee applied for amnesty and was awarded it. Eugene de Kock also applied for amnesty for more than one hundred cases of killing. In at least five of those cases it was found that he had killed persons who had no political ties to the African National Congress, so his crimes could not be given the "political motive" necessary for amnesty. See, for instance, "De Kock Denied Amnesty," *South African Press Association*, May 17, 2001, http://www.news24.com/SouthAfrica/Politics/De-Kock-denied-amnesty-20010517. See also Pumla Gobodo-Madikizela, *A Human Being Died That Night: A South African Woman Confronts the Legacy of Apartheid* (Boston: Mariner Books, 2003).
29. Gobodo-Madikizela, *A Human Being Died*, 120.

30. Sarkin, "Enhancing the Legitimacy," 97.

31. Phelps, *Shattered Voices*, 67.

32. For a particularly chilling examination of what can happen when impunity flourishes for decades after mass killing, see Joshua Oppenheim's documentary about former death squad leaders in Indonesia, *The Act of Killing* (Austin: Drafthouse Films, 2012).

33. Gobodo-Madikizela, *A Human Being Died*, 86.

34. Spelman, *Repair*, 53.

35. Ibid., 55.

36. Phelps, *Shattered Voices*, 66.

37. Tristan Anne Borer, "A Taxonomy of Victims and Perpetrators: Human Rights and Reconciliation in South Africa," *Human Rights Quarterly* 25, no. 4 (2003): 1092.

38. Ibid., 1102.

39. Ibid., 1103.

40. Panu Minkkinen, "Ressentiment as Suffering: On Transitional Justice and the Impossibility of Forgiveness," *Cardozo Studies in Law and Literature* 19, no. 3 (2007): 528–29.

41. Borer, "A Taxonomy," 1111, citing Mahmood Mamdani, "Reconciliation Without Justice," *Southern African Review of Books* 46 (1996).

42. Aryeh Neier, "Rethinking Truth, Justice, and Guilt after Bosnia and Rwanda," in Hesse and Post, *Human Rights in Political Transitions*, 41.

43. Priscilla B. Hayner, *Unspeakable Truths: Confronting State Terror and Atrocity* (New York: Routledge, 2001), 44.

44. For a general survey of some of these themes, see Martha Minow, *Between Vengeance and Forgiveness: Facing History after Genocide and Mass Violence* (Boston: Beacon Press, 1998), 118–47.

45. Ferme, "'Archetypes of Humanitarian Discourse,'" 54.

46. An abridged version of the narrative about time in South Africa and Argentina in this section appears in my article "Speaking Truth to Reconciliation: Political Transition, Recovery, and the Work of Time," *Humanity* 4, no. 1 (2013): 27–48.

47. Jeffrey Herbst, "Mbeki's South Africa," *Foreign Affairs* 84, no. 6 (2005): 99.

48. David Backer, "Watching a Bargain Unravel? A Panel Study of Victims' Attitudes about Transitional Justice in Cape Town, South Africa," *International Journal of Transitional Justice* 4, no. 3 (2010): 453–54. His studies are limited to Cape Town, but, in a field where there is very little systematic empirical evidence of the success of truth commissions over time, the results he discusses begin to offer a richer picture of how justice "ages" in postconflict settings.

49. Ibid., 447.

50. The amendment that allowed for this change in prosecutory discretion was struck down by the North Guateng High Court in December 2008, which "prompted signs of movement in the NPA toward contemplating prosecutions but as yet no indictments," writes Backer in 2010 ("Watching a Bargain Unravel"). See also *Nkadimeng and Others v National Director of Public Prosecutions and Others*, case no. 32709/07, High Court of South Africa, December 12, 2008.

51. Yazir Henry, "Reconciling Reconciliation: A Personal and Public Journey of Testifying before the South African TRC," in *Political Transition: Politics and Cultures*, ed. Paul Gready (London: Pluto Press, 2003), 263.

52. Backer, "Watching a Bargain Unravel," 456.

53. Hayner, *Unspeakable Truths*, 133.

54. Phelps, *Shattered Voices*, 74–97. See also Acuña and Smulovitz, "Guarding the Guardians"; Mark J. Osiel, "Making Public Memory, Publicly," in Hesse and Post, *Human Rights in Political Transitions*, 217–62.

55. Hayner, *Unspeakable Truths*, 171.

56. Ibid., 176.

57. Ibid., 171.

58. David Becker et al., "Therapy with Victims of Political Repression in Chile: The Challenge of Social Reparation," *Journal of Social Issues* 46, no. 3 (1990): 138–39, quoted in O'Connell, "Gambling with the Psyche," 314.

59. O'Connell, "Gambling with the Psyche," 314.

60. Eric Stover and Rachel Shigekane, "Exhumation of Mass Graves: Balancing Legal and Humanitarian Needs," in *My Neighbor, My Enemy: Justice and Community in the Aftermath of Mass Atrocity*, ed. Eric Stover and Harvey Weinstein (Cambridge: Cambridge University Press, 2004), 95, quoted in O'Connell, "Gambling with the Psyche," 314.

61. Hayner, *Unspeakable Truths*, 177. See also Ernesto Verdeja, "Political Violence, Justice, and Reconciliation in South America," in *State Violence and Genocide in Latin America: The Cold War Years*, ed. Marcia Esparza, Henry R Huttenbach, and Daniel Feierstein (New York: Routledge, 2010), 172.

62. An abbreviated version of the argument about anecdotal evidence first appeared in my article "Speaking Truth to Reconciliation."

63. Eric Stover, *The Witnesses: War Crimes and the Promise of Justice in The Hague* (Philadelphia: University of Pennsylvania Press, 2005), 18.

64. Oskar N. T. Thoms, James Ron, and Roland Paris, "State-Level Effects of Transitional Justice: What Do We Know?" *International Journal of Transitional Justice* 4 (2010): 354.

65. O'Connell, "Gambling with the Psyche."

66. Fiona Ross, "On Having Voice and Being Heard: Some After-Effects of Testifying Before the South African Truth and Reconciliation Commission," *Anthropological Theory* 3, no. 3 (2003): 332.

67. See, for instance, Arzt, "Views on the Ground"; Karen Brounéus, "The Trauma of Truth Telling: Effects of Witnessing in the Rwandan Gacaca Courts on Psychological Health," *Journal of Conflict Resolution* 54, no. 3 (2010): 408–37; Rebecca Horn, Simon Charters, and Saleem Vahidy, "Testifying in an International War Crimes Tribunal: The Experience of the Special Court for Sierra Leone," *International Journal of Transitional Justice* 3, no. 1 (2009): 135–49; and Kaminer et al., "The Truth and Reconciliation Commission."

68. Eric Stover, "Witnesses and the Promise of Justice in The Hague," in Stover and Weinstein, *My Neighbor, My Enemy*, 107.

69. Ross, "On Having Voice," 327.

70. Ibid., 333.

71. Kaminer et al., "The Truth and Reconciliation Commission," 375.

72. Brounéus, "The Trauma of Truth Telling," 421. See also Ferme, "'Archetypes of Humanitarian Discourse,'" which argues that the courts were set up in such a way that they pressured "community members to participate . . . by formal and informal surveillance mechanisms that reproduce the fear, paranoia, and mutual mistrust at the origins of the genocide" (50).

73. Judith Herman, "Justice from the Victim's Perspective," *Violence Against Women* 11, no. 5 (2005): 574.

74. O'Connell, "Gambling with the Psyche," 301.

75. It is also not clear that trials facilitate peaceful transition or reconciliation. Edwin Bikundo writes that "there is neither empirical proof nor factual analysis relied on or referred to linking peace and criminal trial, only hopes, promises, suppositions, assumptions and . . . ritualized conduct" ("The International Criminal Court and Africa: Exemplary Justice," *Law and Critique* 23, no. 1 [2012]: 26). Mahdev Mohan points out that it is as yet unproven by empirical research that international courts deter future crime, establish official truths, foster the rule of law, promote reconciliation, or achieve restorative justice ("The Paradox of Victim-Centrism: Victim Participation at the Khmer Rouge Tribunal," *International Criminal Law Review* 9 [2009]: 733–75). And if that is true, we should worry that advocates for these processes might undermine the credibility of the trials by overstating their likely consequences. As time passes, data is collected, and more studies appear, we may develop a better sense of what these institutions do accomplish, what they are able to do for victims and for recovering societies, and also what we should not expect such institutions to accomplish.

76. Sarkin, "Enhancing the Legitimacy," 93.
77. William Burke-White, "Regionalization of International Criminal Law Enforcement: A Preliminary Exploration," *Texas International Law Journal* 38, no. 4 (2003): 735.
78. Ibid.
79. David E. Sokol, "Reduced Victim Participation: A Misstep by the Extraordinary Chambers in the Courts of Cambodia," *Washington University Global Studies Law Review* 10, no. 1 (2011): 180.
80. Ibid., 182. Sokol describes how the court circumscribed victim participation: "On August 27, 2009, the Extraordinary Chambers in the Courts of Cambodia ('ECCC') issued a verbal ruling altering the extent to which victims of the Cambodian conflict are allowed to participate in the prosecution of their tormentors and former members of the Khmer Rouge. Prior to this decision, victims of the conflict were, after joining a Civil Party, allowed to question the Accused on all factual topics before the Trial Chamber. However, following the decision, victims are no longer able to question the Accused on his character or on other matters pertinent to sentencing. At the heart of the decision was a desire to balance the goals of the ECCC with the need to increase efficiency and the right of the Accused to have a fair and just trial as required under international law" (167).
81. Tessa V. Capeloto, "Reconciliation in the Wake of Tragedy: Cambodia's Extraordinary Chambers Undermines the Cambodian Constitution," *Pacific Rim Law and Policy Journal* 17, no. 1 (2008): 123.
82. Susana SáCouto, "Victims and Witnesses," *Justice Initiatives: A Publication of the Open Society Justice Initiative* (spring 2006): 60.
83. SáCouto, "Victims," 61, citing Jonathan Doak, "Victims' Rights in Criminal Trials: Prospects for Participation," *Journal of Law and Society* 32, no. 2 (2005): 308–10.
84. SáCouto, "Victims," 69n18.
85. Similar practices emerge whenever someone makes a claim about torture and cites Elaine Scarry, *The Body in Pain* (Oxford: Oxford University Press, 1987), as "proof" of that claim without considering that Scarry did not author the definitive word on what torture does to human beings. She offered one powerful reading of how worlds and language get destroyed.
86. Judith Herman, *Trauma and Recovery: The Aftermath of Violence—from Domestic Abuse to Political Terror* (New York: Basic Books, 1992), 72. Susan Brison adds, "In the courtroom, what takes priority is the need for credibility as a witness, in order for justice to be done. In the therapist's office, by contrast, it's the need to acknowledge the harm to oneself, in order to heal from it and figure out how to carry on" (*Aftermath: Vio-*

lence and the Remaking of a Self [Princeton: Princeton University Press, 2002], 102).

87. Sokol, "Reduced Victim Participation," 181n93.

88. Kenneth Cupier and Viktor Mayer-Schönberger, "The Dictatorship of Data," *MIT Technology Review*, May 31, 2013, http://www.technologyreview.com/news/514591/the-dictatorship-of-data/.

89. Gobodo-Madikizela, *A Human Being Died*, 125.

90. Ibid.

91. At a conference celebrating the tenth anniversary of the ICC, Alan Whiting, from the ICC's Office of the Prosecutor, admitted that managing expectations is difficult even when an institution is transparent about its processes. He added, "Sometimes inflated expectations help us." But I think he probably meant it helps the court get funding—which matters but doesn't address what happens when victims have inflated expectations. Brenda Hollis, a prosecutor for the Special Court for Sierra Leone and the ICTY, added that it is best to manage expectations from the beginning. She pointed out that some participants and onlookers will always have expectations you cannot meet, but if you do good outreach and explain what you can and cannot do—and listen to them and follow up—you will have done all you can. Whiting and Hollis are quoted or paraphrased from my notes at the conference "Law and the Practice of the International Criminal Court."

92. Christine M. Englebrecht, "The Struggle for 'Ownership of Conflict': An Exploration of Victim Participation and Voice in the Criminal Justice System," *Criminal Justice Review* 36, no. 2 (2011): 129–51.

93. Mohan, "The Paradox," 745.

94. Marie-Bénédicte Dembour and Emily Haslam, "Silencing Hearings? Victim-Witnesses at War Crimes Trials," *European Journal of International Law* 15, no. 1 (2004): 159. Stephen J. Rapp observed that it is part of the job of prosecutors to prep witnesses for what they'll be asked and what isn't an issue—not doing that does them a disservice. His comment speaks not only to the need to educate participants in what an institution can do but also to the limited role a witness plays in a court setting. Rapp is paraphrased from my notes at the conference "Law and the Practice of the International Criminal Court."

95. Dembour and Haslam, "Silencing Hearings," 168.

96. Ibid.

97. O'Connell, "Gambling with the Psyche," 301.

98. Sara Kendall and Sarah Nouwen, "Representational Practices at the International Criminal Court: The Gap between Juridified and Abstract Victimhood,"

University of Cambridge Faculty of Law Research Paper no. 24/2013, August 12, 2013.

99. Rome Statute of the International Criminal Court, July 17, 1998. See http://www.un.org/law/icc/.

100. In the field of humanitarian intervention, for instance, the development of the doctrine of the responsibility to protect is one example of an attempt to make prevention more central to international law—but it will, like any invention of international law, take a lot of time, luck, and cooperative effort to make what it hopes to create a reality. One need not build idealistic doctrines to prevent every conflict, however. Whether or not you think NATO was right to intervene in Kosovo without UN approval, the Kosovo Report reveals that prevention of the conflict was possible. Governments and international institutions were aware of the growing crisis in the region from the early 1990s on, and yet the problem was ignored in the 1995 Dayton agreement facilitated between Bosnia-Herzegovina, Croatia, and Serbia. In addition, little support was offered to the nonviolent resistance movement within Kosovo, a movement that had successfully built its own institutions and prevented large-scale violence until 1997. In terms of human and economic capital—loss of life, money spent, resources expended—it would have been far less expensive to intervene ahead of time to prevent violent conflict. It would also have been a more valuable response for those who lost lives, homes, and communities to the violence and then the bombings. The report of the International Commission on Intervention and State Sovereignty claims, "In Kosovo, almost any kind of preventive activity . . . would have had to be cheaper than the $46 billion the international community is estimated to have committed at the time of fighting the war and following up with peacekeeping and reconstruction" ("The Responsibility to Protect: Report of the International Commission on Intervention and State Sovereignty" [Ottawa: International Development Research Centre, December 2001], 71). See also Independent International Commission on Kosovo, *Kosovo Report: Conflict, International Response, Lessons Learned* (Oxford: Oxford University Press, 2000).

101. The argument about consent and legality first appeared in my article "How Much Does That Weigh? Levinas and the Possibility of Human Rights," in "Reflections on Levinas," special issue, *MonoKL* 8–9 (2010): 661–74.

102. The argument about meaningful human rights first appeared in brief form in my article "Speaking Truth to Reconciliation."

3. HEARING

1. Slightly modified translation of *Ibam forte via Sacra* from Horace, "A Morning Stroll," bk. I, st. 9, in *The Complete Works of Horace*, ed. Casper

J. Kraemer Jr., trans. Hubert Wetmore Wells (New York: Book League of America, 1938).

2. I first told an abbreviated version of the story of Hanna F. at a symposium honoring the work of Linda Ross Meyer at Quinnipiac University School of Law (Hamden, Conn.) in 2011. That short version was then published as "A Hearing: Forgiveness, Resentment and Recovery in Law," *Law Review of the Quinnipiac University School of Law* 30, no. 3 (2012): 517–26. This section is based on and expands arguments made in that article. I am indebted to the participants in that symposium for their response to my early attempts at doing justice to Hanna's testimony.

3. Video testimony of Hanna F., Fortunoff Video Archive for Holocaust Testimonies, Yale University, HVT 0018, interviewed by Laurel Vlock and Miriam Posner, February 11, 1980. All quotations are my transcriptions taken while viewing.

4. Ibid.

5. Lawrence Langer, *Holocaust Testimonies: The Ruins of Memory* (New Haven: Yale University Press, 1991), 64.

6. Hanna F. testimony, 1980.

7. Mary Fabri, clinical psychologist at the Marjorie Kovler Center for the Treatment of Survivors of Torture, quoted in Jamie O'Connell, "Gambling with the Psyche: Does Prosecuting Human Rights Violators Console Their Victims?" *Harvard International Law Journal* 46, no. 2 (2005): 333.

8. Langer, *Holocaust Testimonies*, 202.

9. Antjie Krog, who reported on the TRC, recounts that already in the second week of hearings she felt herself losing language and thought of resigning her post. The next morning a counselor addressed the journalists to warn them that they might experience the same symptoms as victims, finding themselves feeling powerless, without help, without words. Krog writes, "I am shocked to be a textbook case within a mere ten days" (*Country of My Skull: Guilt, Sorrow, and the Limits of Forgiveness in the New South Africa* [New York: Random House, 2007], 51). Krog seems to have undergone something like "critical incident stress debriefing" (CISD), a technique of taking charge of traumatic circumstances by offering counseling to "reduce immediate stress, prevent later adverse psychological sequelae including post-traumatic stress disorder," and so on. Arnold A. P. van Emmerik et al., "Single Session Debriefing After Psychological Trauma: A Meta-analysis," *Lancet* 360, no. 9335 (2002) compared the findings of seven studies on such interventions and found that "CISD has no efficacy in reducing symptoms of post-traumatic stress disorder and other trauma-related symptoms, and in fact suggest that it has a detrimental effect" (769). Possible

reasons for this include CISD getting in the way of "natural" processing of the event or inadvertently leading victims to bypass sources of social support (766).

10. Priscilla B. Hayner, *Unspeakable Truths: Confronting State Terror and Atrocity* (New York: Routledge, 2001), 151.

11. Dori Laub, "Bearing Witness, or the Vicissitudes of Listening," in *Testimony: Crises of Witnessing in Film and Literature*, ed. Shoshanna Felman and Dori Laub (New York: Routledge, 1992), 72.

12. Judith Herman, "Crime and Memory," in *The Trauma Controversy: Philosophical and Interdisciplinary Dialogues*, ed. Kristen Brown Golden and Bettina G. Bergo (Albany: State University of New York Press, 2009), 129.

13. Ibid.

14. James Baldwin, *The Fire Next Time* (New York: Vintage International, 1990), 5.

15. Herman, "Crime and Memory," 135.

16. Ronnie Janoff-Bulman, *Shattered Assumptions: Towards a New Psychology of Trauma* (New York: Free Press, 1992), 78.

17. Ruth Kluger, *Still Alive: A Holocaust Girlhood Remembered* (New York: Feminist Press at the City University of New York, 2003), 17.

18. Jean Améry, "Torture," in *At the Mind's Limits: Contemplations by a Survivor on Auschwitz and Its Realities* (Bloomington: Indiana University Press, 2009), 29.

19. Janoff-Bulman, *Shattered Assumptions*, 89–94.

20. Quoted in Margaret Walker, *Moral Repair: Reconstructing Moral Relations after Wrongdoing* (Cambridge: Cambridge University Press, 2006), 92.

21. Susan Brison, *Aftermath: Violence and the Remaking of a Self* (Princeton: Princeton University Press, 2002), 40.

22. Video testimony of Hanna F., Fortunoff Video Archive for Holocaust Testimonies, Yale University, HVT 971, interviewed by Dana Kline and Lawrence Langer, October 16, 1987. All quotations are my transcriptions taken while viewing.

23. Ibid.

24. Jean Améry writes, of his inability to adjust himself to camp slang, "The intellectual suffered from such expressions as 'grub sarge' or 'to organize' (which designated illegal appropriation of some object); yes, even such set phrases as 'to go on transport' he uttered only with difficulty and hesitatingly" ("At the Mind's Limits," in Améry, *At the Mind's Limits*, 5).

25. Doris Lessing says the following about her father's memories of combat in World War I: "His childhood and young man's memories, kept fluid, were added to, grew, as living memories do. But his war memories were con-

gealed in stories that he told again and again, with the same words and gestures, in stereotyped phrases. . . . This dark region in him, fate-ruled, where nothing was true but horror, was expressed inarticulately, in brief, bitter exclamations of rage, incredulity, betrayal" ("My Father," in *A Small Personal Voice* [New York: Random House, 1975], 87). Quoted in Judith Herman, *Trauma and Recovery: The Aftermath of Violence—from Domestic Abuse to Political Terror* (New York: Basic Books, 1992), 38.

26. Fiona Ross, "On Having Voice and Being Heard: Some After-Effects of Testifying Before the South African Truth and Reconciliation Commission," *Anthropological Theory* 3, no. 3 (September 2003): 335.

27. Ross, "On Having Voice," 335; Martha Minow, *Between Vengeance and Forgiveness: Facing History After Genocide and Mass Violence* (Boston: Beacon Press, 1998); Hayner, *Unspeakable Truths*.

28. Indeed, Pumla Gobodo-Madikizela had not even seen the rape story coming and, once Khutwane described what had happened to her, was drawn in to her own memories of having narrowly escaped sexual violence when she was younger. She writes, of listening to Khutwane's testimony, "I pictured her in the back of the army truck, her body being violated by a white soldier in camouflage uniform, and I feel every detail of her trauma as if it is something that has happened to me: the intrusive hand of the young soldier, the shame of helplessness, and the humiliation all seem like a painful stab deep inside" (*A Human Being Died That Night: A South African Woman Confronts the Legacy of Apartheid* [Boston: Mariner Books, 2003]), 91).

29. Fiona Ross, *Bearing Witness: Women and the Truth and Reconciliation Commission in South Africa* (London: Pluto Press, 2003), 89.

30. Testimony of Yvonne Khutwane, Violation: Torture/Detention, Truth and Reconciliation Commission (South Africa), Case No. CT00530, June 24, 1996, http://www.justice.gov.za/trc/hrvtrans/worcest/ct00530.htm.

31. Susan Brison, a survivor of rape from the United States, makes a similar point about what may happen when a crime is described as rape rather than as something broader: "Although I experienced the murder attempt as a sexual violation, I was initially reluctant to tell people (other than medical and legal personnel) that I had been raped. Using the word 'rape' would have conventionalized what had happened to me, denying the particularity of what I had experienced and invoking in others whatever rape scenario they had already constructed" (Brison, *Aftermath*, 90).

32. Ross, "On Having Voice," 327

33. Ibid.

34. Ibid., 329.

35. Antjie Krog, Nosisi Mpolweni, and Kopano Ratele, *There Was This Goat: Investigating the Truth Commission Testimony of Notrose Nobomvu Konile* (Durban: University of KwaZulu-Natal Press, 2009), 85.

36. Quoted in Thomas Brudholm, *Resentment's Virtue: Jean Améry and the Refusal to Forgive* (Philadelphia: Temple University Press, 2008), 31.

37. Recent works pointing out the limits to discourses of forgiveness in politics, focusing specifically on South Africa's TRC, include Brudholm, *Resentment's Virtue*, and Sonali Chakravarti, *Sing the Rage: Listening to Anger after Mass Violence* (Chicago: University of Chicago Press, 2014).

38. Jan Blommaert, Mary Bock, and Kay McCormick, "Narrative Inequality in the TRC Hearings: On the Hearability of Hidden Transcripts," in *Discourse and Human Rights Violations*, ed. Christine Anthonissen and Jan Blommaert (Amsterdam: Benjamins, 2007), 45.

39. Testimony of Colin de Souza, Nature of Violence: Detention and Assault by Police, Truth and Reconciliation Commission (South Africa), UWC Hearing, Case No. CT/00519, August 5, 1996, http://www.justice.gov.za/trc/hrvtrans/helder/ct00519.htm.

40. Blommaert, Bock, and McCormick, "Narrative Inequality," 54.

41. De Souza testimony.

42. The physical and psychological wounds of trauma sometimes cause lifelong debilitating pain or inability to cope with social settings, such that holding down a regular job is difficult. "Some survivors' psychic pain is so intense that they cannot work or perform ordinary daily tasks" (O'Connell, "Gambling with the Psyche," 306).

43. Blommaert, Bock, and McCormick, "Narrative Inequality," 54.

44. Testimony of Sulejman Crncalo, International Criminal Tribunal for the former Yugoslavia, case against Ratko Mladić (IT-09-92-T), September 28, 2012, http://www.icty.org/x/cases/mladic/trans/en/120928ED.htm.

45. Blommaert, Bock, and McCormick, "Narrative Inequality," 55.

46. Ibid., 54.

47. Ross, "On Having Voice," 334.

48. Blommaert, Bock, and McCormick, "Narrative Inequality," 55.

49. Stuart Grassian, "Psychopathological Effects of Solitary Confinement," *American Journal of Psychiatry* 140, no. 11 (1983): 1453.

50. Ibid., 1452.

51. Ibid.

52. "We Have Invented a New Form of Death": An Interview with Colin Dayan, *Believer* 11, no. 2 (February 2013): 51.

53. "What Is the Experience of Isolation?": An Interview with Lisa Guenther, *Believer* 11, no. 5 (June 2013): 67.

54. Incarceration in general in the United States is part of a larger continuum of ethical loneliness beyond solitary confinement. At a recent graduation ceremony of an Inside-Out course held at SCI-Chester (a state prison in Pennsylvania), inmate-students' reflections on what was meaningful about the course betray a larger social abandonment undergone long before any of them committed crime or were imprisoned. Various of the prisoner-students said things to their teachers and fellow nonprisoner students like, "Before we actually did this, I didn't believe that college students could come in here and work with us as equals, without pre-judging us"; "This is the first time in my life that a teacher paid attention to me": or, simply, "Thank you for coming in here and treating us like human beings." Observed May 1, 2013. I was invited to attend the final class and graduation ceremony of the Haverford College Inside-Out course in order to comment on the students' final presentations.

55. An early, abbreviated version of this section appeared under the title "Hearing" in my article "Speaking Truth to Reconciliation: Political Transition, Recovery, and the Work of Time," *Humanity* 4, no. 1 (2013): 27–48.

56. Levinas's formulation of this point occurs in *Otherwise Than Being: Or Beyond Essence*, trans. Alphonso Lingis (Pittsburgh: Duquesne University Press, 1998): "A thermal, gustative or olfactory sensation is not primarily a cognition of a pain, a savor, or an odor. No doubt it can take on this signification of being a discovery by losing its own sense, becoming an experience of . . . , a consciousness of . . . , 'placing itself' before the being exposed in its theme, in discourse, in which every commencement begins" (65).

57. Levinas, *Otherwise Than Being*, 167. In French: "Exiger qu'une communication ait la certitude d'être entendue, c'est confondre *communication* et *savoir*, effacer la différence, *méconnaître la signifiance de l'un-pour-l'lautre en moi*" (*Autrement qu'être ou au-delà de l'essence* [Paris: Livre de Poche, 2004], 259); emphasis in original.

58. Kathleen Stewart, *Ordinary Affects* (Durham: Duke University Press, 2007), 9.

59. Levinas, *Otherwise Than Being*, 119.

60. Stewart, *Ordinary Affects*, 44.

61. Eve Sedgwick, "Paranoid Reading and Reparative Reading, or, You're So Paranoid, You Probably Think This Essay Is About You," in *Touching Feeling: Affect, Pedagogy, Performativity* (Durham: Duke University Press, 2009), 141.

62. I also discuss Yazir Henry's case in my article "Speaking Truth to Reconciliation."

63. Testimony of Yazir Henry, Nature of Violence: Torture and Detention by Security Police, Truth and Reconciliation Commission (South Africa), UWC Hearing, Case No. CT00405, August 6, 1996, http://www.justice .gov.za/trc/hrvtrans/helder/ct00405.htm.

64. Ibid.

65. Ibid.

66. Ibid.

67. For a good analysis of the limits of the TRC's categories, see Tristan Anne Borer, "A Taxonomy of Victims and Perpetrators: Human Rights and Reconciliation in South Africa," *Human Rights Quarterly* 25, no. 4 (2003): 1088–116.

68. Henry testimony.

69. Yazir Henry, "Reconciling Reconciliation: A Personal and Public Journey of Testifying before the South African TRC," in *Political Transition: Politics and Cultures*, ed. Paul Gready (London: Pluto Press, 2003), 267.

70. Krog, *Country of My Skull*, 70–73, 96.

71. Henry, "Reconciling Reconciliation."

72. Yazir Henry, "Where Healing Begins," in *Looking Back Reaching Forward: Reflections on the Truth and Reconciliation Commission of South Africa*, ed. Charles Villa-Vicencio and Wilhelm Verwoerd (Cape Town: University of Cape Town Press, 2000), 169.

73. On one reading that is the point Hannah Arendt makes in *The Human Condition* (Chicago: University of Chicago Press, 2013) when she discusses "the web of relationships"—none of us is in full control of how our own life's story gets told or heard. But Arendt's observation is attached to a nuanced understanding of what it means to be a person who appears in public at all, and so to say what her observation would mean when applied to testimony in situations of unequal power requires some care—but may shed further light on why creating conditions for successful hearing matters.

74. Ross argues this in "On Having Voice."

75. NAGPRA does not have the power to compel private owners of remains and funerary objects to return them to tribes that claim them—unless the objects are in private museums that have received federal funding. But some norms of voluntary repatriation may be developing because of NAGPRA's putting a spotlight on the problem. See Elazar Barkan, *The Guilt of Nations: Restitution and Negotiating Historical Injustices* (Baltimore: Johns Hopkins University Press, 2000).

76. Debora Threedy, "Claiming the Shields: Law, Anthropology, and the Role of Storytelling in a NAGPRA Repatriation Case Study," *Journal of Land, Resources, and Environmental Law* 29, no. 1 (2009): 96.

77. 25 U.S.C. Section 3002(a)(2)(B), cited in Threedy, "Claiming the Shields," 96.

78. Threedy, "Claiming the Shields," 96, and 25 U.S.C. Sec. 3002(a)(2)(C).

79. Threedy, "Claiming the Shields," 97. Though, for a more nuanced take on whether Western legality can make meaningful room for oral history, see Bradley Bryan, "Legality Against Orality," *Law, Culture and the Humanities* 9, no. 2 (2013): 261–74.

80. Threedy, "Claiming the Shields," 97. See also 25 U.S.C. Section 3005(a)(4) and 43 C.F.R. Section 10.14(e).

81. Barkan, *The Guilt of Nations*, 180.

82. Threedy, "Claiming the Shields," 101. See also Polly Schaafsma, "The Pectol Shields: A Cultural Evaluation; Study Conducted for the Capitol Reef National Park as Part of an Investigation for Repatriation of the Pectol Shields," June 7, 2002. The shields were housed at Capitol Reef National Park before being repatriated. This document summarizes other claims (various of which assert that the shields are Athabaskan, or Navajo, or Ute, or Pueblo, or that they are not) and argues that the shields are Ute in origin, mostly because of where they were found and similarities in design between the shields and known Ute rock art. Schaafsma is a research associate at the Anthropology Museum of New Mexico. The document is available at http://www.azwater.gov/Adjudications/documents/HopiContested CaseDisclosures/Navajo%20Supplemental%20Disclosure/CDV007%5CB NDR002%5C005%5CNN029222.pdf.

83. There was also a claim filed by the Southern Ute and Ute Mountain tribes.

84. See Bryan, "Legality Against Orality," for a gloss on the history of oral history as hearsay and to challenges to that rule in the Canadian context.

85. Threedy, "Claiming the Shields," 110. There are other versions of the story, told by the same man, both because that is how oral history functions and because John Holiday spoke in Navajo through an interpreter to English-speaking interviewers. The story here is the one used by the archaeologist (Kreutzer) who made the decision on the case. Another version of the story appears in John Holiday and Robert McPherson, *A Navajo Legacy: The Life and Teachings of John Holiday* (Norman: University of Oklahoma Press, 2005), as follows: "These shields were huge and had strings attached to them on the inside. The earth shield has the mountains and vegetation depicted on it. The mountain shield has lightning, sunrays and rainbows, while the sky shield has all the heavenly bodies and stars on it. These shields were big, and nothing could penetrate them—neither bullets nor arrows, nor evil and witchcraft. They are shields against all things that can harm a person" (352–53), quoted in Threedy, "Claiming the Shields," 110. Threedy states that she does not know whether this description was recorded before

or after Holiday viewed the shields. Marklyn Chee, a cultural specialist with the Navajo Nation Historic Preservation Department, remarks that a chanter of the tribe "described the shields in great detail, having never seen them." Joe Bauman, "Utah Scientific: Navajo Custody of Shield Fueling Discontent," *Deseret News*, October 10, 2005, http://www.deseretnews.com/article/620152574/Navajo-custody-of-shields-fueling-discontent.html?pg=all.

86. Threedy, "Claiming the Shields," 115. Schaafsma ("The Pectol Shields") also thinks the shields are likely Ute.

87. Ibid., 112.

88. An article by Joe Bauman in the *Deseret News* credits Al Hendricks, superintendent of Capitol Reef National Park, with making the decision, though it does describe Kreutzer's role in determining ownership. See Joe Bauman, "Ute Tribe's Action Preventing Turnover of Shields," *Deseret News*, September 2, 2002, http://www.deseretnews.com/article/934727/Ute-tribes-action-preventing-turnover-of-shields.html?pg=all. Robert S. McPherson and John Fahey, "Seeing Is Believing: The Odyssey of the Pectol Shields," *Utah Historical Quarterly* 76, no. 4 (fall 2008): 357–76, reports that Lawrence Loendorf, Barton A. Wright, Benson L. Lanford, and Polly Schaafsma all prepared independent studies of the shields. They did not come to a consensus on their origins (370).

89. Threedy, "Claiming the Shields," 117.

90. Marianne Constable, *Just Silences: The Limits and Possibilities of Modern Law* (Princeton: Princeton University Press, 2005), 85.

91. Quoted in Threedy, "Claiming the Shields," 118.

92. Constable, *Just Silences*, 80, citing Max Picard, *The World of Silence*, trans. Stanley Godman (South Bend, Ind.: Regnery/Gateway, 1952). An interesting wrinkle in the problem of silence and unspeakability is added by the past of the Pectol shields. Their original finder, Ephraim Pectol, believed that they, along with an animal-skin coat, cap, and apron, were artifacts proving certain aspects of Mormon theology. He was circumspect in his descriptions of why this is so because some Mormon religious practices are also secret. See McPherson and Fahey, "Seeing Is Believing," 360–61.

93. Constable, *Just Silences*, 88.

94. Australian law faces similar difficulty in dealing fairly with some legal claims made by Aboriginal Australians. The Aboriginal and Torres Strait Islander Heritage Protection Act of 1984 acknowledges that some Aboriginal cultural beliefs may not be transmitted to outsiders. In 1994 a group of Ngarrindjeri women invoked the act to prevent construction of a bridge from the mainland to an island called Hindmarsh, which, they claimed, is the site of sacred practices for women. The women asserted that no more than

that could be said to those who were not also women authorized for those practices. A government minister, having commissioned Professor Cheryl Saunders to review confidential materials, "issued a protective order prohibiting construction of the bridge for twenty-five years"—a compromise between absolute privileging of white Australian law and absolute privileging of Aboriginal practice. See Threedy, "Claiming the Shields," 116. However, a federal court quashed the order on appeal by developers, arguing that if the "claimants wanted the protection of the Heritage Act, they had to abide by the requirements of the Act" (116–17). As Threedy points out, "The idea that to obtain the protection promised by the government for sacred sites the claimants had to violate the sacredness of the site can be criticized as presenting a Hobson's choice: maintain the secrecy of the sacred knowledge associated with the site and lose protection of the site itself, or protect the site by disclosing the secret knowledge that makes the site sacred, thereby profaning the sacred. At best, what this conundrum reveals is incommensurability between Western law and indigenous law. The legal system is unable to accept indigenous truth claims on their own terms, without restructuring them according to narrative conventions" (117). Rosanne Kennedy, "Subversive Witnessing: Mediating Indigenous Testimony in Australian Cultural and Legal Institutions," *Women's Studies Quarterly* 36, no. 1/2 (2008): 60, points out that, in Australia, "although Indigenous testimony has been accorded visibility and legitimacy in the cultural sphere, it has not fared well in courts," where cases tried on narrow technical grounds often manage to skirt the deeper issues and render indigenous stories untellable.

95. Threedy, "Claiming the Shields," 117.
96. Ibid., 118.
97. Ibid., 99. See also Bauman, "Utah Scientific."
98. McPherson and Fahey, "Seeing Is Believing," 374.
99. Another possibility: NAGPRA Section 3005(e) allows that, in cases of objects not associated with particular remains and found prior to 1990, when "the federal agency or museum cannot clearly determine which is . . . the most appropriate claimant, the agency or museum may retain such an item until the requesting parties agree . . . or the dispute is otherwise resolved pursuant to the provision of this chapter or by a court of competent jurisdiction." In other words, the park could have passed the buck and refused to make a decision. Threedy points out that this would mean the park would retain stewardship (including the expense of preserving the shields).
100. Lee Ann Kreutzer, "Seeing Is Believing and Hearing Is Believing: Thoughts on Oral Tradition and the Pectol Shields," *Utah Historical Quarterly* 76, no. 4 (fall 2008): 384.

101. McPherson and Fahey, "Seeing Is Believing," 374, citing Andrew Curry, "Tribal Challenges: How the Navajo Nation Is Changing the Face of American Archaeology," *Archaeology* 58 (September/October 2005): 66.

102. Bryan, "Legality Against Orality," 270.

103. Ibid., 272.

104. Ibid., 266.

105. Ibid., 272.

106. Primo Levi, *If Not Now, When?* (New York: Penguin Books, 1995), 9, quoted in Brison, *Aftermath*, 50.

107. Brison, *Aftermath*, 50.

108. Ibid., 51.

109. Henry, "Reconciling Reconciliation"; Henry, "Where Healing Begins."

110. Paul Fussell, *The Great War and Modern Memory* (Oxford: Oxford University Press, 1975), 169–70, quoted in Brison, *Aftermath*, 50–51.

111. Brison, *Aftermath*, 57.

112. Video testimony of Stanley M., Fortunoff Video Archive for Holocaust Testimonies, Yale University, HVT 49, interviewed by Dori Laub, Laurel Vlock, and Nanette Auerhahn, March 10, 1980. All quotations are my transcriptions taken while viewing.

113. Richard von Weizsäcker, president of the Federal Republic of Germany from 1984 to 1994, said the following in a 1985 interview: "When one looks into history 40 or 50 years later it is better as a young person to judge someone for having behaved wrongly if one has also experienced such a situation. The tendency to believe that people then were evil but today they are good is very widespread. And this tendency, naturally, is not good." Quoted in James M. Markham, "Facing Up to Germany's Past," *New York Times Magazine,* June 23, 1985, quoted in Donald J. Shriver, *An Ethic for Enemies: Forgiveness in Politics* (Oxford: Oxford University Press, 1995), 84.

114. Brison, *Aftermath*, 55.

115. Marianne Hirsh, "The Generation of Postmemory," *Poetics Today* 29, no. 1 (2008): 106.

116. Brison, *Aftermath*, 87.

117. Dean Kilpatrick et al., *Rape in America: A Report to the Nation* (Charleston: Medical University of South Carolina, 1992), cited in Sandra Bloom, "An Elephant in the Room: The Impact of Traumatic Stress on Individuals and Groups," in Golden and Bergo, *The Trauma Controversy*, 143–69.

118. Jay G. Silverman et al., "Dating Violence against Adolescent Girls and Associated Substance Use, Unhealthy Weight Control, Sexual Risk Behavior, Pregnancy and Suicidality," *Journal of the American Medical Association* 286, no. 5 (2001): 572–79, cited in Bloom, "An Elephant in the Room."

119. Stewart, *Ordinary Affects*, 1.

120. On "second harm," see Walker, *Moral Repair*, 20, citing Janoff-Bulman, *Shattered Assumptions*, 147, citing Martin Symonds, "The 'Second Injury' to Victims of Violent Acts," *American Journal of Psychoanalysis* 70 (2010): 34–41.

121. Brison, *Aftermath*, 104.

4. REVISION

1. Jean Améry, "Resentments," in *At the Mind's Limits: Contemplations by a Survivor on Auschwitz and Its Realities* (Bloomington: Indiana University Press, 2009), 62–81.

2. The term "revisionary practice" comes from Meir Dan-Cohen, "Revising the Past: On the Metaphysics of Repentance, Forgiveness, and Pardon," in *Forgiveness, Mercy, and Clemency*, ed. Austin Sarat and Nasser Hussain (Stanford: Stanford University Press, 2007).

3. Jean Améry, "Preface to the First Edition, 1966," in *At the Mind's Limits*, xiii.

4. Jeffrie Murphy, "Forgiveness and Resentment," in *Forgiveness and Mercy*, ed. Jeffrie G. Murphy and Jean Hampton (Cambridge: Cambridge University Press, 1988), 16.

5. Friedrich Nietzsche, "On the Genealogy of Morals," in *On the Genealogy of Morals and Ecce Homo,* trans. Walter Kaufmann (New York: Vintage Books, 1989), 1:10.

6. Adam Smith, *The Theory of Moral Sentiments*, ed. Alexander L. Macfie and David D. Raphael (Indianapolis: Liberty Press, 1976), II.iii.I.5, quoted in Charles L. Griswold, *Forgiveness: A Philosophical Exploration* (Cambridge: Cambridge University Press, 2007), 28.

7. Margaret Walker, *Moral Repair: Reconstructing Moral Relations after Wrongdoing* (Cambridge: Cambridge University Press, 2006), 133, and "The Cycle of Violence," in "Human Rights and Negative Emotions," special issue, *Journal of Human Rights* 5, no. 1 (2006): 92.

8. Griswold, *Forgiveness*, 29.

9. Ibid.

10. Walker, *Moral Repair*, 136.

11. Pamela Hieronymi, "Articulating an Uncompromising Forgiveness," *Philosophy and Phenomenological Research* 62, no. 3 (2001): 546.

12. Walker, *Moral Repair*, 122. It is interesting to compare this point with Max Scheler's argument about ressentiment, that the "'common man" is what we might call uppity because he "can only recognize relative values, i.e., values that exist only in relation to other values. Unlike the noble and powerful, the man of *ressentiment* validates himself and his predicament as measurable comparisons in relation to others. . . . This is the basic attribute of what Scheler describes as a careerist upstart or an *arriviste*." (That is Scheler's

position as described in Panu Minkkinen, "Ressentiment as Suffering: On Transitional Justice and the Impossibility of Forgiveness," *Cardozo Studies in Law and Literature* 19, no. 3 [2007]: 522.) On Walker's reading, Scheler's labeling the man of ressentiment as an upstart might itself be a form of resentment.

13. Améry, "Resentments," 68.

14. Ibid.

15. Friedrich Nietzsche, *Thus Spoke Zarathustra*, trans. Walter Kaufmann (New York: Penguin, 1978), 138.

16. Heather Love, *Feeling Backward: Loss and the Politics of Queer History* (Cambridge, Mass.: Harvard University Press, 2007), 1.

17. Ibid.

18. Ibid.

19. Dan-Cohen, "Revising the Past," 117.

20. In a recent interview, Linda Ross Meyer uses the example of garden destruction to make a point about the limits to retributive thinking that runs parallel to Dan-Cohen's argument about revisionary practice: "'Just deserts,' indeed, seem foreign in the context of friendships—you might expect an apology from a friend who runs over your garden, and you might expect her to fix the garden and take you out to dinner. But it is not appropriate to impose on your friend some painful experience that will be equivalent to the pain you suffered. If you did decide to, say, kill your friend's favorite plant in order to even the scales, you would have violated the friendship. Indeed, even if you asked a neutral third party to run over an equivalent part of the friend's garden, it would not do. Instead, the right way to respond to offenses in friendships is to get to work on restoring the garden and the relationship, with a forward-looking spirit of forgiveness that allows for that possibility" ("Nobody 'Deserves' Any of This": An Interview with Linda Ross Meyer, *Believer* 11, no. 7 [September 2013]: 67).

21. Dan-Cohen, "Revising the Past," 127.

22. Améry, "Resentments," 68. The portions of the argument of this section that deal with South Africa first appeared in abbreviated form in my article "A Hearing: Forgiveness, Resentment and Recovery in Law," *Law Review of the Quinnipiac University School of Law* 30, no. 3 (2012): 517–26; Mrs. Kondile's story appears in a longer version in my article "Speaking Truth to Reconciliation: Political Transition, Recovery, and the Work of Time," *Humanity* 4, no. 1 (2013): 27–48.

23. The statement of a senior government spokesman in Zimbabwe voices this problematic idea: "If you don't talk about it, it may die a natural death, so that we can build the society we're trying to build." Quoted in Priscilla B.

Hayner, *Unspeakable Truths: Confronting State Terror and Atrocity* (New York: Routledge, 2001), 55. The Zimbabwean official said this in order to explain why the report of Zimbabwe's truth commission was never released. In answer to that, two Zimbabwean human rights organizations released their own reports.

24. Améry, "Resentments," 72.
25. Kalu was interviewed by Wilhelm Verwoerd for an article in South Africa's *Sunday Independent*, published December 6, 1998. Her words are quoted in Thomas Brudholm, *Resentment's Virtue: Jean Améry and the Refusal to Forgive* (Philadelphia: Temple University Press, 2008), 37.
26. Ibid. 38
27. Améry, "Resentments," 72.
28. Antjie Krog, *Country of My Skull: Guilt, Sorrow, and the Limits of Forgiveness in the New South Africa* (New York: Random House, 2007), 80.
29. Ibid., 143.
30. Améry, "Resentments," 77.
31. Ibid., 78.
32. While the title Améry chose for the collection of essays would translate into *Beyond Guilt and Atonement*, it is published in English under the title *At the Mind's Limits*.
33. In "Resentments," Améry writes, "There seems to be general agreement that the final say on resentments is that of Friedrich Nietzsche, in whose *Genealogy of Morals* we read: '. . . resentment defines such creatures who are denied genuine reaction, that of the deed, and who compensate for it through an imaginary revenge. . . . The resentful person is neither sincere, nor naïve, nor honest and forthright with himself. His soul squints; his mind loves hiding places and back doors; everything concealed gives him the feeling that it is his world, his security, his balm. . . .' Thus spake the man who dreamed of the synthesis of the brute with the superman. He must be answered by those who witnessed the union of the brute with the subhuman; they were present as victims when a certain humankind joyously celebrated a festival of cruelty, as Nietzsche himself expressed it—in anticipation of a few modern anthropological theories" (67).
34. Nietzsche, "Genealogy," 3:15.
35. Jean Améry, "Torture," in *At the Mind's Limits*, 34.
36. Améry, "Resentments," 70.
37. Nietzsche, "Genealogy," 1:14.
38. Améry writes that "I, too, had to determine the quantity of good comrades on the one hand and of the scoundrels and indifferent ones on the other when, in the midst of the German people, I had to reckon every moment

with falling victim to ritual mass murder. Whether I wanted to or not, I had to accept the notion of statistical collective guilt" ("Resentments," 75). He writes elsewhere that he had to be as afraid of any civilian he encountered as he did of the uniformed SS-man (65). Those were the conditions.

39. Nietzsche, "Genealogy," 2:1.
40. Ibid.
41. Video testimony of Count Stanley M., Fortunoff Video Archive for Holocaust Testimonies, Yale University, HVT 49, interviewed by Dori Laub, Laurel Vlock, and Nanette Auerhahn, March 10, 1980. All quotations are my transcriptions taken while viewing.
42. Ibid.
43. Améry, "Resentments," 80.
44. Susan Brison, *Aftermath: Violence and the Remaking of a Self* (Princeton: Princeton University Press, 2002), 103.
45. Améry, "Resentments," 75.
46. Ibid., 78.
47. Walker, *Moral Repair*, 132.
48. Love, *Feeling Backward*, 30.
49. Hannah Arendt, *The Human Condition* (Chicago: University of Chicago Press, 2013), 237.
50. See, for instance, Debra Kaminer et al., "The Truth and Reconciliation Commission in South Africa: Relation to Psychiatric Status and Forgiveness Among Survivors of Human Rights Abuses," *British Journal of Psychiatry* 178 (2001): 375. See also Griswold, *Forgiveness*.
51. Aaron Lazare, *On Apology* (Oxford: Oxford University Press, 2004), 166.
52. Griswold, *Forgiveness*, 49.
53. Quoted in Antjie Krog, Nosisi Mpolweni, and Kopano Ratele, *There Was This Goat: Investigating the Truth Commission Testimony of Notrose Nobomvu Konile* (Durban: University of KwaZulu-Natal Press, 2009), 12.
54. Arendt, *The Human Condition*, 241.
55. Avishai Margalit, *The Ethics of Memory* (Cambridge, Mass.: Harvard University Press, 2002), 193. See also Jean Hampton, "Forgiveness, Resentment, and Hatred," in *Forgiveness and Mercy*, ed. Jeffrie G. Murphy and Jean Hampton, 35–87 (Cambridge: Cambridge University Press, 1988), which argues that forgiveness is "the decision to see a wrongdoer in a new light. Nor is this decision in any way a condonation of a wrong. The forgiver never gives up her opposition to the wrongdoer's action, nor does she even give up her opposition to the wrongdoer's bad character traits. Instead, she revises her judgment of the person himself—where that person is understood to be something other than or more than the character traits of which she does not approve. And she reaches the honest decision that this person

does not merit her moral hatred, because he is still decent despite his action. She does not condone something bad by forgiving him, because the forgiveness is precisely the decision that he isn't bad (even though his action and the character trait that precipitated it are)" (84–85). Hampton agrees with Margalit that forgiveness is a decision, though she also falls closer to Griswold in terms of that decision's relation to the one forgiven.

56. Margalit, *The Ethics of Memory*, 193.

57. Walker makes this point in "Cycle of Violence": "Victims individually do crave vindication but may not always see an opening to seek or demand it. There are many forms and aspects of vindication, not all equally available or relevant to individuals in very different circumstances. Social environments play decisive roles in attributing lesser or greater significance to the offense any victim has suffered, encouraging or discouraging specific interpretations of injury and expectations of responses to injury, and opening or closing avenues of socially supported and legitimated response for victims" (97–98).

58. Margalit, *The Ethics of Memory*, 205.

59. Harry Frankfurt, "Freedom of the Will and the Concept of a Person," in *What Do We Deserve? A Reader on Justice and Desert*, ed. Louis P. Pojman and Owen McLeod, 125–34 (Oxford: Oxford University Press, 1998).

60. Margalit, *The Ethics of Memory*, 205.

61. Walker, *Moral Repair*, 155.

62. Arendt, *The Human Condition*, 243.

63. It is important to remember, however, that Arendt saw real limits to what could be forgiven. Of what Kant calls "radical evil" she writes, "Where the deed dispossesses us of all power, we can indeed only repeat with Jesus: 'It were better for him that a millstone were hanged about his neck and he cast into the sea'" (ibid., 241). She writes this because she believes that we cannot forgive where we cannot punish, and so, if a crime outstrips every idea of proportionality, the perpetrator may be beyond redemption.

64. Pumla Gobodo-Madikizela, *A Human Being Died That Night: A South African Woman Confronts the Legacy of Apartheid* (Boston: Mariner Books, 2003), 101–2.

65. Ibid., 102.

66. Another instance of forgiveness as a possible expression of powerlessness: Women residing in the Old Colony Mennonite settlement, Manitoba Colony, in Bolivia, have been subjected to years of drugging and rape that are often denied or hidden from authorities. Even when eight men were finally sent to jail for the crimes, the rapes continued. And yet the women tend to say that they forgive the rapists because, according to the Old Colony Mennonite belief system, anyone who does not forgive will not go to heaven.

Women residing in Manitoba tend to speak only Low German, do not own property, and are recognized only as the property of their fathers or husbands, and thus it is difficult even for those who might wish to escape to do so. There are no Low German–speaking therapists in the area, and offers from Canadian Mennonite colonies to send therapists have been refused by male elders in Manitoba, so in addition to being trapped, the women are left alone with their trauma. Silence around the crimes is so weighty that in some cases mothers and daughters don't even know that both have been victimized. See "Bolivian Mennonites Jailed for Serial Rapes," *BBC News*, August 26, 2011, http://www.bbc.co.uk/news/world-latin-america-14688458. See also Jean Friedman-Rudovsky, "The Ghost Rapes of Bolivia," *Vice Magazine*, August 5, 2013, http://www.vice.com/read/the-ghost-rapes-of-bolivia-000300-v20n8.

67. This final set of claims about forgiveness and resentment originally appeared in my article "A Hearing."

68. Améry, "Resentments," 77.

69. Ibid., 79.

70. Walker, *Moral Repair*, 129.

71. See Elizabeth Cline, *Overdressed: The Shockingly High Cost of Cheap Fashion* (New York: Portfolio/Penguin, 2012). See also Corrina Goria, ed., *Invisible Hands: Voices from the Global Economy* (San Francisco: McSweeney's, 2014).

72. Goria, *Invisible Hands*.

73. Thomas Pogge, *World Poverty and Human Rights* (Malden, Mass.: Polity Press, 2008), 6.

74. The argument about global responsibility first appeared in my article "How Much Does That Weigh? Levinas and the Possibility of Human Rights," in "Reflections on Levinas," special issue, *MonoKL* 8–9 (2010): 661–74.

75. Derek Summerfield, "Effects of War: Moral Knowledge, Revenge, Reconciliation, and Medicalized Concepts of 'Recovery,' " *British Medical Journal* 325, no. 7372 (2002): 1105.

76. Quoted in Brudholm, *Resentment's Virtue*, 33.

77. James Baldwin, *The Fire Next Time* (New York: Vintage International, 1990), 102.

78. Elizabeth Spelman, *Repair: The Impulse to Restore in a Fragile World* (Boston: Beacon Press, 2002), 95. Conversation around this topic was recently reignited by Ta-Nehisi Coates, "The Case for Reparations," *Atlantic*, May 21, 2014.

79. David Mellor, Di Bretherton, and Lucy Firth, "Aboriginal and Non-Aboriginal Australia: The Dilemma of Apologies, Forgiveness, and Reconciliation," *Peace and Conflict: Journal of Peace Psychology* 13, no. 1 (2007): 30.

80. Summerfield, "Effects of War," 1107.

81. Eve Sedgwick, "Paranoid Reading and Reparative Reading, or, You're So Paranoid, You Probably Think This Essay Is About You," in *Touching Feeling: Affect, Pedagogy, Performativity* (Durham: Duke University Press, 2009), 146.

5. DESERT

1. Teresa Godwin Phelps, *Shattered Voices: Language, Violence, and the Work of Truth Commissions* (Philadelphia: University of Pennsylvania Press, 2011), 13.

2. Jean Améry, "Resentments," in *At the Mind's Limits: Contemplations by a Survivor on Auschwitz and Its Realities* (Bloomington: Indiana University Press, 2009), 79.

3. Margaret Walker, *Moral Repair: Reconstructing Moral Relations after Wrongdoing* (Cambridge: Cambridge University Press, 2006).

4. Linda Ross Meyer, "Nobody 'Deserves' Any of This": An Interview with Linda Ross Meyer, *Believer* 11, no. 7 (September 2013): 23. See also Linda Ross Meyer, *The Justice of Mercy* (Ann Arbor: University of Michigan Press, 2010).

5. Quoted in Phelps, *Shattered Voices*, 12.

6. Jeffrie Murphy, "The Retributive Emotions," in *Forgiveness and Mercy*, ed. Jeffrie G. Murphy and Jean Hampton (Cambridge: Cambridge University Press, 1988), 2–3. Claire Katz points out that this is a very Christian way of understanding the problem. She writes, "The suppression of emotions from anger to eros has much to do with the suppression and degradation of the body over the elevation of the soul. You don't see this—or at least not very much of it—in Judaism."

7. Phelps, *Shattered Voices*, 17.

8. William Shakespeare, *The Tragedy of Hamlet: Prince of Denmark*, ed. Sylvan Barnet (New York: Signet, 1998), act 1, scene 5, lines 23–25.

9. Ibid., act 5, scene 2, lines 345–49.

10. Phelps, *Shattered Voices*, 36.

11. Ibid., 1, 35.

12. And yet Hamlet is haunted by the story of Hecuba's loss of Priam in *The Iliad*. Hecuba, or the actor playing her, weeps for her husband's death and rends her garments and throws herself on the ground. Hamlet wonders why the actor should be so capable of fictional grief when Hamlet himself is not capable of his own real grief, and he wonders as well whether or why he himself should be so affected by a scene of grief so far from his own. About this Levinas writes, "Why does the other concern me? What is Hecuba to me? Am I my brother's keeper? These questions have meaning only if one has already supposed that the ego is concerned only with itself. . . . In this

hypothesis it indeed remains incomprehensible that the absolute outside-of-me, the other, would concern me. But in the 'prehistory' of the ego posited for itself there speaks a responsibility" (*Otherwise Than Being: Or Beyond Essence*, trans. Alphonso Lingis [Pittsburgh: Duquesne University Press, 1998], 117). Hamlet's subjection to the affect of a fictional grief presses on him with his own sense of the need to respond to past injustice. And it also gives him an idea about how to proceed. At the end of the scene Hamlet decides to use a *story* to ensnare Claudius: "the play's the thing/wherein I'll catch the conscience of the King" (act 2, scene 2, lines 616–17).

13. Nils Christie, "Conflicts as Property," *British Journal of Criminology* 17, no. 1 (1977): 3.

14. Elizabeth Spelman, *Repair: The Impulse to Restore in a Fragile World* (Boston: Beacon Press, 2002), 56.

15. Judith Herman in an interview by Priscilla B. Hayner, quoted in Hayner, *Unspeakable Truths*, 147.

16. Christie, "Conflicts as Property," 7.

17. Spelman, *Repair*, 64.

18. Paul Tullis, "Can Forgiveness Play a Role in Criminal Justice?" *New York Times Magazine*, January 4, 2013, http://www.nytimes.com/2013/01/06/magazine/can-forgiveness-play-a-role-in-criminal-justice.html?pagewanted=all&_r=0.

19. Ibid.

20. Ibid.

21. Ibid.

22. Ibid.

23. Ibid.

24. Ibid.

25. Ibid.

26. See, for instance, Sarah Cobb, "The Domestication of Violence in Mediation," *Law and Society Review* 31, no. 3 (1997): 397–440.

27. Christie, "Conflicts as Property," 10.

28. Tullis, "Can Forgiveness Play a Role?"

29. For instance, one could make a good argument that many prisoners in the United States and elsewhere were made ethically lonely by structural injustice long before they ended up in prison.

30. However, it is not at all the case that all are accepted, or that reintegration goes smoothly. See Erin K. Baines, "The Haunting of Alice: Local Approaches to Justice and Reconciliation in Northern Uganda," *International Journal of Transitional Justice* 1, no. 1 (2007): 91–114. See also Erin K. Baines, "Complex Political Perpetrators: Reflections on Dominic Ongwen," *Journal of Modern African Studies* 47, no. 2 (2009): 163–91.

31. Kamari Maxine Clarke makes a similar argument in the context of the ICC's intervention in African conflicts in *Fictions of Justice: The International Criminal Court and the Challenge of Legal Pluralism in Sub-Saharan Africa* (Cambridge: Cambridge University Press, 2009).

32. Baines, "Complex Political Perpetrators," 164.

33. See Mariane C. Ferme, "'Archetypes of Humanitarian Discourse': Child Soldiers, Forced Marriage, and the Framing of Communities in Post-Conflict Sierra Leone," *Humanity* 4, no. 1 (spring 2013): 55ff., for a good reading of how children who act as soldiers both do and do not possess meaningful agency in their actions.

34. Ferme (ibid., 61, 63) makes a similar point about child soldiers in Sierra Leone and uses it to back her claim that, for some, returning "home" after such conflict is not the welcome option it would be for someone whose home life had been safe. For some survivors, whether perpetrator or victim, being freed to start a new life elsewhere—being freed to have other choices—is the only good outcome of the violence.

35. Baines, "The Haunting of Alice," 91–92.

36. Ferme, "'Archetypes of Human Discourse,'" 59.

37. Baines, "Complex Political Perpetrators," 180.

38. Ibid., 182.

39. Ibid., 186.

40. Ongwen's case is made even more complicated by the attitudes of Acholi victims in Uganda. Though they have suffered most at the hands of the Lord's Resistance Army, they do not want the rebels to be indicted by a domestic or international court, not only because they think that will make the fighting last longer but also because they have their own rituals of reconciliation for incorporating returned soldiers back into the community. See Baines, "The Haunting of Alice."

41. In 2009, 39.4 percent, according to the U.S. Bureau of Justice Statistics.

42. See, for instance, M. Marit Rehavi and Sonja Starr, "Racial Disparity in Federal Criminal Charging and Its Sentencing Consequences," University of Michigan Law School, Program in Law and Economics Working Paper No. 12–002, May 7, 2012.

43. Derek R. Brookes, "The Possibility of a Correctional Ethic," in *Discretion, Community, and Correctional Ethics*, ed. John Kleinig and Margaret Leland Smith (Lanham, Md.: Rowman and Littlefield, 2001), 51.

44. John P. Pittman, "The Case for Abolition and the Reality of Race," in Kleinig and Smith, *Discretion, Community, and Correctional Ethics*, 72.

45. Pittman, "The Case for Abolition," 76, citing David Goldberg, "Surplus Value: The Political Economy of Prisons and Policing," in *States of Confinement:*

Policing, Detention, and Prisons, ed. Joy James (New York: St. Martin's Press, 2000), 220.

46. Ibid.

47. Ibid.

48. "What Is the Experience of Isolation?": An Interview with Lisa Guenther, *Believer* 11, no. 5 (June 2013): 69.

49. Ibid.

50. Antjie Krog, Nosisi Mpolweni, and Kopano Ratele, *There Was This Goat: Investigating the Truth Commission Testimony of Notrose Nobomvu Konile* (Durban: University of KwaZulu-Natal Press, 2009), 12.

51. See the section discussing Yvonne Khutwane in chapter 3 for more on the imposition of form in TRC testimony.

52. Krog, Mpolweni, and Ratele, *There Was This Goat*, 45.

53. Jean Améry, "At the Mind's Limits," in *At the Mind's Limits*, 2.

54. Krog, Mpolweni, and Ratele, *There Was This Goat*, 61.

55. Judith Butler, *Precarious Life: The Powers of Mourning and Violence* (New York: Verso, 2006), 22.

56. *Long Night's Journey into Day*, directed by Deborah Hoffmann and Frances Reid (San Francisco: Iris Films, 2000). There is a complexity of conditions of guilt in the Konile case. Though Thapelo Mbelo is the only one who officially asked for Mrs. Konile's forgiveness and is the one she turned her back on in the amnesty hearing, he didn't actually kill Zabonke. Sergeant Riaan Bellingan (who got amnesty but treated the process with disdain—to such an extent that Commissioner Gobodo-Madikizela said that she would prefer he not get amnesty) killed Zabonke, acting under orders from Eugene de Kock (who ended up in prison rather than receiving amnesty).

57. Krog, Mpolweni, and Ratele, *There Was This Goat*, 145.

58. Ibid., 46.

59. Antjie Krog, *Country of My Skull: Guilt, Sorrow, and the Limits of Forgiveness in the New South Africa* (New York: Random House, 2007).

60. Yazir Henry notes that Krog took liberties with his story, bending and editing it to a narrative of betrayal rather than the more complex story he told: "Not only do I question the intentions of writers such as Antjie Krog; I assert that their work has, in various ways and with serious personal consequences to myself, impacted negatively upon my life. Serious thought needs to be given to the ethics of appropriating testimony for poetic license, media freedom, academic commentary and discourse analysis" ("Reconciling Reconciliation: A Personal and Public Journey of Testifying before the South African TRC," in *Political Transition: Politics and Cultures*, ed. Paul Gready [London: Pluto Press, 2003], 266). Henry's personal experience reflects the argument I try to make in chapter 3 about hearing.

61. Krog, Mpolweni, and Ratele, *There Was This Goat*, 39.

62. Ibid.

63. Lee Ann Kreutzer, "Seeing Is Believing and Hearing Is Believing: Thoughts on Oral Tradition and the Pectol Shields," *Utah Historical Quarterly* 76, no. 4 (fall 2008): 382.

64. Rustom Bharucha, "Between Truth and Reconciliation: Experiments in Theatre and Public Culture," *Economic and Political Weekly* 36, no. 39 (2001): 3766.

65. She may or may not know that that is also the name of a book by Thomas L. Dumm, *A Politics of the Ordinary* (New York: New York University Press, 1999).

66. Kathleen Stewart, *Ordinary Affects* (Durham: Duke University Press, 2007), 15.

67. From "Notes Toward a Supreme Fiction," section 4, "It must give pleasure," in *The Collected Poems of Wallace Stevens* (New York: Vintage Books, 1990), 401.

Epilogue

1. "Political Cartoonist Not Sure How to Convey That Sack in Senator's Hand Is Full of Money," *Onion*, August 19, 2013, http://www.theonion.com/articles/political-cartoonist-not-sure-how-to-convey-that-l,33545/.

2. Most of the content of this epilogue first appeared in my article "Speaking Truth to Reconciliation: Political Transition, Recovery, and the Work of Time," *Humanity* 4, no. 1 (2013): 27–48.

Index

multiple uses of, 131–33; pressure on victims to forgive, 121–23, 134–35, 201–2n66; and sacrifice of individuality, 121, 122; as second-order desire, 132–33; and unequal social relations, 134–35, 201–2n66. *See also* resentment

Fortunoff Video Archive for Holocaust Testimonies, 72, 79, 107, 127

Frankfurt, Harry, 132

Fransch, Anton, 94

freedom, 20, 23–26, 127, 128, 161, 162, 169

friendship, 24, 30, 113, 129, 143, 171, 198n20

Fromm-Reichmann, Frieda, 30

Fussell, Paul, 106

future, 7, 8, 32, 37, 39, 44, 53, 60, 61, 66, 93, 108, 110, 113, 116–17, 135, 137, 140–42, 147, 153, 156, 167, 168, 171–72. *See also* world-building

genocide, 40, 76, 104, 137–38, 177n1, 179n13, 183n72. *See also* Holocaust

Germany, 196n113; and collective guilt, 28, 78; and evil of Nazism, 13–14; and public consciousness of war guilt, 11, 123, 129, 136, 137, 179n13; and silence on war experiences, 76, 112–13, 123, 129, 137; victim participation in trials, 57. *See also* Améry, Jean; Hanna F.; Holocaust; Levinas, Emmanuel; Stanley M.

Gill, Anton, 12

goat dream of Notrose Nobomvu Konile, 158–65

Gobodo-Madikizela, Pumla, 44, 45, 47, 60, 82, 134, 189n28

Goldston, James A., 42

Grassian, Stuart, 88–89

Griswold, Charles, 114, 131, 133

Grosmaire, Ann, 150–53

Grosmaire, Kate, 150–51

Guenther, Lisa, 89–90, 158

Hamlet (Shakespeare), 142, 147, 148, 170, 203–4n12

Hampton, Jean, 200–201n55

Hanna F. (Holocaust survivor), 72–81, 96, 105

Haslam, Emily, 62

Hayner, Priscilla, 75, 81, 198–99n23

hearing, 69–111; duty to hear and respond beyond what is wanted or expected, 6–7, 28, 70, 75, 80, 105–7, 109–10; learning to hear, 109–11, 165; and reparative reading, 69–70, 104; transcripts of testimony vs. hearing in person, 87–88; and willingness of audience to be interrupted, 70, 74, 106, 169

hearing, failure of, 2, 6, 7, 8, 32, 70, 103, 157, 165, 166, 170; and apartheid survivors, 27, 32, 81–90, 94–97, 105–6, 158–65, 206n60 (*see also* de Souza, Colin; Henry, Yazir; Khutwane, Yvonne; Kondile, Charity; Konile, Notrose Nobomvu); and communication, 90–94; and debate over Native American ownership of Pectol shields, 97–105, 165–66, 194n92; and ethical loneliness, 1–2, 9, 70; failure of hearing in institutions designed for hearing, 6, 70, 73, 83 (*see also specific institutions and testimonies*); and Holocaust survivors, 12, 32, 72–81, 105, 107, 128 (*see also* Améry, Jean; Hanna F.; Stanley M.); and limitations of trials and truth commissions, 41–44, 47, 48; and misunderstandings about autonomy of the self, 11; need for reflection on limits of hearing, 7, 8, 103; and rape and assault survivors, 81–83, 89–90,

limitations of, 46–48, 166; and narrowing the range of possible lies, 178n4; Ngewu's testimony, 131; questionable therapeutic value of testifying before, 54–55; and site of repair beyond the victim, 138–40; testimony procedure, 83–84; trauma symptoms in stenographers, journalists, etc., 75, 187n9

truth commissions, 45–49; and amnesty, 46, 47, 49; and barriers to recovery due to perceived absence of justice, 39; benefits of, 45–46, 48; conflicting goals of nation-building and individual recovery, 6, 83–84; disadvantages and limitations of, 46–49; and forgiveness, 84; goals of, 5, 178n4; inflated expectations for, 60–65; and lack of state capacity for adequate response, 147–48; lack of substantial proof for healing of survivors, 6, 54; and restorative justice, 38; and retributive justice, 38; as revisionary practice, 112; rules and procedures determining what counts as harm and what counts as truth, 48; transcripts of testimony vs. hearing in person, 87–88; value compared to criminal trials, 38–39; and victim-perpetrators, 96. *See also* National Commission on the Disappearance of Persons; Truth and Reconciliation Commission

Tullis, Paul, 152, 153

Ubuntu, 160, 161, 163, 164
Uganda, 153–56, 179n14, 205n40
United States: apologies for slavery, 139; criminal offenses as offenses against the state, not the victim, 61; debate over Native American ownership of Pectol shields, 97–105, 165–66;

ethical loneliness and structural injustices, 157–58, 204n29; incarceration in, 88–89, 143, 157–58, 191n54; mediation between families of killer and victim, 150–53

Unspeakable Truths (Hayner), 81
Ute Indian Tribe, 99–105, 165–66

victims: and disadvantages of criminal trials, 40–44, 148–49, 183n72; and evidence of repair, 53–60; and hybrid of retributive and restorative goals, 152–53; ICC's rhetoric of victimhood, 63–64; lack of substantial proof for healing value of truth commissions and trials, 6, 54–55, 57–58; needs and desires of, 61–62, 66–67, 149, 201n57 (*see also* Améry, Jean); *parties civiles*, 41, 57, 64; psychological impact of testifying, 54, 57, 62–63, 183n72; sites of repair beyond the victim, 137–41; and subsidiary prosecution, 57–58; victim participants at ICC, 64; victim-perpetrators, 96, 153–56. *See also* desert; forgetting; forgiveness; intersubjectivity of the self; recovery; resentment; self; trauma

von Weizsäcker, Richard, 196n113

Walker, Margaret, 22, 29, 114–15, 130, 133, 136–37, 143, 177n46, 201n57
Walpole penitentiary, 88–89
weariness, as resistance to existence, 17, 18, 22, 169
Western culture: and assumption of self's autonomy, 4, 7, 160, 161 (*see also* autonomy of the self); and debate over Pectol shield ownership, 99–105; failure to account for larger context of wrongdoing, 155; incommensurability with Australian indigenous law,

GPSR Authorized Representative: Easy Access System Europe, Mustamäe tee
50, 10621 Tallinn, Estonia, gpsr.requests@easproject.com

www.ingramcontent.com/pod-product-compliance
Lightning Source LLC
Chambersburg PA
CBHW032044040426
42334CB00039B/1130